GERONTECHNOLOGY

GERONTECHNOLOGY

Growing Old in a Technological Society

Edited by

GARI LESNOFF-CARAVAGLIA, PH.D.

CHARLES C THOMAS • PUBLISHER, LTD.
Springfield • Illinois • U.S.A.

Published and Distributed Throughout the World by

CHARLES C THOMAS • PUBLISHER, LTD.
2600 South First Street
Springfield, Illinois 62704

©2007 by CHARLES C THOMAS • PUBLISHER, LTD.

ISBN 13 978-0-398-07692-4 (hard)   ISBN 10 0-398-07692-8 (hard)
ISBN 13 978-0-398-07693-1 (paper) ISBN 10 0-398-07693-6 (paper)

Library of Congress Catalog Card Number: 200604-9382

Printed in the United States of America
SR-R-3

Library of Congress Cataloging-in-Publication Data

Gerontechnology : growing old in a technological society / edited by Gari Lesnoff-Caravaglia.
　　p. cm.
　Includes bibliographical references and index.
　ISBN 0-398-07692-8 -- ISBN 0-398-07693-6 (pbk.)
　1. Older people--Care--Technological innovations. 2. Self-help devices for people with disabilities. 3. Gerontology--Technological innovations. 4. Geriatrics--Technological innovations.
I. Lesnoff-Caravaglia, Gari.

RA564.8.G4721 2007
618.970028--dc22

　　　　　　　　　　　　　　　　　　　　　　　　　　　　　　2006049382

CONTRIBUTORS

Rodney Diaz, M.D.

Assistant Professor
Department of Otolaryngology
University of California–Davis
Davis, California

Michael Fischer, O.D., FA.A.O.

Director of Low Vision Services
Lighthouse International, New York
Optometric Consultant, Northport Virginia Medical Center
Adjunct Assistant Clinical Professor
SUNY College of Optometry

James L. Fozard, Ph.D.

School of Aging Studies
University of South Florida
Tampa, Florida

William D. Kearns, Ph.D.

Department of Aging and Mental Health
Louis de la Parte Florida Mental Health Institute
University of South Florida
Tampa, Florida

Gari Lesnoff-Caravaglia, Ph.D.

Professor, School of Health Sciences
Ohio University
Athens, Ohio

Cynthia R. Marling, Ph.D.

Assistant Professor
School of Electrical Engineering and Computer Science
Ohio University
Athens, Ohio

Arunkumar Pennathur, Ph.D.

Associate Professor, Industrial Engineering Program
University of Texas at El Paso
El Paso, Texas

Joelle Pineau, Ph.D.

McGill University, School of Computer Science
Montreal, Quebec, Canada

Rozanne M. Puleo, M.S., R.C.E.P.

Age-Lab – Ideas + Technology for Quality Living
Massachusetts Institute of Technology
Cambridge, Massachusetts

Nicholas Roy, Ph.D.

Massachusetts Institute of Technology
Computer Science and Artificial Intelligence Laboratory
Cambridge, Massachusetts

Eric W. Sargent, M.D., F.A.C.S.

Otologist/Neurotologist, Michigan Ear Institute
Farmington Hills, Michigan
Clinical Associate Professor, Department of Otolaryngology
Wayne State University School of Medicine
Detroit, Michigan

Cynthia Stuen, D.S.W.

Senior Vice President for Education
Lighthouse International
New York, New York

PREFACE

Awareness of the potential role of technology to extend the independence of older adults has grown significantly in the past decades. As two critical trends converge—the global aging of the older population and the rapid acceleration of technological development—they will have a marked effect upon all spheres of human experiencing. The presence of an increasingly older population calls for a reevaluation of the meaning of life, death, and the quality and nature of human experience. Aging does not occur in isolation but is a reflection of societal attitudes and resulting practical outcomes. Such practical responses are principally the purview of engineering, technology, and the biomedical sciences. The societal attitudes represent the ethical, philosophical, and social bases of the culture. Together they provide the inevitable link between the fields of gerontology and technology: Gerontechnology.

Gerontechnology, as an expression of the practical and the theoretical, forces an examination of the contemporary world, its immediate needs, and future trends. For gerontologists this has meant a conscious assessment of the role of technology in the ameliorating, prolonging, and concluding of human life. For engineers and developers of technologies, the presence of increasing numbers of persons over the age of 65 has forged a new vision of the role of technology in the practical pursuit of healthy and rewarding long life.

The six sections of the book detail this relationship. The first two chapters of Part I describe the multifaceted convergence of technology and aging, as well as the problems and challenges it presents. Part II serves as an introduction to both gerontologists and engineers to the nature of the aging process and potential areas of technological intervention. These four chapters cover the age-related changes due to disease or senescence inherent in human aging and outline specific health issues. The effects of lifestyle and the environment upon gerontechnology are given particular attention.

Part III addresses the problems and processes of invention, particularly ergonomics, which lead to the development of technologies specifically designed for the enhancement of the lives of the older population. The chapter on interventions and modifications of the environment has particular significance for the altering of the human environment in ways that can complement and enrich the experience of growing older.

Major factors in successful aging are the special senses, specifically vision and hearing. Part IV explores the range of sensory interventions currently available, as well as describing those that hold promise for future older populations. Chapters in Part IV explore problematic issues and innovative methods for their resolution.

Part V focuses on automation through the employment of robots and advanced forms of transportation. The utilization of robots to increase the independence of older persons is the subject of Chapter 11; while in Chapter 12, personal mobility, as well as technological assistive mobility devices are given attention. Issues of transportation are discussed from the perspectives of their effects upon lifestyle and well-being. Both chapters delineate areas of future research efforts.

In the closing section, Part VI, Chapter 13 is devoted to discussion of information processing communication, an essential ingredient in the growth and direction of Gerontechnology. The final chapter examines the effects of the constant and continuing interplay between technology and aging. It also analyzes human experience from the perspective of the extraordinary framework for living provided by the growth of an aging population and the advanced technologies which have led to the conceptualization of *Gerontechnology.*

The prevalent belief is that all aspects of human life should be open to their potential realization by all persons, regardless of age. Consequently, age, in and of itself, is not a condition for determining the breadth or scope of life experience. Thus, Gerontechnology may be viewed as directly providing new life and new opportunities to those reaching advanced ages–the herald of a new age for all men and women.

This volume was developed under the auspices of an 1804 Grant sponsored by Ohio University. The assistance provided by my Research Assistant, Rebecca Brashears, is gratefully acknowledged.

Gari Lesnoff-Caravaglia, Ph.D.

CONTENTS

GERONTECHNOLOGY

PART I

Chapter 1

GERONTECHNOLOGY: THE LINKING OF GERONTOLOGY AND TECHNOLOGY

Gari Lesnoff-Caravaglia

INTRODUCTION

The application of technology to gerontology is not simply the enlisting of current methods to alleviate existing problems. The response must be a revolutionary conceptual view that takes into account the fact that the coupling of an aging population with the advances of science and technology herald a new frontier.

The designing and marketing of new technologies and assistive devices to enhance the independence of the elderly is, in itself, a radical departure from the long-held position of regarding the elderly as a group that would not be the major target for expensive medical, engineering, environmental, or lifestyle interventions. The old were to continue to grow old and to gradually die. Intervention was not regarded as critical. The illnesses of old age were of natural causation and were to take their course. This stance is well illustrated by the overworked statement: What do you expect at your age? To decline was natural, to experience sensory loss was unavoidable, and to become increasingly dependent upon family and society was an unfortunate inevitability.

The view that older persons could and preferred to remain active and productive, and would actively seek health counsel and aid in order to become advocates on their own behalf, has caught the world by surprise. It appears that a futuristic prediction has come true. Many such futuristic predictions, however, did not take into account an increasingly older and healthier population that would alter the nature of aging.

The future has traditionally always belonged to the young. That societies should concern themselves in creating a future for the old is unprecedented, not only in thought, but is a reversal of the entire Western tradition which is built upon a youthful future-time orientation.

The linkage of gerontology, the multidisciplinary scientific study of aging, with technology has led to a new focus within education and research: Gerontechnology. The current demographic and technological explosion is closely linked to scientific information on the aging process. The quality of health care, housing, the environment, employment, transportation, information services, and recreational activities will continue to be heavily influenced by scientific and technological advances. Many of these developments have already demonstrated a potential to enhance the quality of life of older persons, but the application of scientific findings to the development of specific technological products is yet largely unexplored and underdeveloped.

Health

Health is a major determinant of well-being. Delivery of health services, technological advances in biomedical research and engineering, and advances in understanding the importance of nutrition in the later years have each contributed to the increasing longevity of men and women. As people live longer, the quality of life becomes a pressing issue. Technological innovations must not simply delay death but must facilitate daily activities and the enjoyment of life (Bang, Bien, & Stefanov, 2004). Areas of concern that call for continued attention include advances that allow individuals with arthritis, vision and hearing loss, cardiovascular disease, or amputations to remain in the community in an independent and productive capacity.

Home Health Care

There is a growing and persistent interest on the part of the elderly in maintaining control over their lives and in selecting lifestyles built upon personal choice. Further, expectations have increased with respect to the number and types of technological interventions that people are willing to have introduced into their homes (Hughes, 2004). While lower health care costs can be one deciding factor in favor of such home health care interventions, what is equally significant is the fact that older individuals increasingly balk at admission to health care facilities such as hospitals and nursing homes which deprive them of personal control.

While the experience of a life long lived alters older individuals' needs and wishes, their increasing sophistication and knowledge of their own health status and the health care system convinces them that most traditional health care settings are inappropriate. The changes in health care alternatives over which societies slowly and painfully deliberate, have led older individuals to opt for systems based on personal choice. As the educational level, political acumen, and economic status of the elderly continue to rise, the demand by the elderly for health care within the home setting or within the community also rises. At the same time, their conventional fear of authority figures such as doctors, lawyers, bureaucrats, and overbearing adult children has diminished. For many, appropriate health care and the home environment have become synonymous.

Housing and Environment

Housing and the larger environment constitute critical determinants of the lifestyle of an older person. Many individuals perceive their visual world with less clarity while others have difficulty with mobility when climbing stairs, rising out of chairs or tubs, reaching for objects, or carrying out many routine, but important tasks. Often these changes are due to irreversible physiological processes, but the environment may either exaggerate or minimize the functional limitations commonly associated with old age (National Research Council, 2003).

An important component of adapting environments to older persons is the implementation of technological innovations. Bathroom devices increase safety, while kitchen modifications may encourage preparation of food and ultimately better nutrition. Large print may allow more communication with the outside world, and clearly demarcated steps and curbs may promote a greater willingness to venture beyond the confines of one's home. Transportation systems encourage access to the larger community and support continuation of a network of social relations. A supportive environment which removes or minimizes barriers allows older persons to live with greater independence, security, and dignity ("Rocket Science," 2004).

Employment

Employment of older workers will become increasingly frequent as the work force itself ages. Technological innovations designed for older employees not only increase productivity and safety in the workplace but also provide the community with valuable resources. Whether older people work full-time or part-time at a new or continued career, they represent a potentially significant consumer group. Older workers can benefit from technological advancements both by their meaningful involvement in the work-force and by their capacity to consume products and services.

Learning and Recreation

Learning is often defined as comprising four categories of skill: surviving (learning for economic sufficiency); coping (learning for practical life skills); giving (learning for community contribution), and growing (learning as part of life span development). Recreation, in many respects, is an important aspect of personal growth and frequently involves an investment in both innovative products as well as services, such as those offered through travel or continuing education. Technological innovations designed to advance learning are sophisticated and readily available. However, the needs of the older learner must remain a central focus in the design and development of such products.

In general, the role of technology will become increasingly important in the lives of older persons. Research efforts must be broadened to examine the needs of the well elderly in addition to those who suffer from impairments (Lesnoff-Caravaglia, 1999). Underlying the development of new products and services is the opportunity to facilitate and to enrich life in the later years and to promote the interactions between two major revolutions ongoing in the United States and the world at large: the aging of the population and the advancement of technology. The four basic concerns of older persons encompass: health care, housing and the environment, employment, and recreational and educational opportunities.

Global Aging

At the initiation of the twenty-first century, it became quite clear that one of the major and preeminent worldwide phenomena was that of global aging. Lowered fertility rates and improved health and longevity have generated growing numbers of proportions of older populations throughout most of the world. After the year 2020, the numbers and proportions of elderly, especially nonagenarians and centenarians, will rise rapidly in most developed and many developing nations. The projected increase is primarily the result of high fertility rates following World War II (Baby Boomers). The elderly population will continue to expand and will reflect a larger proportion of each nation's total population in the future.

Rapidly expanding numbers of very old people represent a social phenomenon without historical precedent, and one that is bound to alter previously held stereotypes of older people. The growth of nonagenarians and centenarians is crucial to determinations of public policy in regard to gerontechnology due to the fact that individual needs and social responsibilities change considerably with increased age.

The contemporary world can be described as increasingly aged and interdependent. As the Baby Boomers, common to many nations, begin to number among the elderly by the year 2020, there will be a significant leap by 2040 in the proportion of the world's population that is aged. The characteristics of this aging population, along with their strengths and requirements, will be felt throughout the global economy (Andrews, 1998).

In the United States, the nation's older population is expected to more than double by the year 2050. The composition of that population will be more racially and ethnically diverse than generations before them, thus intensifying the need for flexible and sensitive provision of services at all levels (Montemagno & Roco, 2004).

The Older Population

The older population is made up principally of females, most of whom live alone. They remain in the community setting for as long as possible. Most are unemployed, and many live under reduced economic circumstances. Some suffer from two or more debilitating chronic illnesses. Despite societal changes, the lives of such older persons continue unchanged; and, as they continue to age, their only expectation is eventual institutionalization or death.

The general apathy toward the aging process and older persons leads to premature aging, wherein persons become more prone to exhibit behavior patterns and disease symptoms which are generally characteristic of much older persons. Persons of 70 appear 90; those 90 appear 110 or older. There is a concomitant lack of fit between the person and the environment. The environment, unadapted to the physiological and psychological needs and concerns of older persons is antiquated, and thus provides little by way of accommodation of older adults. Such lack of accommodation with respect to the environment causes older persons to assume stereotypical postures and behaviors (Oram, 1997; Shotton, 2003). Older persons are not encouraged to develop skills to deal with the environment, and the rigidity of the environment promotes the onset and growth of disease.

Gerontechnology

Freedom and independence have been promised through the adaptation of technologies to offset the debilities of age. These have yet to be forthcoming. The home environment of many persons has changed little from the post-World War II era. The Smart House, which has long been promised, that would incorporate various facets of modern technology and would permit older persons to remain in their own homes and within the community setting indefinitely has not, at this juncture, even enabled older persons to change a light bulb safely. The Smart Nursing Home has not gone beyond the incorporation of bathroom grab bars. Smart Hospitals are nonexistent in terms of daily patient care, and the care marshaled out to patients is best characterized as "reluctant care."

The Process of Aging

Biological changes are inevitable as part of senescence or the aging process. This is true of animate and inanimate entities. However, the nature of this process is poorly understood.

While it is not unusual to see an old human being, aged animals exist only in captivity. Wild animals do not usually reach extreme old age or even what in humans is referred to as middle age. Wild animals thus resemble ancient or prehistoric human beings who rarely, if ever, saw an old person. Of the three hundred Neanderthals found, only one may have been a postmenopausal woman (Hayflick, 1994).

Not only physical vigor, but also less obvious powers such as the ability to resist disease and the physiological capacity of many major organs, peak and then decrease in both human beings and other animals following sexual maturation. Some of the more obvious normal age changes include loss of strength and stamina, farsightedness, new hair growth in ears and nostrils, decline in short-term memory, balding, loss of bone mass, decrease in height, hearing loss, and menopause. Although most of these changes can be viewed externally, they have their origins at levels not readily perceived by the senses (Hayflick, 1994).

Normal age changes make humans more vulnerable to diseases that in youth would be more easily repulsed. As the immune system ages, it becomes less efficient in defending the body and more likely to make errors in defense. It may mistake normal proteins in the body for foreign proteins, thus producing antibodies against its own cells (Ross, 1995). The result is an autoimmune disease.

The diseases associated with old age are not part of the normal aging process. Cancer, heart disease, Alzheimer's disease, and strokes become more prevalent as persons age because of the reduced capacity to repel them. Often their long maturation permits them to manifest themselves in old age, although they are initiated at much younger ages (Hazzard et al., 1999). Some diseases such as herpes and tuberculosis can be dormant for many years and become reactivated in old age. This increase in vulnerability results from the normal aging process.

The improper understanding of the aging process leads to the physiological losses experienced in old age and, ultimately, death. Unless more attention is paid to the fundamental processes of aging, the fate of everyone fortunate enough to become old will be death on or around his or her hundredth birthday. The true causes of those deaths will probably be unknown because of lack of basic research that would increase the knowledge of the fundamental aging process and insights into how to reduce human vulnerability to the current causes of death (Hayflick, 1994).

No current theory has provided an adequate explanation as to why people age, or how they age. Efforts to retard or slow the aging process have suggested lowering the caloric intake, sleeping in colder environments, or developing special diets. The large scale effects of the aging process are pronounced at all levels, including the cellular.

Biological Aging

There are a number of older persons who function very well into advanced old age, and because of better lifestyle choices and increased income, educational level, and accessibility of new medical technologies, their number will continue to grow. Those who are well endowed with respect to genetic structure and have experienced the advantages of good health throughout the life span will very likely enjoy a healthy old age.

There are inevitable biological changes which occur as an individual becomes older. Such changes, however, are not the result of disease but are more aptly attributed to the aging process known as senescence. This term refers to the bodily changes that occur, and the limitations which such changes may engender. This term is not to be confused with the word "senile," which is often used as a pejorative term to describe older persons who may be suffering from physical or mental dysfunctions.

There are some diseases which are more likely to occur as a person continues to age. This does not mean that persons will necessarily suffer from such diseases. Diseases which may have had their onset in early periods of life manifest themselves as persons live to reach advanced old age. Such diseases can be the result of unhealthful lifestyles followed by the individual for a number of years. Cancers and diseases of the circulatory system are among those that manifest themselves in old age. The use of a number of medications to treat the multiple chronic diseases sometimes suffered by older persons can also lead to additional health problems. Drug dosages and uses in older persons have not been sufficiently studied.

The prevalence of health risk factors increases as individuals age. Some individuals are at risk for chronic conditions because of factors that cannot be modified, such as genetic predisposition, gender, and age. Risk factors related to health behaviors, however, can be modified. The majority of adults have risk factors for chronic conditions because of their health-related behaviors (Backman & Hentinen, 2001). Individuals who modify their health-related behaviors can reduce the risk of developing chronic conditions and enhance the quality of their lives. Such modifications include weight reduction, physical activity, lowering cholesterol levels and alcohol consumption, and not smoking.

Many modifiable risk factors are associated with chronic diseases such as hypertension, heart disease, diabetes, cancer, and stroke. There is a close association between excess weight and an increased risk of dying from heart disease or cancer (Spirduso, Francis, & MacRae, 2005). Obesity and smoking are the leading causes of preventable death (Calle, Thun, Poetrelli, Rodriguez, & Health, 1999). Adults at risk for chronic conditions are much more limited in their activities of daily living (ADLs), such as bathing, dressing, eating, toileting, and walking. The elderly have a higher rate of heart disease than any other age group. A healthy lifestyle can significantly reduce the risk of heart disease. Coronary heart disease is the leading cause of premature, permanent disability in older persons (Manuck, Jennings, Rabin, & Baum, 2000).

Arthritis is quite common in old age, and approximately half of the elderly population suffers from this chronic condition. Arthritis, or joint inflammation, affects a larger proportion of older women. Many need assistance to accomplish activities associated with daily living. Use of a social worker, adult day care, rehabilitation services, transportation, chronic pain management programs, and Meals on Wheels is significantly higher for the elderly who have arthritis.

The incidence of hip fractures is rising in many countries as the population continues to age. For example, the number of hip fractures in elderly Finnish men and women is increasing at a rate that cannot be explained merely by demographic changes. The precise reasons for this are unknown, but deterioration in age-adjusted bone-mineral density and strength, with accompanying increase in the age-adjusted incidence of injurious falls of the elderly, could partly account for the development (Kannus, Niemei, Parkkari, Palvanen, Vuori, & Jaumlrvinen, 1999).

Sex and Aging

The elderly of the future will have considerably more time to devote to interpersonal relationships, leading to a consequent increased interest in personal appearance. Cosmetic surgery offers opportunities to maintain a personal image based on personal preference. After the age of 80, the health status of individuals appears to reach a plateau, and few serious disabilities occur for at least another decade.

Since the elderly will have followed healthier lifestyles, their physical condition will be superior to that of the older population of today. Older persons today exhibit what can be termed as "premature aging," which is brought on by stress, improper diet, unhealthful living conditions and habits, and unsound work patterns. An amelioration of the total environment will not only prolong life, but can add immeasurably to the maintaining of youthfulness. In some cultures, long-living men who have led healthful lifestyles are found to possess viable sperm at the age of 100. Women in such environments menstruate until the age of 60 or later (Lesnoff-Caravaglia & Klys, 1987). With the more recent advances in conception and the added possibilities of "rent a womb," there is now the possibility for women to give birth and to nurture children at ages much older than had been thought possible. Through uterus replacement, there is the potential to eliminate menopause altogether.

The sex life of the future may be characterized as being "age independent" and, once sexual maturity is attained, not tied by function to any particular period of chronological age. The enjoyment of family and intimacy may take on entirely new configurations (Gott, 2005). Romance until death may well be the norm.

Biological Systems

Diseased conditions of one part of the body can seriously compromise several other systems. When oral health is compromised due to the presence of periodontal disease, one out of every four persons will lose all of his or her teeth by the age of 60 (Pathy, 1998). Oral bacteria also may be linked to stroke, heart attack, respiratory illness, gastrointestinal problems, and severe systemic infections because poor oral health becomes more common as persons age.

Older persons suffering from high levels of stress are especially prone to Alzheimer's disease and depression, both of which severely affect memory. While the types of stress differ among individuals, well-known causes often include illness, financial concerns, the death of loved ones, and resonating fears with regard to one's own health (Spirduso, Francis, & MacRae, 2005).

Increased Longevity

Advances in medical knowledge, combined with better dietary and sanitary measures, have led to an increase in life expectancy. An increase in the number of elderly people is accompanied by a greater incidence of the health disorders of the aged.

A conspicuous feature of an aged population is the range, or variability, of function seen in any given age group. An individual, age 70, who is near death and has many systems failing to maintain homeostasis, provides a notable contrast with those of the same age and in good health who may expect to live another 10 to 30 years. This variability is not trivial to the understanding of age changes. It is not surprising, for example, that older persons have nutritional needs and metabolic characteristics that are different and more limiting than those of their youth. If there is no particular value to the species in these functions lasting in optimal form beyond the reproductive period of life, then some may deteriorate as aging occurs, while others randomly persist.

Gerontologists, who study all aspects of aging, and geriatricians, the biomedical group interested in the health of the aged, must look at the aged as a population in which some of the physiological characteristics of the young continue, but in which other characteristics become altered in an irregular way and require further exploration (Tyson, 1999).

Life Expectancy and Life Span

There has been a gradual increase in life expectancy over time. If an individual had reached the age of 50 in early 1900s, this individual was considered to be old. People of that age were regarded in the same light as are people today who are 125 years of age.

There were a number of reasons to account for the earlier shorter life expectancy. The standard of living was lower, there were more environmental dangers, and women died in child birth more often. Currently, health concerns have been more successfully resolved due, in part, to the presence of advanced technologies allowing people to experience new health care interventions. Health care intervention has changed, along with the educational levels of the population. It was not until after World War II that many people had access to professional schools and institutions of higher learning. This was largely due to the G.I. Bill which provided such opportunity for war veterans. Better education, better jobs, and higher incomes all led to increases in life expectancy.

Gender differences with respect to life expectancy continue to persist. Life expectancy for females is approximately six to ten years greater than it is for males (Ferraro, 1997). Environmental factors for women differ from those of men. Men are more prone to experience industrial accidents, to become exposed to toxic substances, to be involved in greater numbers in automobile accidents, to participate in greater numbers in suicidal and homicidal deaths, and to engage in unhealthful lifestyles that include the abuse of alcohol and tobacco. All of these factors significantly reduce life expectancy. As a result, in most industrialized societies, the life expectancy for women exceeds that of men.

Life span, on the other hand, is species determined. The life span for the human species for some time had been considered as 100 years, but the figure now accepted is 125 years. There are mice that live six months and insects that live only hours. The average life span for the cat is approximately 25 years, the dog 30 years, the horse approximately 60 years, some turtles 125 years, and some birds 100 years. Aging, however, is experienced at different rates by individuals, and the rate of aging is affected by a wide variety of factors including heredity, lifestyle, economics, and the environment.

Technology, Religion, and Wars

The role of wars and religion in shaping the development of science and technology with respect to health care services and health and social services was of utmost significance (Ferraro, 1997). Early hospitals were constructed in the shape of a cross, and the religious precept of providing care to the needy bolstered the influence of religious groups. Monks were the first nurses. Subsequently, the establishment of nursing orders of nuns led to their specializing in nursing care.

Medical information was spread through wars, and soldiers often returned from distant lands with new knowledge in health care and new interventions. This was a significant contribution of the Crusades, which, although a religious war, resulted in bringing new medical knowledge from the East and North Africa to the European continent. The American Civil War was also a time for new medical discoveries. Anesthetics, surgery, embalming (preparing dead soldiers to send back to their families), and rehabilitation, including prosthetic devices and artificial limbs, were all prompted by the exigencies of war.

It was World War II, however, that revolutionized health care. The MASH units of World War II were largely responsible for the introduction of radical surgeries and treatment modalities in the care of the wounded. Providing care with minimal medical assistance or medication called for extensive innovation. Having to make do with just what was available proved to be a remarkable new training ground for many health care units. Emergency room service was altered significantly following World War II. Prior to that time, patients were picked up in a hearse, not in an ambulance. This daring spirit is what sparked the burgeoning of advanced health care technologies following World War II (Lesnoff-Caravaglia, 2001).

Aging and Terminology

Demarcations that specify age groupings are exceedingly important if older adults are to receive adequate health and social services. The labeling of populations through the use of euphemisms has led to the stereotyping of older persons and confusion in research findings.

Researchers have confounded their studies by dividing older persons into amorphous categories such as the "young old," "the old old," "the oldest old," "the frail elderly," "the well elderly," and "the long-living" (Spirduso, Francis, & MacRae, 2005). Others have facetiously referred to older age groups as "the slow go, "the no-go," and "the go-go;" or simply "the risky" and "the frisky" (Lesnoff-Caravaglia, 2000).

Dictionary terms do exist that permit the appropriate designation of terms to employ in describing older population groups according to age. They include:

Septuagenarians	70–79
Octogenarians	80–89
Nonagenarians	90–99
Centenarians	100–109
Centedecinarians	110–119
Centeventenarians	120–129
Centetrentenarians	130–139

The last three designations are neologisms coined to meet modern exigencies to properly define older age groups. A further advantage to the use of such nomenclature is that these terms have a Latin base and allow for international understanding and utilization.

Aging and Demography

A proper assessment of population growth and change is vital to proper planning for the needs and concerns of society. One such change which has decided ramifications for health care services is that the sector of the population that is aged 85 and older is growing at a rapid rate. This population group also suffers from multiple health problems and occasions greater costs in terms of health expenditures. Research on maintaining health in old age is also of economic interest in order to offset costs of hospitalization and long-term care.

The chronic, nonfatal disorders of longevity destroy the quality of life and drain society's resources. A full 80 percent of all deaths occur after age 65. People over the age of 85 are now the fastest growing segment of the population. Dementia, arthritis, diminished hearing and visual acuity, incontinence, and hip fractures all continue to occur at approximately the same age as they did in the past.

The extension of life expectancy has meant that persons, through appropriate prevention and intervention strategies, can live with such health problems and disabilities over longer periods of time. Furthermore, it is possible to defer disease and to minimize dysfunction.

Additional years of life spent bedfast or in an institutional setting are not the anticipated rewards of long life. While it is accepted that aging contributes to increased vulnerability to disease and disability, it is vital to understand what precedes or leads to particular types of dysfunction. The three major precursors to disease, which can be significantly altered through extensive research efforts, include genetics, aging, and the environment. To postpone dysfunction may, in the case of aging, carry greater significance with respect to life enhancement than the possibility for cure.

REFERENCES

Andrews, G. R. (Ed). (1998). Ageing beyond 2000: One world one future. *Australian Journal on Ageing, 17* (1), Supplement.

Backman, K., & Hentinen, M. (2001). Factors associated with the self-care of home-dwelling elderly. *Scandinavian Journal of Caring Science, 15,* 195–202.

Bang, W., Bien, Z., & Stefanov, D. H. (2004). The smarthouse for older persons and persons with physical disabilities: structure, technology, arrangements, and perspectives. *IEEE Transactions on Neural Systems and Rehabilitation Engineering, 12* (2), 228–250.

Calle, E., Thun, M., Petrelli, J., Rodriguez, C., & Health, C. (1999). Body-mass index and mortality in a prospective cohort of U.S. adults. *The New England Journal of Medicine, 341* (15), 1097–1105.

Ferraro, K. F. (Ed.). (1997). *Gerontology: Perspectives and issues* (2nd Ed.). New York: Springer.

Gott, M. (2005). *Sexuality, sexual health and ageing.* Maidenhead, England: Open University Press.

Hayflick, L. (1994). *How and why we age.* New York: Ballantine.

Hazzard, W. R. et al. (Eds.). (1999). *Principles of geriatric medicine and gerontology* (4th Ed). New York: McGraw-Hill, Health Professions Division.

Hughes, T. P. (2004). *Human-built world: How to think about technology and culture.* Chicago: University of Chicago Press.

Kannus, P., Niemi, S., Parkkari, J., Palvanen, M., Vuori, I., & Jaumlrvinen, M. (1999). Hip fractures in Finland between 1970 and 1997 and predictors for the future. *Lancet, 353* (9155), 802–805.

Lesnoff-Caravaglia, G. (1999). Ethical issues in a high-tech society. In T. Fusco Johnson (Ed.), *Handbook on ethical issues in aging* (pp. 271–288). Westport, CT: Greenwood Press.

Lesnoff-Caravaglia, G. (2000). *Health aspects of aging.* Springfield, IL: C. C Thomas Publishers, Ltd.

Lesnoff-Caravaglia, G. (2001). *Aging and public health.* Springfield, IL: C. C Thomas Publishers, Ltd.

Lesnoff-Caravaglia, G. & Klys, M. (1987). Lifestyle and longevity. In G. Lesnoff-Caravaglia (Ed.), *Realistic expectations for long life* (pp. 35–48). New York: Human Sciences Press.

Manuck, S. B., Jennings, R., Rabin, B.S., & Baum, A. (Eds.) (2000). *Behavior, health, and aging.* Mahwah, NJ: Lawrence Erlbaum Associates.

Montemagno, C. D., & Roco, M.C. (Eds.). (2004). *The coevolution of human potential and converging technologies.* New York: New York Academy of Sciences.

National Research Council (2003). *Technology for adaptive aging.* Washington D.C.: The Washington Academies Press.

Oram, J. J. (1997). *Caring for the fourth age.* London: Armelle.

Pathy, J. (Ed.). (1998). *Principles and practices of geriatric medicine* (3rd Ed.). Chichester, England: Wiley.

Rocket science to help Britain's elderly (2004, January 28). *Biotech Weekly,* p. 261.

Ross, I. K. (1995). *Aging of cells, humans & societies.* Dubuque, IA: Wm. C. Brown Publishers.

Shotton, L. (2003). The role of older people in our communities. *Nursing Ethics, 10* (1), 4–17.

Spirduso, W. W., Francis, K. L, & MacRae, P. G. (2005). *Physical dimensions of aging* (2nd Ed.). Champaign, IL: Human Kinetics.

Tyson, S. R. (1999). *Gerontological nursing care.* Philadelphia: Saunders.

Chapter 2

GERONTECHNOLOGY: THE CHALLENGE

GARI LESNOFF-CARAVAGLIA

There appears to be a new turn in the wheel of evolutionary progress. The increased and increasing adoption of technologies within everyday life contains an evolutionary aura, while the presence of technology is a decided spur toward advancing human growth and independence. Such an evolutionary aspect has encouraged a realistic assessment of what must be devised in order for older persons to continue to survive into advanced old age without the benefits of continued augmentative human growth and in the face of potential physical and mental decline. Although there is something remarkable about contemplating oneself as a centeventenarian, this feeling is coupled with a surge of fear that one might well continue to exist just as a shell of one's former self (Spirduso, Francis, & MacRae, 2005).

To offset such a possibility, the new mechanisms for survival are both person-oriented and environment-oriented. Person-oriented changes include adaptations such as dentures and organ transplants; whereas, adaptation to the environment has taken on a wide variety of constructs derived principally from computer technology. Such significant advances have been achieved through the mimicking of nature and the extending of human capabilities through artificial means.

The process of matching technological advances to human needs continues to move this evolutionary process forward. Marshall McLuhan was correct when he described wheels as extensions of feet, microphones as extensions of ears, and cameras as extensions of eyes (Alcorn, 1986). The technological evolutionary process has a long history, but it is only by virtue of the changes in demographic structure that the focus has become human survival. It was only partially in jest that Bernard Isaacs, the noted British geriatrician, entitled one of his books *Survival of the Unfittest*. The challenge of this age and whatever age may surface in the future (such as the gerobotic age) is that of harnessing or yoking together two contemporary phenomena: extreme human longevity and persistent and promiscuous technological advances (Bodoff, 2003).

The evolvement of modern science was due not so much by the acquisition of new knowledge about the world, but as a new way of thinking about that world in the broadest sense (Hatton & Plouffe, 1997). The discovery of innovative practical applications stems largely from such new connections or relationships. Demographic alterations, such as the emerging older population, provide new ground for adaptation or exploration.

Contemporary deliberations regarding the effects of technology upon society have their roots in debates that originated as far back as seven centuries. It is important to recognize that long before the dramatic changes precipitated by the Industrial Revolution could be firmly implanted on a large scale, such changes had to be foreshadowed by a slowly evolving reorientation of human values, habits, ideas, and goals. One of the major changes in lifestyle was brought on in the middle of the eighteenth century with the introduction of glass. The discovery of glass led to the lighting first of places of business, then homes with natural light through the placement of glass panes as windows. This led to their usage in instruments such as the microscope without which there could have been little by way of modern science or medicine. The invention of the printing press and electricity possessed the same capacity for irrevocable life alteration.

Just as the introduction of the stethoscope permitted the physician the ability to judge what went on in the patient internally, the microscope led to the determination of more secret bodily functions and structures. In fact, physicians became so enamored of their ability to ausculate and to learn of the bodily functions, that they often discredited the information offered by the patients themselves as to their health condition. The knowledge gained by listening and examination was considered to be far superior (Lesnoff-Caravaglia, 2000).

The reliance upon the machine, however, to provide information, to monitor human beings, to propel them about, to feed them, to virtually control every aspect of human life does not preclude its use as an instrument to determine death. Modern developments in life-sustaining technologies, their use or nonuse, has played a major role in health care practice (Hjorth, 2000).

Viewing the growth of technology as springing from a network of relationships tied to a host of additional cultural factors leads to a better understanding of the present applications of technology, the areas of technological growth and expansion currently being fostered, and the present attitude about present and future possible uses of technology. This view also broadens the understanding of the ways in which technology has altered not only the exterior but the interior worlds of human experiencing. Such a broad view allows for an evaluation of the level of acceptance or rejection of technology, along with the range of fears that technological expansion has engendered (Armitage, 2000).

The presence of large numbers of persons aged 65 or older in the nation is leading to changes as novel and dramatic as those experienced during the First Industrial Revolution. The initiation of such changes occurred at the end of the nineteenth century, became evident in the twentieth century, and will continue to fashion life in the twenty-first century, resulting in a Second Industrial Revolution.

As larger portions of the population experience diminished capacities in coping with the activities of daily life, there has been a concomitant decrease in the labor force of persons capable or willing to assist with such tasks. The adoption of new lifestyles, geographical distance, divorce, death, or the advanced ages of adult children has diminished the presence of support groups in the home such as children, spouses, or relatives. Thus the reliance upon people as an appropriate resource is less and less a viable alternative. The lack of personnel to provide such services spurred the development of technologies as methods of intervention (Armstrong & Frueh, 2003).

Technological innovation has irretrievably altered the course of human lives. It continues, however, to evoke strong positive and negative reactions. The introduction of a new technology brings in its wake the possibility of unforeseen inherent occurrences and the potential for accidents or malfunction.

Increases in life expectancy to ages of 125 and beyond can also potentially embody the notion of the unforeseen, in that advances in technology are largely responsible for increases in life expectancy (Schulz-Aellen, 1997). The effects of such life extension upon society and the individual have yet to be determined. The advent of legislation regarding "mercy killing" or the termination of one's own life in some nations may lead to new views of what constitutes "life" and the appropriate timing of death. Also, the future may hold totally new diseases and disabilities which result from the increases in life expectancy. There may well be future references to the "accident" of old age.

Technology: The Practical Application of Science

The practical application of science can be at either the levels of high technology or low technology. On occasion, simple solutions on the level of low technology, such as redesigning tools or altering home environments, have more practical outcomes. Some high technology streams, such as genetics, robotics, informatics, and, in particular, communication technology provide the potential for very powerful and controversial applications (Sivard, Bradley, Chadwick, & Higgins, 2004). For example, the science of genetics is leading to the possibility of predicting such conditions as heart disease and Alzheimer's disease.

In industrial applications, robotics has meant freeing labor from unwanted repetitive tasks, as well as freeing up labor for more important tasks. It has also been instrumental in effecting speed of production in areas such as automobile manufacture. Such applications of robotics can be used to meet human needs, as well. The most important feature of the application of robotics so far is that it has provided a certain amount of dignity for the individual who is helped. It offers the promise of being able to do things for oneself that normally require a caregiver to perform. For example, fetch-and-carry systems could routinely deliver various supplies to the rooms of some nursing home residents. A robotic system, Helpmate, is being used in hospitals to deliver late trays and to perform errands.

Communication is probably the most important feature of human experience in that it mitigates isolation and prevents depression. Although many of today's elderly have had limited experience with computers, they are increasingly receptive to using the new technology, either "as is" or when tailored to their needs. The elderly of the future are likely to be more open to using computers because of exposure to them throughout their lifetimes, as well as their recognition of the empowerment aspects inherent in being abreast of new technology (Thompson, 2003). This also serves to explain the omnipresence of the cellular phone.

Computer-Assisted Health Instruction

The use of computer-assisted health instruction is a logical extension of self-care and self-help (Hummert & Nussbaum, 2001). The growing use of information technologies for educating the public about maintaining health, and preventing or treating disease, is rapidly increasing the number of software programs on health education and management (Carbonara, 2005). The relevance of this technological phenomenon for use by and for the elderly has not yet been widely recognized in either the private or public sector; however, the use of information technologies, particularly the microcomputer, could help the elderly maintain independent living, and is likely to be particularly effective when used in conjunction with physicians and other health care providers.

Future computer use by patients is expected to reach beyond providing them with information about their health status to become a virtual "hospital on the wrist." The concept of the hospital on the wrist includes a computer, a microminiature analyzer, and drug reservoirs with electronic probes. It is capable of monitoring changes in the body, measuring vital signs, analyzing blood and enzymes, cardiac monitoring, and comparing findings with expected values for the individual wearing it. The device would be able to communicate with computers of the wearer's physician as well as with computers in hospitals or other medical institutions and could administer drugs directly through the skin. It could also signal the patient when direct medical care was needed.

As envisioned, the hospital on the wrist does not offer the patient total medical autonomy but includes interactions between the patient, his or her computer, and the computers of health professionals. Computers and telecommunications now in use by patients for health purposes are oriented to assisting physicians and other health professionals with patient management in various health settings (Hummert & Nussbaum, 2001; Bangert & Doktor, 2005).

Computer-assisted health care that complements professional care may enable chronically ill people to remain in their homes when they wish to do so. A number of factors point to an increase in the proportion of the chronically ill population who may choose home care over institutional care in the future. Moreover, advances in medical technology now allow services to be provided at home that once required an institutional setting. Reductions in size and complexity have made many machines portable. Telecommunication equipment connecting patients and health professionals can facilitate their interaction and enhance the quality of care.

"Smart" sensors that incorporate microprocessors currently sense and measure blood pressure, pulse rates, body temperature, blood glucose, and electrical activity of the heart. Measurements of other physical functions have been developed for use in rehabilitating handicapped patients. Those that have the potential for computer-based processing may be applicable for monitoring the health status of segments of the older population. Computer technology can enable hospital-based approaches for managing chronic diseases to be expanded to the home.

Computers that monitor household functions such as turning on and off lights, radios, and televisions, and providing wake-up service by voice synthesizers that speak preprogrammed messages, could be programmed to remind elderly persons of medication times, diet and medical care practices, and physician and other health professional visits. Devices could be programmed to track medicinal intake and periodically dispense medicines. A bedside automated programmable dispensing machine has been developed for use in hospitals that may be adaptable for use in the home (Thilmany, 2004).

Medical Devices and Instrumentation for the Elderly

The human body is endowed from birth with many natural defenses, including autoimmunity and redundancy of tissues, organs, and parts, enabling it to resist the changes that come with age, disease, and trauma. As human beings age, such natural defenses gradually fail and may require replacements. The growing number of medical devices and instrumentation that has characterized modern health care, along with transplants, may well substitute for loss of such natural defenses. This may also pave the way for the technological control of human bodily functions.

Society has rejected two of the most obvious remedies of the past, hiding the disability or hiding the disabled. Alternatives are now available in aids that are attractive, and that would be used without reservation, and, in some cases, even with pride. Such aids run the gamut from the vast array of visual aids to prosthetic devices and footgear.

Technological advances in the medical-device area have had a profound impact on patient survival and improved quality of life. The benefits have been particularly notable for chronic diseases or dysfunctions that become more prevalent with increasing age. Technologies that have increased life expectancy include advances in public hygiene and sanitation, reductions in infectious diseases, and continued improvement and accessibility of general health care. Today's medical devices can improve the functioning of, and, in some instances, replace body parts that have deteriorated due to age or disease. Some examples include dental prostheses that are utilized in cases of tooth loss, artificial knees, hip prostheses, and mechanical aids that help with problems of mobility.

The most significant contributions have been made in the area of implantable systems. These include intraocular lenses, heart valves, urethral sphincters, penile implants, cochlear implants, electrical pain control, cardiac pacemakers, defibrillators, artificial joints, and drug pumps. In each instance, the intent is to return the patient to a situation as close to normal as the state of the art permits. By virtue of their being implanted, these devices become relatively transparent to the patient. They tend to free the patient of the responsibility as well as the emotional involvement that may accompany the disease.

The use of body parts from cadavers has occasioned ethical dilemmas, but has also acted as an incentive for the production of mechanical substitutes. The use of a cadaver hand has followed this practice. Recent developments in the artificial hand, the cyberhand, which restores movement and the sense of touch to the fingers, is one such advance. Such a device also allows for handwriting and activities such as turning a book page.

With the advances in home health care, the older population can receive intravenous medications in a home setting instead of the hospital. This helps prevent environmental confusion in that companionship and security in familiar surroundings are available. Services such as homemakers allow older persons to maintain mobility in the household. Video and audio cassettes are helpful in rehabilitation. Large type is available in health instruction magazines and with medical instructions.

Ethical dilemmas abound with respect to when, where, and how to utilize such medical interventions. They involve the deliberations of physicians, social workers, and third-party payers who become, in fact, gatekeepers in terms of health care allocation (Lehoux, Saint-Arnaud, & Richard, 2004). When would a person be considered too old to be given a particular device? What is the rationale for keeping older persons alive when they suffer from irreversible brain disease or dementia? The responses to such questions become increasingly more complex as medical technology and science continue to advance and to provide alternative treatment possibilities. Technology now can control the timing and quality of individual demise.

The Brave "Old" World

The crisis in health care personnel has led to an even closer scrutiny of the potential uses of technology in health care environments. If there are insufficient numbers of persons available to perform services, machines (robots) must do the work. For example, with the reduction in adequate numbers of personnel, clerical work often performed by nurses can be more efficiently accomplished by computers, allowing nurses more time for one-on-one nursing care (Hein, 2001).

Another example is in the lifting and moving of patients. This can be more easily and safely accomplished through appropriate devices, thus reducing the number of staff required, as well as lessening the severity of back problems sustained by health care personnel. The debate with respect to "high touch versus high tech" has virtually vanished from the scene because it is now patently clear that it is possible to increase high touch only when aided by the presence of high tech.

Lifestyles of caregivers, such as family members, can be appreciably ameliorated through the introduction of technologies in the home environment. One such advance is the development of a wearable computer system with a hands-free operation interface for the use of home health caregivers (Mizuno et al., 2005). The ability to remain in control of one's life even in very advanced old age allows for individual dignity and self-esteem. Both elements are significant factors in the maintenance of physical and psychological well-being.

States of dependency are made up of a variety of factors. They include experiencing multiple chronic symptoms; a limitation on personal options; dependency on the physical environment that was once taken for granted; and dependency on persons drawn from the family unit or public agencies. To grow old and to be well has not been a common human experience. Increases in life expectancy means that persons can live long lives without experiencing many limitations. Once they begin to experience some restrictions, dependency becomes a source of deep and abiding frustration.

Shrinking of the Personal World

Just as the expansion of the world is a gradual and often overwhelming experience for the young child, the subtle contraction of the world and one's capability to experience it is also fraught with fear and questioning on the part of older persons. Older individuals tend to use less and less of what can be termed the total environment. This gradual restriction often begins when the person leaves the world of work at retirement. A second point at which there is a reduced level of participation in the outside world occurs when the individual experiences the onset of a chronic illness. Further restrictions occur as the individual ages and sensory deficits, such as vision or hearing losses, become more intensified. Such physical alterations can, at times, be sufficiently severe to constitute a need to alter individual lifestyle (Latham, Bogner, Hamilton, & Blanarovich, 1999). A frequent change is to limit outside activities, with a concomitant increased usage of the home environment.

Home environments are utilized at a much higher rate by older persons due to physical constraints, economic difficulties, and even psychological conditions such as fear (Pearce, 1998). The location of the residence of the person plays an important role in the perception of safety within the environment and the view of the outside environment as being essentially hostile. Such a restriction to the home environment leads to what can be termed as "basic-needs orientation." Requirements for the carrying out of activities of daily living (ADLs) take on increasing importance as the limitations due to senescent changes and disabilities due to disease continue to escalate (Arthur, Clarke, Jagger, & Spiers, 2001).

Independence in this shrinking environment continues to be eroded, and there is the necessary enlistment of outside resources. The entrance of other family members, health care personnel, social service agencies, and a host of other assistive groups into the individual's private life means the lessening of decision-making power by the older person. As the individual gradually loses control of his or her personal life due to illness, immobility, or sensory loss, the control of that life is assumed by outside agencies. Such a decrease in control is usually followed by further constrictions of the individual world.

The types of activities that usually suffer some restriction generally fall into the categories of instrumental activities of daily living (IADLs) or activities of daily living (ADLs). Although many of these activities are considered routine, their performance reflects upon individual functional capabilities. Problems in the performance of such activities are frequently the basis for a determination as to whether or not the person can live independently and whether institutionalization needs to be considered.

One intervention that can help offset some problems is the development of augmentative technologies that permit persons to perform many of the activities necessary for independent living. Decreasing abilities to use particular appliances, to utilize the entire living space, or to provide for the accommodation of sensory losses, reduced mobility, and the reduction in physical strength can all be counteracted by modifications of existing homes or the construction of homes that are prosthetic in nature. The conventional home may be a lethal environment for the older person.

A simple series of inexpensive alterations such as adding more lighting or including press-on or motion sensor light switches; adding dual-sided banisters on stairways; creating adjustable countertops; implementing lever controlled door knobs; laying carpets with a tight weave to prevent tripping; or installing safety bars or hand-held showers in the bathroom, can make such a choice a reality. Since the elderly spend more time at home than any other demographic group, a constant upgrading or retrofitting of their homes to keep up with changing capabilities is an important health issue.

Physical movement also is restricted as the environment shrinks. Contrary to the dictates of human health requirements, older persons become more sedentary and engage in less exercise. Part of this reduced physical activity results from reduced participation in the environment because of physical or environmental barriers. Environmental barriers can include the structure of the home, its layout, and the presence of stairs. Storage space and appliances may be difficult to access or use, thus cutting back on the person's activity.

Shrinkage of the environment due to the nature of the environment itself means that there is a lack of fit between the person and the environment. Such a lack of consonance means that the person is less stimulated by the environment and finds it to be more of a frustration. Increasingly, drawing away from the environment and curtailing their ability to manipulate the environment to their own best advantage results in persons losing control of their lives, and, eventually, of themselves. Both physical and mental deterioration may result, and it is at this juncture that a loss of interest in life may manifest itself. Coupled with such negative views of the self are the feelings of impotence and uselessness, which can lead to suicidal ideation.

Aging and Technology: The New Frontier

The technological advances that have resulted in a significant extension of the life expectancy have also contributed to the improvement in the quality of life. Specifically, these advances have dramatically enhanced the ability to be mobile. Mobility that is conducive to walking, as well as small-muscle coordination, is essential to the activities of daily living.

Surgical technology can improve eyesight, retard joint degeneration, and reduce deafness. Pharmaceutical technology has improved the medications for the maintenance of chronic conditions and the elimination of acute ones. Advances in science, technology, and medicine have allowed for research into cellular and molecular behavior which is resulting in the potential retarding of aging and in facilitating the maintenance of health. Technology can be viewed as the stimulus for maintaining youthful, spontaneous, and efficient behaviors.

The development of technology and its use fosters behavior and responses in the elderly that are reflective of the expected norm. As technology produces assistive devices with greater accuracy and sensitivity, it works inherently to achieve growthful responses in individuals that can then be interpreted as improving healthy behavior in older persons.

Assistive devices at the macro and micro levels are geared essentially to maintain the status quo. Aging, however, should not be geared toward normative behavior. Rather, this is the time of life when uniqueness, individuality, interests, and enthusiasms untempered by responsibilities and spontaneous expression of feeling can best come forth. Technology helps in this, of course. Nonetheless, it is assistive rather than an end in itself. It reduces physical difficulties but needs to allow the emergence of the person, one more unique and satisfying than previously known. Rather than retard aging, technology can move individuals to a level of aging not yet achieved, but one that is now possible.

There are currently strategies being practiced to delay osteoporosis and hip fracture. Hip fracture is closely related to osteoporosis and progressive bone degeneration. Such interventions include modification in diets and exercise, therapeutic regimens using hormones, medications and vitamins, and, finally, taking precautions to avoid falls (Spirduso, Francis, & MacRae, 2005). Further research can lead to the uncovering of mechanisms which slow down what is now considered as a normal pattern of bone loss with age.

Aging-dependent diseases are those which rise steadily with age, accumulating as people live longer. Such diseases and conditions include cerebrovascular disease, dementias, vision loss, hearing loss, Type II diabetes and altered glucose metabolism; hip fracture, osteoporosis, Parkinson's disease, specific infections such as pneumococcal pneumonia; constipation, incontinence, signs of depression, social isolation, living alone, widowhood, or institutionalization. Aging can be considered as a series of risk factors providing fertile soil for numerous events. With age comes the occurrence of more than one aging-dependent disease or condition.

There is a second class of diseases and conditions that can be termed age-dependent. Such diseases occur at a certain time in life and, if an individual passes through the susceptible period, the disease is much less likely to develop. Age-dependent diseases are slow viruses which, by definition, produce diseases in which there is no immune component. In age-dependent disease it is important to expand on the possibilities of postponement of onset by keeping people in the critical age from succumbing to the disease. By delaying onset, it is possible to prevent the illness.

Diseases that are candidates for postponement include Alzheimer's disease and related dementias, loss of vision and hearing, arthritis, incontinence, and osteoporosis. Postponement of these diseases would have a greatly beneficial effect upon late life (Jacobsen, 2002). What is needed is information on how to slow down some of the physiological and structural elements which increase susceptibility to these diseases. A major goal would be achieved in solely postponing such events, without achieving a total cure, particularly for those diseases which do not kill but compromise the quality of life.

The increase in life expectancy necessitates that researchers direct more of their efforts toward diseases which make aging a burdensome experience. Unfortunately, there is the potential for living longer, but sicker.

Muscle weakness that accompanies advanced age increases the risk of falling and fracture. The very old and frail experience skeletal muscle atrophy as a result of disuse, disease, undernutrition, and the effects of senescence. Sarcopenia, defined as the age-related loss in skeletal muscle mass, results in decreased strength and aerobic capacity, and thus functional capacity (Spirduso, Francis, & MacRae, 2005). Through physical exercise and training, primarily resistance training, it may be possible to prevent sarcopenia and the associated abnormalities such as noninsulin dependent diabetes mellitus (NIDDM), coronary artery disease, hypertension, osteoporosis, and obesity. An exercise program can increase muscle strength and endurance at any age. There is no pharmacological intervention that holds a greater promise of improving health and promoting independence in the elderly than does exercise. Functional capacity in old age is more the result of lifestyle rather than chronology.

It may not be clear as to what holistic, social, or intellectual achievements can be attained by the elderly. It is patently clear, though, that without a responsive, supportive environment and without stimulation of growth-related qualities, those achievements will be less. Such an environment must recognize that the individual, regardless of age, is growing, changing, and evolving. The concept of evolving is key as it shapes and gives purpose to the use of technology. This continued evolution is largely uncharted and unexpected in aging individuals. The current expectations about aging include a continued, expected decline that can be bolstered and minimized through various supports now available, or, at best, that those elderly who are healthy and have sufficient financial means will lead satisfactory lives.

It is also important to bear in mind that the elderly are not the handicapped. Their concerns and problems may stem from similar dysfunctions, but the problems of the elderly are precipitated and experienced in old age and are often brought on by the process of normal aging. In addition, there is insufficient anthropometric data on the elderly. Not enough is known about reaching capabilities or the strength potential of older persons. Functional body measurements are needed that define not only what the elderly are, but what they can do in terms of body movements, ambulation, arm and leg reaches, and task performance—the kinds of data needed by engineers who deal with the design of housing, health and chronic-care facilities, transport vehicles, appliances and equipment, and prostheses. Most of the studies done in these areas have been based on males in their mid-twenties, leaving a serious research gap. This is particularly true of the development of wheelchairs.

In order to provide for a continuity of experience for older persons, surveys or assessments of homes must be an ongoing activity. Such inventories or assessments can evaluate what is presently available to the individual, as well as what can be added to the environment to ensure greater independence. A degree of choice must be afforded the older person with respect to either the inclusion or dismissal of particular technologies. As changes are required to adequately accommodate the needs of older persons, home arrangements and the additions of technologies need to be a steady feature of the provision of care. Since accidents figure so prominently in the health care of older persons, safety is an important aspect of all home assessments and contributes to the reduction of overall health care expenditures.

Providers of services to the elderly can also utilize many of the housekeeping technologies, with the added bonus of having those chores that are boring, repetitious, demeaning, or overly fatiguing performed through mechanical means. The presence of technological devices can significantly add to the interpersonal exchanges between caregiver and client due to less time being given to routine activities. The cost of such home health care would be markedly reduced due to lower labor costs.

Losses in Old Age

The range of losses experienced by older persons cannot be equated with losses experienced at any other time in an individual's personal history. Many of these losses are of a permanent nature and strike at the very heart of personal identity: work role, social role, loss of sensory acuity, the death of nearly everyone one has known, and an alteration in the relationship between the self and the environment. When physical, economic, and familial changes are the norm, individuals begin to question their personal identity. Neighborhood changes are often viewed as a form of death. Once initiated, many of these changes are irreversible.

Another factor that has important implications for the acceptance and use of technologies is the fact that the older population is made up principally of females. Females generally have received little exposure to things mechanical or technical.

The Environment

The fit or lack of fit between the person and the environment has a determining effect upon when aging occurs and how the process is made manifest. The environment as the locus for aging provides a significant point of interaction that largely influences why particular changes are experienced with advancing age. Environments that do not adequately match the needs and interests of the elderly often serve to accelerate the aging process, resulting in premature aging. Prosthetic environments that are malleable to the needs and interests of the elderly can be regarded as augmentative in that they serve to extend the capacities of aging persons and are geared toward promoting continued maximal functioning.

Traditional home, institutional, and work environments can maximize or restrict optimal functioning in the elderly. The incorporation of both high and low technologies in such key settings can offset the decrements of age. Electronic cottages permit people to continue to conduct a variety of occupational roles while remaining in the home setting.

Through an electronically controlled environment, control can be exerted through the interaction with a finger, an eye, or a voice. Behavior is accommodated to the type of control to be effected and the capabilities of the user. The only exceptions might be the acts of eating, washing, dressing, or toileting. The blind or paralyzed person can be viewed as the model for the visually or mobilely disabled occupant of the intelligent home (Virilio, 2000). A remote control provides the power to control the domestic environment. The user's energy and motor body triggers the utilization of the domestic functions. Environmental control can lead to a sedentary society with the home activity analogous to the activity of astronauts moving around in high orbit (Virilio, 2000). This can produce a type of fixedness resulting in a seated or couched individual as a prototype of the future.

In much the same way that the experience of a life long lived is altering the needs and wishes of the elderly, their own increasing sophistication and knowledge of their own health status and the health care system convince them that most traditional health care settings are inappropriate. As the educational level, political acumen, and economic status of the elderly continue to rise, the demand for health care within the home setting or the community will also increase.

Not only does technology provide the freedom for the making of personal decisions, but it also frees caregivers from routine activities and allows for more time to be spent in meaningful personal interactions (Engelhardt, 1989). Examples of ways in which robotics can be used in health care settings include the following: transfer of patients (lifting), housekeeping, ambulation, physical therapy, depuddler (cleaning of human and pet wastes), surveillance, physician assistance, nursing assistance, patient assistance, fetch and carry, and cognitive rehabilitation. The successful utilization of such technologies rests largely on attitudes of caregivers, patients, and family members (Harwin, 1997; Forlizzi, DiSalvo, & Gemperle, 2004; Songmin & Yoshiro, 2004).

The robotic systems that will best serve the needs of the most severely disabled individuals will be those that have a high degree of machine intelligence. The need for sensitive and delicate touch will be mandatory in a robotic aid intended to help lift or to transfer a paralyzed patient whose body or garments must be handled with a confident but gentle touch.

Automated Guided Vehicle Systems technology is already performing materials-handling tasks in industry. This same technology can be utilized in an institutional health care environment to transport meals, drinks, and personal items to patients. Such a mobile robotic device could also move from patient to patient, collect vital-signs data, and, with two way communication, provide a link with the centralized nursing station. Robots can perform tasks that health care providers find boring, repetitive, degrading, or dangerous. Robotic technologies hold the possibility for playing a role in both patient therapy and therapist training. A system that can deliver range-of-motion exercises for muscle maintenance, if properly designed, can also serve as a teaching tool for student therapists because it could be programmed to mimic certain disabilities.

There are currently a number of technologies that have broad applicability and not only serve in a rehabilitative capacity, but provide freedom for a broad range of activities. Examples of technologies with such liberating features include eyeglasses, hearing aids, pacemakers, talking books, and Kurzweil reading machines. Furthermore, devices such as eyeglasses have no side effects and open up a broad arena of activities for the user in the vocational as well as avocational spheres of life. Devices for the elderly must find such a broad market base in order to ensure their development, utilization, and acceptability as ordinary features of life.

Equally important are those features of daily life that can promote and encourage the taking on of responsibilities by patients. One such possibility lies in the development of reminding technologies. In developing reminding technologies, it is important to place sufficient emphasis upon the reaction of the older person to the technology. Such concern must focus upon how the information is delivered, that is, whether the speed is appropriate, and whether the rate at which the information is given is meaningful. Whether such information is accepted to the point of provoking action or a response may be related to the gender or language of the speaker.

It is even conceivable that robots can be designed that can make the environment so sensitive that it can provide respite care. Sensitive monitoring instruments can serve to offset accidents and to develop an environment that focuses upon intervention and prevention rather than simply custodial or policing care. One robot can fulfill a variety of functions from cleaning spills to paper shredding; there is now the possibility that robots can even reproduce themselves by way of programs of replication.

Technology and Long-term Care

The relationship between technology and aging underscores the importance of functional ability for maintaining the independence of the elderly, along with maximizing their options and improving their quality of life. The growth of the aging population is likely to increase the demand for long-term care and the need for assistance, principally for those aged 85 and older who face a combination of incapacitating and largely unavoidable infirmities (Stoil, 2004).

With the increase in life expectancy, individuals will increasingly survive into ages where the prevalence of chronic and debilitating conditions rises significantly. Eighty percent or more of persons over the age of 65 have at least one identifiable chronic disease or condition, the most common being arthritis, impaired hearing or vision, diabetes, chronic heart conditions, respiratory problems, and some degree of mental failure. Technological advances potentially provide a means for dealing with at least some of the disabilities often associated with aging and which frequently lead to the need for costly long-term care (Hutlock, 2003).

The health of the caregivers and the health of the care receiver must be jointly considered. That which benefits the caregiver can also result in lower staff turnover. For example, the technology that can be employed for patient lifting and moving may not be immediately perceived as having such a beneficial effect, but the reciprocal nature of the provision and the receipt of care are too often lost. The incorporation of technology into long-term care settings thus plays a dual role that enhances the environment from both the perspective of the patient and the care provider.

Gerontechnology

What the blend of aging and technology can look like is largely dependent upon attitudes toward the elderly and the appropriate utilization of technologies in areas such as home heath care, education, work/retirement schemes, and adaptive lifestyles. As the population continues to age, it is likely that increasing numbers of those aged 85 or older will face incapacitating and largely unavoidable infirmities.

Most current projections regarding the impact of an aging population, however, assume an elderly population with characteristics similar to those of persons living in the present day, such as withdrawal from the work force, declining health, increased need for hospitalization and nursing care, and other characteristics that suggest a highly dependent 65 and older age group. Improved health care, increased understanding of the physiology of aging, and continued advances in technology may well alter the characteristics of the elderly of the future. In addition, applications of computers, robotics, telecommunications, and other technical innovations in the home and workplace may provide new opportunities for increasing independence, productivity, and quality of life for the elderly.

When the contemporary world is looked upon from a historical perspective, it is clear that there has been an evolutionary progression. Planes have become the wings dreamed of by Daedalus, and people do walk on water, albeit on the decks of ships. Astronauts have explored the moon and found that it was not made of green cheese, and scientists have discovered that it is not brownies who curdle milk, but bacteria (Mumford, 1963).

New mysteries are being constantly uncovered in the world of the computer, robotics, and a host of other systems with equally complex features. Once a technology is invented, it usually advances to be perfected again and again. The process of aging is equally irrevocable; populations will continue to age in large numbers. The late premier of the former Soviet Union, Nikita Khruschev, was quoted as having observed that the world has moved, in one generation, from the outhouse to outer space (Lesnoff-Caravaglia, 1999).

REFERENCES

Alcorn, P. A. (1986). *Social issues in technology: A format for investigation.* Englewood Cliffs, NJ: Prentice Hall.

Armitage, J. (Ed.). (2000). *Paul Virilio. From modernism to hypomodernism and beyond.* Thousand Oaks, CA: Sage.

Armstrong, M. L., & Frueh, S. (2003). *Telecommunications for nurses: Providing successful distance education and telehealth* (2nd Ed.). New York: Springer Publishing.

Arthur, A. J., Clarke, M., Jagger, C., & Spiers, N. A. (2001). Patterns of onset of disability in activities of daily living with age. *JAGS, 49,* 404–409.

Bangert, D. C., & Doktor, R. (Eds.). (2005). *Human and organizational dynamics in e-health.* Oxford, England: Radcliffe.

Bodoff, R. (2003, January). New technology should serve the elderly. *Nursing Homes: Long Term Care Management, 52* (1), 6.

Carbonara, D. D. (Ed.). (2005). *Technology literacy applications in learning environments.* Hershey, PA: Information Science Publishers.

Engelhardt, K. G. (1989). Health and human service Robotics: A multi-dimensional perspective. *International Journal of Technology and Aging, 2* (1), 6–41.

Forlizzi, J., DiSalvo, C., & Gemperle, F. (2004, March). Assistive robotics and an ecology of elders living independently in their homes. *Human–Computer Interaction, 19* (1/2), 25–59.

Harwin, W. S. (1997). Robots with a gentle touch: Advances in assistive robotics and prosthetics. *Technology & Health Care, 7* (6), 411–417.

Hatton, J., & Plouffe, P. B. (1997). *Science and its ways of knowing.* Upper Saddle River, NJ: Prentice Hall.

Hein, E. C. (Ed.). (2001). *Nursing issues in the 21st century: Perspectives from the literature.* Philadelphia: Lippincott.

Hjorth, L. S. (Ed.). (2000). *Technology and society: A bridge to the 21st century.* Upper Saddle River, NJ: Prentice Hall.

Hummert, M. L., & Nussbaum, J. F. (Eds.). (2001). *Aging, communication, and health: Linking research and practice for successful aging.* Mahwah, NJ: Lawrence Erlbaum Associates.

Hutlock, T. (2003, October). The 'smart technology' future is now. *Nursing Homes: Long Term Care Management, 52* (10), 84–90.

Jacobsen, J. S. (2002, April). Alzheimer's disease: An overview of current and emerging therapeutic strategies. *Current Topics in Medicinal Chemistry, 2* (4), 343–352.

Lathan, C. E., Bogner, M. S., Hamilton, D., & Blanarovich, A. (1999). Human-centered design of home care technologies. *NeuroRehabilitation, 12* (1), 3–10.

Lehoux, P., Saint-Arnaud, J., & Richard, L. (2004, July). The use of technology at home: What patient manuals say and sell vs. what patients face and fear. *Sociology of Health & Illness, 26* (5), 617–644.

Lesnoff-Caravaglia, G. (1999). Ethical issues in a high-tech society. In T. Fusco Johnson (Ed.), *Handbook on ethical issues in aging* (pp. 271–288). Westport, CT: Greenwood Press.

Lesnoff-Caravaglia, G. (2000). *Health aspects of aging.* Springfield, IL: C. C Thomas, Publisher, Ltd.

Mizuno, F., Hayasaka, T., Tsubota, K., Wada, S., & Yamaguchi, T.(2005). Development of a wearable computer system with a hands-free operation interface for the use of home health caregiver. *Technology & Health Care, 13* (4), 293–300.

Mumford, L. (1963). *Technics and civilization.* New York: Harcourt, Brace & World.

Pearce, B. W. (1998). *A complete guide: Senior living communities.* Baltimore: The Johns Hopkins University Press.

Schultz-Aellen, M. (1997). *Aging and human longevity.* Cambridge, MA: Birkhauser Baston.

Sivard, A., Bradley, P., Chadwick, P., & Higgins, H. (2004, November). The challenge of designing in-body communications. *Embedded Systems Programming, 17* (11), 20–27.

Songmin, J. H., & Yoshiro; T. K. (2004). Human-assistance robotic system based on distributed computing technology. *Advanced Robotics, 18* (5), 515–532.

Spirduso, W. W., Francis, K. L., & MacRae, P. G. (2005). *Physical dimensions of aging* (2nd Ed.). Champaign, IL: Human Kinetics.

Stoil, M.J. (2004, May). Technology as a solution–and a policy problem? *Nursing Homes: Long Term Care Management, 53* (5), 12–16.

Thilmany, J. (2004). Aids for the elderly. *Mechanical Engineering, 126* (4), 10–14.

Thompson, T. L. (Ed.). (2003). *Handbook of health communication.* Mahwah, NJ: Lawrence Erlbaum Associates.

Virilio, P. (2000). *Polar inertia.* (P. Camiller, Trans.). Thousand Oaks, CA: Sage.

PART II

Chapter 3

AGE-RELATED CHANGES WITHIN BIOLOGICAL SYSTEMS: INTEGUMENTARY, SKELETAL, AND MUSCULAR

GARI LESNOFF-CARAVAGLIA

Although the systems within the body are described as separate systems, they do not operate independently but often share or complement bodily functions. They are treated as separate systems in order to understand their functioning for didactic purposes. They are, however, intimately interconnected. For example, what happens to the respiratory system can affect the digestive system; which, in turn, can affect the general balance of the organism or the homeostasis of the body. Such interrelationships between body systems are also an important consideration in introducing technologies whether in the administration of medications, applications of prostheses, the performance of surgery, or alterations in the human environment (Ham, Sloane, & Warshaw, 2002).

THE INTEGUMENTARY SYSTEM

Outward signs of aging, such as the graying of hair, the wrinkling of skin, or stooped posture, do not necessarily indicate the level of energy or activity of which an individual may be capable (Chop & Robnett, 1999).

The integumentary system involves the entire surface of the body through skin, hair or nails. The first reaction to the environment is reflected through the skin. The sensing of heat or cold causes the body to approach or to withdraw. Sweat glands, which are important to the maintenance of appropriate body temperature, are located in the skin. In addition, the skin serves as a barrier to prevent the intrusion of foreign substances into the body such as toxins or poisons. It serves as a protection against the bites of insects and the infiltration of microorganisms. The skin not only serves as a barrier, it can also serve as a useful surface for the administration of certain medications because of their easy absorption through the skin (Spence, 1995).

Along with the network of sweat glands, there is also a layer of blood vessels which help in the regulating of temperature and in the homeostasis of the body. When the body temperature rises, the blood vessels dilate and spread out to provide more blood closer to the surface of the skin. The moisture provided by the sweat glands covers the surface of the body which is then evaporated, and the body is cooled. In older persons this temperature regulating system operates less efficiently, and this explains, in part, why when temperatures rise, there is an increase in the incidence of older persons suffering from heat stroke or dying.

Heat, cold, and sensitivity to pain and touch are relayed to the brain through the skin. Since the skin surface reacts easily to drug absorption, it is often used to counteract illness such as motion sickness or to alter smoking habits. Skin patches are effective because the skin can absorb the chemical compounds that make up the drug. Anything that passes through the skin eventually enters the blood stream, and, consequently, does not need to be injected or taken orally. Furthermore, it provides a constant dosage for a long period of time. Use of the skin for treatment is particularly important in medicating older persons who may have difficulty in swallowing (Sunderkotter, Kalden, & Luger, 1997).

Because of its location on the body surface, the integumentary system is influenced by environmental factors as well as changes within the body. Wrinkles and sagging skin appear, and the skin tends to become thinner, less pliable, and dryer. There is a generalized loss of fat from the hypodermis beneath the skin, which, coupled with diminished elasticity, causes the skin to become loose resulting in folds and wrinkles to become prominent. This fat loss causes the body framework to become more obvious, which can give an emaciated appearance to some older persons.

Although the number of pigment-producing cells diminishes significantly with age, those remaining move closer together to form dark age spots (Ross, 1995). Nails become thicker and curved, while growing more slowly. There is a generalized loss of hair, and the remaining hair tends to lose its color and to appear gray.

Overall, the integumentary system comprises the skin, hair, nails, and various glands located in the skin (Pathy, 1998). All of these components help maintain a stable internal environment (homeostasis) within the body so that the various cells composing the body are able to function normally.

Epidermis and Dermis

The epidermis, as the superficial portion of the skin, is generally quite thin, but increases in thickness in areas where there may be unusual pressure or friction. Two such bodily surfaces are the soles of the feet and the palms of the hands. Prolonged pressure can result in the formation of calluses or corns. The color of the skin is determined primarily by the pigment called melanin which is located within the epidermis.

Beneath the epidermis lies the dermis which contains sweat glands and oil-secreting sebaceous glands. The secretions of the sebaceous glands provide the lubrication for the epidermis to allow for smoother movements, particularly in areas such as the fingers. Information regarding environmental stimuli, which lead to sensations of touch, pressure, pain, and temperature changes, is provided to the nervous system through specialized receptors in the dermis.

Aging and the Integumentary System

The health of the older individual is not seriously compromised by changes that occur in the skin with age. The skin gradually becomes thinner, and the number of immune cells in the skin diminishes (Pathy, 1998). With these changes in mind, the skin can become more susceptible to chemical irritants.

Due to water and fat composition changes, the skin will start to wrinkle and sag. Scales or uneven patches of rough skin, as well as growths on the skin itself, may appear. The skin surface is then prone to crack or break easily.

Another change that occurs is a gradual reduction in the number of sweat glands and sebaceous glands. As a result, older persons tend to sweat less, and their skin can become dry and parchment-like. An additional consequence of the reduction in sweat glands and the inability to perspire is that older persons are less able to regulate body temperature. Such inefficient body temperature regulation can lead to heat exhaustion. Monitoring exposure to the sun then becomes significant due to such reductions in function. Older persons should also be encouraged to drink increased amounts of water.

Because of the generalized reduction in blood flow to the skin, the skin surface of older persons may also appear cooler than in younger individuals. Compromised thermoregulation makes the older person more susceptible to hyperthermia (heat exhaustion) and hypothermia (reduced body temperature) (Tyson, 1999). Hypothermia can be life-threatening.

Foot Problems

The growth of the fingernails and toenails is compromised by the lowered skin temperature and may grow more slowly. Nails may become brittle, and crack or break easily. Due to deposition of calcium, the fingernails and toenails may become discolored, thicker, and develop ridges. There also may be curving of the toenails. Such changes are particularly problematic for women whose cosmetic care often includes painting and attention to the fingernails and toenails.

Lack of appropriate care can result in reduced mobility and dependence. The assistance of a podiatrist who specializes in care of the feet can be sought before problems become serious. Podiatrists can also recommend special shoes or shoe alterations to accommodate foot problems. Many institutions have arrangements by which podiatrists make regular visits to residents, and there are podiatrists, much like dentists, who have traveling units equipped to care for patients in various locations.

Poor Circulation

The effects of decreased circulation are often first seen in the feet because they are the part of the body farthest from the heart. As a result of this lack of blood flow, the skin may become dry and more susceptible to infection and varicose veins and numbness may also occur. Support hose can be helpful for problems of circulation. Lotions or creams can be applied to moisturize the skin, particularly after bathing.

Depending on the extent of the circulatory problem, patients are often referred to a vascular specialist for further evaluation.

Hair

As persons age, there is a generalized loss of body hair, particularly on the head. Men and women with a genetic predisposition toward baldness will find an increase in hair loss with age. There is also a reduction in the presence of overall body hair, including the underarm and pubic areas. On some parts of the body there appears to be an increase in the proliferation of hair. This is particularly true of older men. They experience extensive growth of hair in the nostrils and ears. The hair in the eyebrows, not only grows longer, but can also extend in different directions. Women may experience an increase in facial hair with the growth of a mustache or beard. Removal of such hair growth is easily accomplished through a variety of cosmetic procedures.

Changes in hair color is due to a gradual reduction of pigment in the hair with aging. Heredity may play a role in the amount of hair color lost and at what age the change occurs. The hair coloring which is a mixture of dark and gray, resulting in the salt and pepper effect, is hair that still retains some pigment. The very white hair that is sometimes seen in persons in their seventies or eighties is hair from which pigment is totally absent.

In addition, there often is a reduced sensitivity to touch in regions of the skin that are no longer covered by hair. There are also indications of a decline in the sensitivity of temperature receptors. As a result, persons can be burned by touching extremely hot objects, such as cooking utensils. The finer sensations of touch such as the smoothness or roughness of surfaces seems to diminish, as well as responses to textures such as silk or satin.

Hypodermal Changes

With age, the hypodermis, located just beneath the skin, exhibits a generalized loss of fat from the subcutaneous tissue. This loss is usually most obvious in the face and the limbs. The loss of subcutaneous fat is a major cause of wrinkles and is responsible for the emaciated appearance of some older persons. It also results in a loss of body padding which allows bony prominences to protrude causing discomfort and potential skin problems.

The gradual loss of subcutaneous fat also means that the body is not insulated as well, and that greater amounts of body heat can escape. Due to the loss of fat and diminished blood supply to the skin, older persons may require warmer environments to feel comfortable.

On the whole, the protective aspects of the integumentary system are compromised as persons age. The thinning or lack of hair interferes with its heating and cooling function while the reduction in fat eliminates the body's protective padding. The loss of sweat glands affects thermal regulation, and the loss of oil glands diminishes facile movement.

Dysfunctions

DECUBITUS ULCERS: Immobility can lead to decubitus ulcers, or pressure sores. This condition is often found in persons who are bedfast for long periods of time (Pathy, 1998). People who utilize wheelchairs for extended periods of time are also subject to this condition. In older persons, this is a common problem due to the generalized loss of fat that consequently exposes bony structures. Furthermore, since the circulatory system is less efficient in old age, there is a reduction in blood supply to the skin. These are the primary factors that predispose older persons to develop pressure sores.

The sores generally develop in areas where the skin is under constant pressure such as the hips or heels. Leaning on one side for long periods of time or resting on an elbow can result in the development of pressure sores. In addition, remaining in one position for a long period of time or rubbing the skin against sheets and blankets can irritate the skin. In some cases, pressure sores can result in lesions so deep that craters develop in the skin exposing bone and tissue causing further danger of infection. With proper care and treatment, the sores can be eliminated, but the problem can reoccur due to the immobility of the patient. Improving nutritional levels can be beneficial in treatment programs of these patients.

In addition, turning of the patient and constant surveillance are important. Care of patients whose treatments require prolonged bed rest, such as those on respirators or residents in long-term care facilities, can become particularly problematic. This is a concern since there has been an increase of persons aged 85 and older who are more often hospitalized and utilize long-term care facilities.

To ameliorate the problem, special bed mattresses made of materials which allow for a more responsive give to the weight of the person can also be utilized. Such mattresses have been developed using water, spun glass, air, or plastic materials. In general, preventive health measures that ensure against prolonged immobility are the best forms of intervention.

SENILE PRURITUS: With the loss of oil-secreting glands and sweat glands, there is a reduction in the water content of the skin as well as its motility. This causes the skin to become drier and less resilient resulting in breaks or tiny cracks in the skin or senile pruritus (itching). Because the skin itches, people tend to scratch the area, bringing about further skin damage. Environmental factors can also add to the problem, such as high temperatures or strong wind. Frequent bathing also serves to dry the skin and can worsen the condition.

Skin color also seems to play a role in the number of skin diseases to which the person may become subject. For instance, light-skinned, fair-haired persons appear to suffer more from such disorders than do persons who have darker skin and dark-hair.

PLASTIC OR COSMETIC SURGERY: Plastic or cosmetic surgery is a method commonly resorted to in order to obviate the signs of aging and to restore an image of youth. Plastic surgery can be performed on virtually all parts of the body, as well as the face. Both men and women resort to such treatment. Removal of wrinkles, altering facial structure, removal of unwanted pouches or sagging skin are some of the alterations sought. Breasts, hips, thighs, arms and legs can all be altered through surgery. For both sexes, the removal of fat through liposuction is a common procedure, as is hair replacement caused by baldness. Some areas of the body are more easily altered than others, and some procedures when repeated too frequently can create problems in health or appearance.

As the population continues to age, marriages between generations are becoming commonplace. Both older men and women marry or develop relationships with much younger partners. As a result, when there is disparity in age between couples, and, consequently, one partner ages more rapidly than the other, cosmetic surgery is often the sought remedy. Overall, plastic surgery can provide a more youthful appearance, but it does not delay the aging process.

Mobility and Independence Aids

Proper footcare plays an important role in the mobility of older persons. Pedal problems, if left untreated, can lead to a decrease in walking or general activity. This, in turn, can create an increase in cardiovascular problems, and a decrease in circulation and muscle tone.

Diabetics with proper instructions, footcare, and positive attitudes can often improve lower extremity maintenance and thus possibly avoid amputation. Arthritic deformities can be modified with minor surgical procedures and resilient footwear. In many cases, orthotic devices and jogging and walking shoes can arrest certain deformities. Some accommodative devices help to distribute weight from painful areas to healthier regions of the foot. Advances have been made in the use of mobility aids, such as crutches, canes, portable walkers, as well as answering devices, such as cellular phones (National Research Council, 2003). Such advances in mobility are extremely important because without mobility or foot health virtually every system in the body deteriorates.

Over the years, materials for shoegear and prosthetic/orthotic devices have improved primarily in the areas of flexibility and resilience, and have become increasingly lightweight. Tread sole of shoegear can increase walking safety in the winter months and materials designed with perforations tend to decrease perspiration problems. Additionally, aerosols containing emollients and dermatological medications and powders obviate the need for bending over, and, hence, are of great value in geriatrics. Other advances include velcro on prosthetics and shoegear, which has been revolutionary for arthritics who are unable to tie laces easily. Even artificial limbs have advanced beyond a functional basis in which care is taken to match the limbs so that shoe sizes will be the same for each limb.

Overall, advances in technology regarding podiatric gerontology and foot health may be considered in three dimensions. The first is the detection and identification of these conditions with a degree of accuracy and timeliness. The second is the added challenge in today's world of cost-effective treatment that is both economical and widely available. Finally, the third is providing patients under custodial care or in long-term care institutions with mobility and independence aids that allow for the activities of daily living to be completed with minimal restriction and reduction of costs (Arthur et al., 2001). The maintenance of mobility and activity adds both to the quality and length of life.

THE SKELETAL SYSTEM

The skeletal system provides the structure for the body and is made up of bone and cartilage. Bones not only serve as structural support for the soft tissues of the body, but most of the body muscles are attached to bones. The skeletal system, through special movable joints, allows the body to move in a variety of ways.

In addition, the skeletal system provides a protective function. Many of the internal vital organs of the body are housed in or are surrounded by bony structures. In addition, the brain and the spinal cord are protected by the skull and the vertebral column. The rib cage effectively surrounds the heart and the lungs. Such protective functions can be easily provided by bone because it is very hard and resilient.

Changes in the skeletal system with age can have profound implications with respect to a person's lifestyle. Mobility may be compromised due to the stiffening of joints and pain associated with the initiation or carrying out of even simple movements. Standing erect or maintaining an upright posture may be difficult due to structural changes in the vertebral column. Since bones become more brittle and fragile with age, the protective functions of the skeletal system may be diminished.

People do not necessarily have to experience a fall to break a bone; brittle bones crush easily in a movement as simple as turning the body from one side to the other (Pathy, 1998). The breaking of a hip, for example, can have serious consequences for an older person. It may result in the individual's having to move from an independent lifestyle to placement in a nursing home setting. The breaking of a hip bone may have rendered it impossible for the person to continue to function adequately within the home environment. Such changes are psychologically damaging as well as physically debilitating since most older persons prefer living in their own homes for as long as possible.

Age-related alterations in the skeletal system can be offset by appropriate exercise programs and the establishment of balanced nutritional practices over the life span (Oram, 1997).

Bone

Bones vary in shape according to the exigencies of the body and can be short, flat, irregular, and long. New bone continues to be formed as old bone is broken down or reabsorbed throughout the life span. The continuous cycle of formation and reabsorption of bone replaces the old and more brittle matrix, and remodels the bones to match the bodily needs over time. For example, when people gain weight their bone becomes thicker and stronger to meet the changed bodily requirements.

A major factor in the development of bone is proper nutrition (Spirduso, Francis, & MacRae, 2005). The consumption of vegetables is important to proper bone formation. Women begin to lose calcium from their bones as early as age 30. This is the age when many women begin to go on diets and to limit the amount of calcium they absorb. Such dietary changes hold more serious consequences for women because they are more prone to diseases of the bone, such as osteoporosis. This disease results in porosity of the bones, and, although men are susceptible to this disease as well, it affects women at a higher rate, especially following menopause (Spirduso, Francis, & MacRae, 2005).

Older persons frequently do not follow a balanced diet. This may be due to loss of appetite, depression, or simply the condition of their teeth which makes chewing difficult. Many of the vegetables which harbor ingredients important to bone formation are eschewed by older persons because they have difficulty in masticating due to ill-fitting dentures or the total absence of teeth (edentulous). Dairy foods may be avoided because of lactose intolerance.

Cartilage

While the skeletal system is largely made up of bone, cartilage is important in terms of structural support and in the efficient movement of joints. Lack of exercise more often is the causative factor in the development of stiffness in joints (Pathy, 1998). Sedentary lifestyles are largely responsible for such stiffness.

Activities to prevent joint stiffness need not be strenuous. Gardening is an activity which is relaxing and causes persons to move about, reach, and stretch. Nursing homes, particularly in Europe, frequently provide gardens for residents that can be cared for from a variety of levels, including a reclining position, standing, or sitting in a wheelchair. People do not have to be excluded from activities because of a health problem or disability; the challenge lies in discovering new outlets that can continue to enhance life or finding ways to adapt the environment so as to meet the individual's new needs. Even bedfast patients can participate in exercises through activities geared toward their particular capabilities.

Dysfunctions

As persons age, the loss of calcium from bone is the major change in the skeletal system. Women experience such losses in greater severity than do men, with the amount of calcium in the bones steadily decreasing beginning at approximately the age of 30. For men, such losses in calcium are not initiated until the age of 60 or older. The rate of calcium loss can be reduced through regular participation in exercise programs.

The smooth functioning of the various movable joints of the body relies on the cartilage in the skeletal system. Joints are covered with an articular cartilage which during movement, rub together. As people age, the cartilages of joints may become thinner, with the result of bone rubbing against bone. Such changes can lead to pain and discomfort and can restrict the movement of the joint. Even movements like rising from a chair can be executed by some older persons with great difficulty. Unfortunately, once older persons encounter some difficulty in movement or experience some pain associated with such movement, they tend not to use that limb or that part of the body. In actuality, they should be encouraged to continue the limb's use, but there is usually great resistance. It is disuse of the body that often creates problems of movement in old age. The body, by and large, is underused by most people.

As people grow older, there is also a rigidity that takes place in the bone structure that can hamper movement. For example, the respiratory system can function less efficiently because of the growing rigidity of the rib cage and reduced expansion of the lungs upon breathing. The inspiration and expiration of the lungs can be restricted.

There is also a change in the intervertebral discs with age. They begin to flatten causing persons to lose height resulting in persons becoming shorter in old age.

Arthritis

Arthritis is a major source of discomfort and disability for many older persons. It is one of the oldest known diseases. Arthritis is a general term that refers to various types of inflammation or degenerative changes that occur in joints.

The most important risk factor for arthritis is age. Other factors include: body type (risk is increased in stocky individuals, decreased in tall thin people); race (risk is increased in Caucasians over African Americans, Asians and Native Americans); diabetes (which may be partially controllable when due to obesity); and, genetic traits (one possible form is influenced by sex chromosomes; another involves many genes) (Pathy, 1998). Some of the controllable risk factors include obesity and exercise. Many orthopedic surgeons fear that the current popularity of jogging and other vigorous exercises may exacerbate osteoarthritis. With this in mind, overexercise can worsen the condition of those who have the disease.

The three most common types of arthritis are osteoarthritis (the most common), rheumatoid arthritis (second most common), and gouty arthritis. Osteoarthritis is so common that for many years it was considered a normal aspect of aging. Limb joints are most affected by this disease, especially those responsible for weight-bearing (hips and knees), the vertebrae, and (for unknown reasons) the joints closest to the tips of the fingers (Spirduso, Francis, & MacRae, 2005).

The progression of osteoarthritis can be retarded, and its symptoms can be ameliorated by simple interventions such as the use of a cane, by adapting beds and chairs for easier entry and exit, and arranging living space to avoid use of stairs. In addition, utensils and furniture that compensate for limited function, especially of the hand and major joints of the legs, could greatly improve independent functioning. The design of computer keyboards can be refined to make them accessible to those whose hand mobility is restricted by this disease.

The most common drug therapy is the use of high doses of aspirin. Extensive use of aspirin, however, can lead to hearing loss. Total joint replacement is a relatively new surgical technique made possible by technological advances in low-friction materials, biocompatible plastics and metals, and the development of cements that can function in bone. The joint most commonly replaced is the hip, but some medical centers also perform knee replacement surgery and surgery on other joints, such as fingers and shoulders. The majority of total hip replacements performed annually in the United States are conducted on persons over the age of 65. Hip replacement is now a routine procedure which can reduce pain and improve mobility.

Osteoporosis

Osteoporosis ("porous bone") is a major chronic disorder of older people, principally women following menopause. White and Asian women are at higher risk than Black women who tend to have greater bone density (Pathy, 1998). A family history of osteoporosis also increases the risk of the disorder, as does a slight frame. Although men are subject to this disease, when contracted by men, the disease seems to progress much more slowly than it does in women.

Osteoporosis is defined as a condition in which total bone mass is decreased while bone volume is unchanged; therefore, the density of the bone decreases. This thinning of the bone increases its fragility and makes it more susceptible to fracture. Activities and stresses that would not harm normal bone can result in fractures of osteoporotic bone (Avioli, 2000). Loss of bone mass occurs in all people as they age, but the rate of loss is higher in women for about 10 years immediately following menopause. This period of rapid loss causes women to be especially subject to vertebral and wrist fractures. Diet is one of the major modifiable lifestyle factors which may affect progression of bone loss (Spirduso, Francis, & MacRae, 2005). The role of physical activity in preventing bone loss has yet to be determined.

Osteoporosis is an important cause of morbidity and mortality in the elderly. It appears to be the underlying cause of about two-thirds of hip fractures in older people. Osteoporosis is also one of the most common causes of back pain in older persons (Taylor et al., 2004). The pain is due to the partial or complete collapse of a vertebra. Persons sometimes associate the onset of pain with pushing or lifting heavy weights, but it often starts spontaneously and has no definite precipitating, aggravating, or relieving factors. The pain is difficult to control and potent analgesia is sometimes required.

Greater life expectancy and rising health care costs are expected to sharply increase the costs related to hip fractures. Fractures of the wrist are common, as are vertebral fractures. It is estimated that 25 percent of white women have at least one vertebral fracture by the age of 60. Most of these fractures are compression fractures or "crush fractures" in which the vertebra simply collapses from the weight of maintaining the body in the upright position.

Such loss of bone can result in diminished height, stooped posture, pain, and tooth loss (Pathy, 1998). It can cause curvature of the spine and backache as vertebrae are eroded and compressed. The disease often causes a general reduction in the strength of bones, making them more easily fractured. Fracture and compression of the vertebrae produces the hunched back (widow's or dowager's hump) and shortening of the trunk. Because of the curvature of the spine, respiration can be adversely affected. Overall, hip fractures are more common among older women.

Over the course of time, lifestyles can be markedly changed as movement is decreased, and general mobility is affected. Such gradual bodily disuse fosters the development of additional chronic disease, and, may, ultimately lead to death. Some skeletal changes are due to senescence; but others, however, are the result of lifestyle, including smoking.

Future Possible Interventions

There is increased attention being given to the potentially large market presented by an aging population for prosthetic devices. Companies that produce prosthetic devices could also greatly improve the functioning of arthritic individuals. Designers of chairs, stairways, beds, telephones, and computer keyboards are likely to continue to adapt their designs for use by the growing numbers of those affected by arthritis. Development of "smart" technologies to assist in daily activities should prove highly marketable to this large subpopulation.

Prosthetic Joints for the Elderly

Stairs, revolving doors, heavy doors, high curbs, small curbs, low chairs, narrow passageways, tiny toilet booths, and all the other hazards impeding access and transportation conspire against those who have difficulty in moving. Together, these hazards and decrements disproportionately affect those with musculoskeletal or motor impairment (Mann et al., 1995; Ciol et al., 2003).

Joint replacements have radically changed the outcome of locomotor dysfunction in the elderly. Most patients are able to walk without canes or crutches several months following the operation. Most patients report that pain is almost totally relieved and that the joint is functional, with its motion materially enhanced. An elderly person does not hold joints in the same position as a younger person. For example, many of the elderly have natural mild flexion stances of hips and knees. However, with appropriate postsurgery therapy, even these normal deficits can be overcome and gait can be returned to a premorbid state—in fact, to a state more closely resembling that of much younger persons.

The prosthetic replacement of various joints have been more successful than any other treatment in improving the quality of life for the older person who has locomotor impairment. Such interventions have reduced the amount of time needed for bed rest, spared the patient prolonged hospitalization that can lead to disorientation, potentially increased the individual's life expectancy, and decreased the amount of discomfort.

THE MUSCULAR SYSTEM

Much like the skeletal system which contains numerous bones, varying in size to suit particular bodily functions, the muscular system consists of a variety of muscles to help execute bodily movements. People smile, walk, move about, and blink their eyes, using a number of muscles without much regard to the complex coordination that permits such activity to occur. Muscles are constantly in use.

Changes in the muscular system can affect many parts of the body simultaneously; such changes can also cause negative reactions with regard to a person's self-esteem (Pathy, 1998). Body image is a very important factor in how individuals view themselves and is an integral part of personal identity. The inability to perform certain movements as persons age can lead to serious depressive states (Daley & Spinks, 2000).

The skeletal system and the muscular system are interminably linked. It is their dual coordinative functions that permit persons to move about easily and to perform small to gross movements. As an individual ages, there is a gradual reduction in strength and endurance, and certain movements may not be as well coordinated. There is a reduced functional capability and an increased likelihood of falling ("Daily Activities," 1998; Spirduso, Francis, & MacRae, 2005). Such changes can be minimized through a program of regular exercise (Fiatarone Singh, 2000).

Mobility and Independence Aids

Persons with limitations in movement can more conveniently engage in swimming as a means of exercise. A mini-pool that is four meters long and two meters wide can be installed in a room of the home, the garage, or in the office. This pool is equipped with a motorized paddle-wheel that creates a constant artificial current. The swimmer moves against the current or wave either by remaining in the same spot or by swimming the short pool length. The force of the current can be regulated through a control panel. This system allows the exerciser to move against the flow of water or to exercise by moving only a few meters or actually remaining stationary. The swimmer has the sensation of the water coming toward him or her as a wave in the sea.

The Seattle Foot (TM) is probably one of the most advanced simulators of human function. It is an artificial foot intended to be attached to a below-knee or above-knee prosthesis. The prosthetic foot contains a plastic keel within a cosmetic, anatomically detailed foam foot. This incredibly lifelike foot is designed so that the amputee can even wear sandals and thongs. The spring keel stores and releases energy as an amputee applies and removes force. In this manner, natural shock absorption and forward thrust are provided to the prosthetic leg. This allows activities such as walking, running, or jumping to be performed. Different keel spring rates are available to tailor the prosthesis to the individual. The Seattle Foot offers great promise to amputees. This intervention even allows persons to engage in sports activities, such as basketball.

For patients with Alzheimer's disease and related problems, radioemitting devices may be worn to facilitate locating or finding these individuals when they are walking about the facility or the grounds for exercise. In a similar vein, telephone devices that dial automatically by squeezing may be used.

Personal emergency response systems are now in common use. An emergency response system allows an individual to seek by pressing a small personal help button. This help button is worn on a chain around the neck or on a wrist strap. When pressed, the help button can link the individual to the Emergency Medical System, if needed. Such devices increase independence and security and are conducive to the maintenance of continuity in personal lifestyle which can include independent movement and exercise (Shumway-Cook et al., 2003).

Over the years, major technological advances have been made in the diagnosis, treatment, and aides to mobility regarding aging in general and podiatric gerontology in particular. The positive effects of these technologies include improved physical fitness, decreased mortality, improved home health care delivery, increased leisure, and the possibility of second or multiple careers for persons as they age (Thilmany, 2004; Ciol et al., 2003). Robotics are also becoming increasingly important in tasks such as ambulation, housekeeping, physical therapy, surveillance, and mental stimulation (Coles, 2004; Edwards, 2004).

Ambulation Aids

Physically impaired older patients must be carefully prepared in the use of ambulatory aids. Those with lower extremity weakness or other impairment frequently benefit from walkers, canes, crutches, and wheelchairs. These devices, however, might not help–and may even be harmful–if they are given to persons physically incapable of using them or untrained in their proper use.

To determine whether a person will be able to use a device, it is important to evaluate the person's general condition and specific gait disability. It is futile to expect an individual to ambulate with crutches, cane, or walker if he or she lacks sufficient strength to do so. Muscle strength must be evaluated with particular ambulation needs in mind (Hammel & Nochajski, 2000; Murtagh & Hubert, 2004).

People must also be taught to operate a wheelchair properly and safely. Both the older person and the family must be cautioned about prolonged sitting and the possible dangers of pressure sores and flexion contracture of the knees and hips (Jagger et al., 2001).

REFERENCES

Avioli, L.V. (Ed.). (2000). *The Osteoporotic syndrome: Detection, prevention, and treatment* (4th Ed.). Millbrae, CA: Academic Press.

Chop, W. C., & Robnett, R. H. (1999). *Gerontology for the health care professional.* Philadelphia: F.A. Davis.

Ciol, M.A., Cook, A., Ferrucci, L., Guralnik, J.M., Patla, A. & Stewart, A.(2003). Environmental components of mobility disability in community-living older persons. *JAGS, 51* (3), 393–398.

Coles, C. (2004, May–June). Robots and sensors help make seniors mobile. *The Futurist,* pp. 12–14.

Daily activities help older persons maintain their strength. (1998). *Geriatrics, 53* (2), 15–17.

Daley, M. J., & Spinks, W. L. (2000). Exercise, mobility, and aging. *Sports Medicine, 29* (1), 1–12.

Edwards, C. (2004, July 19). Ready to buy a home robot? *Business Week,* p. 84–89.

Fiatarone Singh, M. A. (2000). *Exercise, nutrition, and the older woman: Wellness for women over fifty.* Boca Raton, FL: CRC Press.

Ham, R. J., Sloane, P. D., & Warshaw, G. A. (Eds.) (2002). *Primary care geriatrics: A case-based approach* (4th Ed.). St. Louis: Mosby.

Hammel, J., & Nochajski, S. M. (Eds.). (2000). *Aging and developmental disability: Current research, programming, and practice implications.* Binghamton, NY: Hawthorne Press.

Jagger, C., Arthur, A. J., Spiers, N. A., & Clarke, M. (2001). Patterns of onset of disability in activities of daily living with age. *JAGS, 49,* 404–409.

Mann, W. C., Hurran, D., & Tomita, M. (1995). Assistive devices used by home-based elderly persons with arthritis. *The American Journal of Occupational Therapy, 49* (8), 810–819.

Murtagh, K. N., & Hubert, H. B. (2004). Gender differences in physical disability among an elderly cohort. *American Journal of Public Health, 94* (8), 1406–1411.

National Research Council (2003). *Technology for adaptive aging.* Washington D.C.: The Washington Academies Press.

Oram, J. J. (1997). *Caring for the fourth age.* London: Armelle.

Pathy, J. (Ed.). (1998). *Principles and practices of geriatric medicine* (3rd Ed.). Chichester, England: John Wiley.

Shumway-Cook, A., Patla, A., Stewart, A. Ferrucci, L., Ciol, M.A., & Guralnik, J. M.(2003). Environmental components of mobility disability in community-living older persons. *JAGS, 51* (3), 393–398.

Spence, A. P. (1995). *Biology of human aging* (2nd Ed.). Englewood Cliffs, NJ: Prentice Hall.

Spirduso, W. W., Francis, K. L., & MacRae, P. G. (2005). *Physical dimensions of aging* (2nd Ed.). Champaign, IL: Human Kinetics.

Sunderkotter, C., Kalden, H., & Luger, T. (1997). Aging and the skin immune system. *ARCH Dermatology, 133,* 1256–1261.

Taylor, B. C., Schreiner, P. J., Stone, K. L., Fink, H. A., Cummings, S. R., Nevitt, M. C., et al. (2004, September). Long-term prediction of incident hip fracture risk in elderly white women: Study of osteoporotic fractures. *Journal of the American Geriatrics Society, 52* (9), 1479–1486.

Thilmany, J. (2004). Aids for the elderly. *Mechanical Engineering, 126* (4), 10–14.

Tyson, S. R. (1999). *Gerontological nursing care.* Philadelphia: Saunders.

Chapter 4

AGE-RELATED CHANGES WITHIN BIOLOGICAL SYSTEMS: CIRCULATORY, RESPIRATORY, AND DIGESTIVE

GARI LESNOFF-CARAVAGLIA

THE CIRCULATORY SYSTEM

The circulatory system has a direct effect upon the total functioning of the body and incorporates several very different components. The supplying of the body with nutrients and the carrying off of waste deposits is essential to body maintenance. The heart (myocardium) is the key to this functioning. The lymphatic system also assists in this process through its filtering processes and the deneutralizing of toxins carried out by organs such as the liver, tonsils, and the spleen. This constant process throughout the body is carried on by the propelling of the blood through the veins and arteries by the rhythmic beating of the heart.

The importance of the circulatory system is intensified in old age. Diseases of the circulatory system become increasingly a problem as they significantly affect all bodily systems. The major causes of death in the United States and many developed countries are from diseases of the heart and the blood vessels (Spirduso, Francis, & MacRae, 2005). The two primary causes of death, heart disease and stroke, are both the result of circulatory system dysfunction. Those who survive the onslaught of such diseases can be left with a variety of disabilities. For instance, some persons may experience a total change in lifestyle, including abandonment of work roles and recreational pursuits. Interpersonal relationships can also be affected. Dependency becomes a significant factor, and transfer from life in the community to an institutional setting may become a reality for more severely disabled persons (Kart, 1997). Home health care can provide assistance in the private home setting, but such services are frequently unavailable or too costly for many older individuals.

It is quite likely that disease and lifestyle may have a greater influence on cardiovascular function than does aging. In fact, elevated blood pressure, inappropriate blood lipoprotein patterns, obesity, smoking and glucose intolerance are also strong predictors of coronary risk in the elderly (Schlenker, 1998). Such lifestyle factors when prevalent throughout the lifespan manifest their consequences in old age. Not only the diseases that people contract, but the medications used to treat these diseases can ultimately affect the cardiovascular system.

Atherosclerosis and Arteriosclerosis

Atherosclerosis is the disease that prevents the coronary arteries from supplying adequate blood flow to the heart. The formation of and enlargement of material called "plaque" in the walls of the arteries causes the coronary arteries to become narrower and thus reduces blood flow (Manuck, Jennings, Rabin, & Baum, 2000). It also stiffens arteries, much like old bicycle tires, reducing their ability to dilate when more oxygen is needed by the heart muscle. Plaques can also contribute to the formation of clots which can completely prevent blood flow. When blood flow to the body drops, the performance of all organs deteriorates. The brain, kidneys, lungs, and heart are especially in danger because these organs require a high level of blood flow. A low level of oxygen can lead to the death of the heart muscle, resulting in a myocardial infarction (heart attack).

As the life expectancy of the general population increases, more people can be expected to develop atherosclerotic occlusive disease. Although the cause of atherosclerosis is not known, its frequent association with the degenerative aging process is widely accepted.

Cardiovascular diseases in combination with other major diseases can present serious health problems. Persons suffering from diabetes, for example, may experience reduced blood flow to the extremities which can lead to the development of gangrene and limb amputation. Amputees are frequently older persons, and the clientele of rehabilitation centers increasingly include the elderly.

Hypertension

Hypertension, or high blood pressure, is a problem of all age groups, but it is found more commonly among older persons. It is also known as the silent killer. In older persons, hypertension is generally linked to atherosclerosis and arteriosclerosis. Blood pressure represents the force exerted by blood flowing against vessel walls and created by the pumping action of the heart. Elevated blood pressure is potentially serious because it can contribute to heart attack, heart failure, stroke, renal failure, or rupture of blood vessels.

It is generally accepted that high blood pressure is not an automatic consequence of aging and need not be as prevalent as it is in well-developed countries. Lifestyle factors contribute more to the development of hypertension and heart disease than does aging. Among these factors are obesity, lack of exercise, excessive intake of salt, and smoking (Spirduso, Francis, & MacRae, 2005).

Coronary Artery Disease

Coronary artery disease results when insufficient blood flows through the coronary arteries to the heart muscle. Ischemic heart disease results when tissue does not receive a supply of blood sufficient to maintain its cells. The reduced blood flow is due to a narrowing or constriction of the coronary arteries caused by plaque formation.

Such decreases in coronary artery blood flow in old age increase the likelihood of coronary artery disease. In fact, it is the major cause of heart problems and death among the elderly. There is also an increased incidence of coronary artery disease among postmenopausal women which may be caused by sudden increases in blood cholesterol levels (Ham, Sloane, & Warshaw, 2002).

The symptoms that result from a sudden blockage of a coronary artery are considered a heart attack. A blocked coronary artery can be treated through bypass surgery in which a portion of an artery from another region of the body is grafted to the coronary artery and used to direct blood around the blocked portion. Another treatment procedure involves the injection of chemicals to dissolve the clot to restore blood flow, while, at the same time, a small catheter with a miniature balloon on its tip is entered through the vessel to the location of the clot. The balloon is inflated which then compresses the clot and opens the vessel.

This procedure is known as balloon angioplasty. Still another method is one by which laser beams transmitted through fine glass fibers within a catheter remove the clot.

Coronary heart disease is more dependent on age in women than in men; women are usually 10 years older than men when any coronary manifestations first appear, and myocardial infarction occurs as much as 20 years later. One in 8 or 9 American women aged 45–64 years has clinical evidence of coronary heart disease, and this increases to 1 in 3 in women older than 65 years. Coronary heart disease is the leading cause of death in women in the United States (Spence, 1995).

Congestive Heart Failure

A condition in which the heart cannot pump enough blood to meet bodily needs is known as congestive heart failure or cardiac insufficiency. The condition which becomes more common and serious with age is the result of other cardiovascular diseases that have damaged the heart to the extent that it no longer functions adequately (Aronow & Tresch, 1997).

Because the heart cannot pump efficiently, blood collects in tissues. Edema (swelling) of the legs and ankles is common. When fluid backs up into the lungs, shortness of breath results and people have difficulty breathing, particularly in supine positions. Congestive heart failure does not have a favorable prognosis. Drugs, however, that increase the contractile strength of the cardiac muscle and eliminate excess fluid from the body are helpful. Modification of diet, along with rest, is frequently recommended. Surgical interventions including repair of defective valves or other structural problems can also reduce the severity of heart failure (Bosworth et al., 2004). Since the heart is the key to the smooth and efficient functioning of all systems, muscular activity can be limited and participation in a variety of vocational or recreational activities may well be restricted.

Technology and Interventions

The functioning of the circulatory system is compromised by presence of diseases which are frequently initiated by unhealthy lifestyles (Oram, 1997). Environmental factors continue to be an additional concern with regard to the maintenance of the equilibrium of the circulatory system. Unhealthy work environments can wreak havoc upon a person's circulatory system which can result in serious debility in the later years of life or can shorten life expectancy. One example is black lung which affects both the respiratory and circulatory systems of miners as a result of breathing in coal dust.

Some medical and surgical interventions are not indicated for older persons because their health is already compromised by other diseases from which they may be suffering. Bypass surgery, laser treatments, or angioplasty may not be recommended for some patients, but there are patients of advanced ages whose health can permit the use of more radical interventions (Deaton & Grady, 2005). Ethical dilemmas with respect to the cost of such interventions and the appropriateness of their utilization continue to surface as the population continues to age and more people request such interventions.

Overall, the process of aging alters the structure of the heart and contributes to primary cardiac dysfunction. The incidence of heart failure has increased progressively over the past three decades, and it now comprises a major source of morbidity and mortality in the American population, especially as the population ages. In patients over the age of 65, heart failure has now become the most common diagnostic related group category (DRG) for hospitalized patients (Davidson et al., 2004). This increase in the incidence of heart failure has occurred despite major advances in the treatment of what has been thought to be primary etiological factors initiating the problem, namely hypertension, valvular disease, and ischemic heart disease. The passage of years allows primary abnormalities such as coronary atherosclerosis to play a progressively increasing role in the evolution of the disease (Gehi, Pinney, & Gass, 2005).

Surgical Interventions

A healthy lifestyle and medical checkups are the principal ways to ensure a healthy cardiovascular system. However, when a cardiac problem is diagnosed, in addition to an appropriate diet and sufficient exercise, the use of drugs is frequently the next step. When such remedies are no longer effective, then surgical intervention is necessary.

If the problem involves cardiac insufficiency, new pathways can be used to furnish the obstructed area by using arteries from other areas, such as the stomach. This intervention is not without its problematic aspects, but it is one method for revitalizing the pumping action of the heart.

Another surgical intervention is to cut away the enlarged portions of the heart that complicate the cardiac problem, and thus reducing the size of the heart. Replacement of part of the heart, especially the left ventricle, with an artificial ventricle to which the blood is diverted is yet another possibility.

Heart transplant remains the best solution to date. This intervention enjoys a high success rate (95% probability of survival for the first year, and 70% for the next eleven years). Unfortunately, there are extensive patient waiting lists (Spence, 1995). The use of laser interventions is particularly helpful with older persons for whom traditional surgery may prove to be too great a risk.

THE RESPIRATORY SYSTEM

The primary function of the respiratory system is to transport oxygen to the bloodstream as well as remove carbon dioxide from the bloodstream (Spirduso, Francis, & MacRae, 2005). All cells within the body require a continuous supply of oxygen to carry out their various metabolic activities, and the carbon dioxide that results from these activities must be removed. The organs of the respiratory system, in conjunction with those of the circulatory system, carry out these functions.

The organs of the respiratory system are affected more by environmental factors than are the organs of most other body systems. The principal organs of the respiratory system are the two lungs. Respiratory organs are constantly exposed to environmental factors, such as various pollutants in the air. The frequency of such onslaughts, along with respiratory infections, may well contribute to the premature aging of the human organism (Phillips & Hnatiuk, 1998).

The respiratory system includes many protective devices to offset the intrusion of foreign particles. One of these is the cilia or hairs found principally in the nasal passages, with some in the throat and the mouth. These hairs serve to keep out potentially harmful substances. Habits of breathing through the mouth can diminish the effectiveness of such protective measures.

An additional problem is presented by the fact that the ear, nose, mouth, and throat are all interlinked. Diseases in one area can spread easily to another, and because they are homogeneous areas–all dark and moist–they encourage the growth of bacteria and can move from one part to another almost endlessly. All of these passages interconnect so that an infection of the throat can easily move to the ear.

For proper functioning, clean air, oxygen, must be taken into the body, while carbon dioxide is released from the body. This process of taking in air is known as inspiration, and the letting out of stale air is expiration. In breathing in, the thoracic cavity is increased, and in breathing out, the thoracic cavity is diminished. The lungs, the diaphragm, and muscles are involved in this process. The rib cage which provides a protective covering to the lungs is also resilient and provides a certain "give" during inspiration and expiration. In older persons, such elasticity of the rib cage is lessened due to increased rigidity of the skeletal system, and the thoracic cavity does not expand and contract to the same degree. What is referred to as vital capacity is the amount of air that the person can take in during inspiration, and the amount of air the individual exhales during expiration.

Alterations with Aging

One sign of aging of the individual is when the person has difficulty in performing activities at the same rate or level at which they were able to perform when somewhat younger. People who are accustomed to running a number of miles per day, find that they can run fewer miles within the same time frame as they become older. Due to breathing problems, they are able to swim fewer laps. This does not indicate that persons as they grow older should eliminate certain activities, but rather that they perform them at less strenuous levels. According to the Italian geriatrician, Francesco Antonini, older persons should not be told not to climb mountains, but they should be exhorted to select smaller mountains. It is the level of the activity that should be the measure of what the person can accomplish.

STRUCTURAL CHANGES: The general structural changes which affect the body as people age also alter the functioning of the respiratory system. Postural changes can affect the efficacy of the respiratory system. Erect posture has important psychological benefits, as well as improving respiratory functioning. People who develop habits of sitting in hunched positions or slumped in chairs or who do not stand erect develop rounding of the shoulders and a narrowing of the chest cavity.

The posture of some older persons is so bent that they appear to be facing the ground, rather than facing forward. This accentuated downward posture gave rise to the saying that the grave is already beckoning the person. Such postural changes which cramp the lungs have a direct effect on the breathing capacity of the person.

Loss in height is common due to changes in the vertebrae, and persons who are in their nineties and 100s are much shorter than they were when younger. Stooping because of a dowager's hump makes women appear even shorter.

The rounding of the thoracic region of the vertebral column is due to the loss of calcium and a gradual weakening of muscles of the neck and back. These changes reduce the volume of the thoracic cavity, and it becomes difficult for the lungs to expand (Spirduso, Francis, & MacRae, 2005). Thus, breathing becomes more laborious for the older person. Since the cartilage that connects the ribs to the spinal column and sternum tends to calcify, joints become stiffer with age. These combined changes in the skeletal and respiratory systems make respiration more difficult and less efficient.

With age, more muscular work is required to move air into and out of the lungs, and older persons tend to rely more on the diaphragm for inspiration. Older persons may find it more difficult to breathe when lying on their backs. This position increases intra-abdominal pressure, which, coupled with the stiffness of the rib cage, makes it difficult to increase the volume of the thoracic cavity and to ventilate the lungs adequately. It is easier for older persons to breathe if they are elevated or supported by layers of pillows. It is also important to rotate persons who sleep on their sides or on their stomachs to prevent suffocation. Breathing is compromised by the presence of various disease states, along with senescence.

Caution also has to be exercised in feeding persons who are bedfast due to the fact that breathing and swallowing are quasi-simultaneous actions. The breathing of persons in prone positions is already compromised, and the ingestion of food may create additional complications. Choking or the aspiration of food into the lungs can lead to serious consequences such as pneumonia or death.

Dysfunctions

Older persons are frequently subject to diseases of the respiratory system. This is due to the limited respiratory reserve capacity and the development of dyspnea on exertion. It may also be aggravated by several changes in the respiratory system probably associated with the aging process. Older persons are also particularly vulnerable to developing respiratory tract infections (Tyson, 1999).

Years of exposure to unhealthful environmental factors, such as air pollution and smoking, are also contributing factors. Prolonged residence in industrialized cities can have baneful effects on the respiratory system.

Pulmonary disorders are divided into two categories: restrictive diseases or obstructive diseases. Restrictive diseases reduce the expansion of the lungs; whereas, obstructive diseases cause the respiratory airways to become compromised resulting in an increased resistance to air flow (Adams, 1998).

CHRONIC OBSTRUCTIVE PULMONARY DISEASE: The two most common chronic obstructive pulmonary diseases are chronic bronchitis and emphysema. Persons with these disorders tend to have a decrease in respiratory muscle efficiency paired with an increase in the actual work required in breathing. As the disease progresses the ability to lead a normal life is diminished due to the extreme physical exhaustion which occurs during most forms of physical exertion. Later in the disease, even the smallest amount of exertion in everyday tasks can lead to exhaustion and shortness of breath (Resnikoff & Ries, 1998). Nutrition intervention is needed in severe COPD as resulting exhaustion may cause dyspnea and extreme fatigue making it difficult for the person to make and eat meals (Chapman & Winter, 1996).

Environmental factors and age are primary causes of COPD. In about 80 percent of the cases, cigarette smoking is considered to be a large contributing factor. There are, however, some indications of possible genetic predisposition. With COPD, the person often assumes a stooped posture, even leaning on the elbows when in a sitting position. Breathing becomes labored and is often through pursed lips. The two most common chronic obstructive pulmonary diseases are emphysema and chronic bronchitis. Others include pneumonia, tuberculosis, pulmonary embolism, environmental factors, and lung cancer (Celli, 1998).

LUNG CANCER: Lung cancer is the leading cause of cancer deaths in the United States. Lung cancer risk increases with the intensity and duration of cigarette smoking, the depth of inhalation, and the tar and nicotine content of the cigarettes. The overall survival rates for patients with all stages of lung cancer are low. Patients with lung cancer may not receive surgical treatment if their preoperative pulmonary function tests reveal chronic obstructive pulmonary disease (COPD). Nearly 90 percent of patients with lung cancer also have COPD, and 20 percent of these patients have severe pulmonary dysfunction (Yohannes & Hardy, 2003).

Technology and Interventions

Recent advances in video technology and endoscopic instrumentation have expanded the use of thoracoscopy from diagnosis to treatment of pulmonary disease. Because of advances in endoscopic surgical equipment and anesthetic technology, surgical treatment via thoracoscopy is now possible. Thoracoscopy was introduced more than 80 years ago for the diagnosis of pleural disease. This technique was limited until recent advances allowed thoracic surgeons to have greater visualization and mobility within the chest. The advent of miniaturized video cameras, placed on the tip of a flexible thorascope, has enabled multiple persons to simultaneously view this procedure via television.

THE DIGESTIVE SYSTEM

Much like other systems within the body, the digestive system relies upon other bodily systems to function appropriately. The digestive system generally presents few major problems to older persons. The threat of cancer of the digestive system, however, increases with age. Frequent complaints, nonetheless, center about gastrointestinal disorders such as indigestion, heartburn, loss of appetite, and constipation.

The digestive system is essentially a long tube known as the gastrointestinal tract that extends from the mouth to the anus. The main function of the digestive system is to change the composition of food to a form that can be assimilated by the body cells.

Dysfunctions

CANCER: One of the more serious problems of the digestive system is the rise in the numbers of malignant cancers (carcinomas) of the digestive system with age. Dietary components being evaluated in relation to cancer risk include total kilocalorics, fat, fiber, iron, selenium, calcium, ascorbic acid, beta carotene, and vitamins E and A (Schlenker, 1998).

Cancer of the esophagus is most common among men who smoke; stomach cancer is more common in men over the age of 60. Some symptoms of stomach cancer include loss of appetite, weight loss, and a general feeling of malaise. Since the symptoms are nonspecific, the diagnosis of cancer of the digestive tract is difficult and problematic. Persons may not consult a physician until the disease has substantially progressed. Furthermore, people resort to self-medication for extended periods of time which can be more damaging than beneficial. Medical advice is often sought after the disease progresses to a more advanced stage and symptoms become more severe.

FECAL INCONTINENCE: Fecal incontinence is not as common as urinary incontinence. It has, however, severe traumatic psychological effects on the person and drastically curtails social contacts. The diminished capability to regulate one's bowel movements is a problem for many older persons, particularly residents in long-term care facilities.

Health problems related to fecal incontinence can be obviated through proper procedures of hygiene. It can, however, be very damaging to an individual's self-esteem. Fecal incontinence is an impairment of the ability to control the external anal sphincter and the striated muscles forming the pelvic floor. Such loss of control can result from diseases such as cancer or neurological problems. Some persons experience fecal incontinence during phases of an illness (Oram, 1997). Not infrequently, fecal incontinence is drug induced.

WATER BALANCE: An important aspect of overall nutrition is water balance. Several factors conspire to put older people at a relatively high risk of dehydration. For example, older people have a lower capacity to conserve water through the kidneys, as well as a significantly lower sensation of thirst. This is particularly problematic in acute illnesses accompanied with fever, such as common colds and flu, which increase the risk of dehydration even further (Aspen Reference Group, 1998). Dehydration can also increase the risk of flu-related complications (such as sinusitis and pneumonia).

Older persons should consume about one and a half to two quarts of fluid per day. Relatively little is known about the effects of age on requirements for specific nutrients (Fiatarone Singh, 2000).

ORAL HEALTH: A common problem for older persons is oral health care. Many persons lose their teeth by the age of 65, or wear or require dentures. While oral health care has improved, and older persons are more conscious of its importance, major concern still exists with regard to periodontal or gum disease. Periodontal disease is an inflammation which can destroy the periodontal membrane that lines the tooth socket. The absence of teeth or the wearing of uncomfortable dentures compromises the older person's ability to chew. Periodontal disease, responsible for 30 percent of tooth loss in elderly people, is both treatable and preventable (Schlenker, 1998).

With age, there is also a reduction in the amount of saliva present in the oral cavity. The role of saliva in oral health care is to cleanse the mouth and teeth. The sensation of taste can be altered when sufficient amounts of saliva are no longer present.

Oral health is an essential factor in maintaining the general health and well-being of the elderly. The ability to chew and enjoy favorite foods adds much to the older person's pleasure in eating and desire to eat (Schlenker, 1998). With this in mind, poor oral health has been shown to be a major contributor to malnutrition, loss of strength, poor general health, and facial disfigurement. Furthermore, when oral health declines, embarrassment and social withdrawal often follow (Kiyak, 2004). Without social relationships, a downward spiral of self-esteem and general health is likely.

Tooth loss, gum disease, and reduced flow of saliva are some of the oral health problems that influence food choices and may adversely affect nutrient intake (Schlenker, 1998). These oral problems may be higher predictors of inadequate nutrition than demographic factors such as living alone. As teeth are lost, the nutritional quality of the diet often declines.

Technology, Prevention, and Intervention

Dental caries (decay) in adults can be reduced through proper nutrition, removal of dental plaque through brushing and flossing, and use of fluoride. Improved dental hygiene has decreased the incidence of caries overall; however, with more older people retaining their teeth, caries have become a lifelong problem (Schlenker, 1998). In some cases, dental implants have now been used successfully.

When proper medical precautions are taken, comprehensive dental care is as possible for an older patient, as it is for a younger patient.

With appropriate treatment such as root canal therapy, implants, crowns and bridges, and periodontal treatment, older persons can keep their teeth for a lifetime. Even if teeth are lost, a dental prosthesis such as a complete or partial denture can be provided. Although a prosthesis rarely equates with one's own teeth, an individual can learn to use it effectively.

Dental Devices for the Elderly

The popularity of dental prostheses increased only very slowly because of the popular myth that losing teeth was a natural adjunct to growing old. It was not considered unattractive or unhealthy for a person to be partially or completely edentulous. Increases in economic status and public entitlement for dental care have reduced the percentage of lost teeth per person. Nonetheless, the increases in population and in life expectancy have created a greater need and desire for dental prostheses. Currently, there are approximately 35 million people who are edentulous in one form or another; another 15 million who have lost more than 75 percent of their teeth will become completely edentulous within the next decade.

In addition to contributing to proper nutrition, the dental prosthesis also provides better control and modification of the airflow for speech and respiratory function. Prolonged chewing made possible by the prosthesis may improve secretion. The movement of food within the mouth also stimulates the taste buds and releases odors that stimulate the olfactory receptors (Schlenker, 1998).

Moreover, the aesthetic improvement is associated with a significant improvement in self-esteem and more active social participation. A dental prosthesis is successful when it facilitates normal speaking, chewing, and swallowing; does no harm to the residual tissues; is serviceable, can be altered or adjusted to compensate for changing biologic processes; and maintains tissues in good health with minimum additional costs.

REFERENCES

Adams, F. V. (1998). *The breathing disorders source book.* Los Angeles: Lowell House.
Aronow, W. & Tresch, D. (1997). Treatment of congestive heart failure in older persons. *JAGS,* *45* (10), 1252–1257.

Aspen Reference Group. (1998). *Dieticians' patient education manual.* Gaithersburg, MD: Aspen Reference Group.

Bosworth, H. B., Steinhauser, K. E., Orr, M., Lindquist, J. H., Grambow, S. C. & Oddone, E. Z. (2004). Congestive heart failure patients' perceptions of quality of life: Integration of physical and psychosocial factors. *Aging & Mental Health, 8* (1), 83–91.

Celli, B. R. (1998). Pathophysiology of chronic obstructive pulmonary disease. *Respiratory Care Clinics of North America, 2* (3), 359–370.

Chapman, K., & Winter, L. (1996). COPD: Using nutrition to prevent respiratory function decline. *Geriatrics, 51* (12), 37–42.

Davidson, P. M., Introna, K., Cockburn, J., Davis, J. M., Rees, D., Gorman, D. et al. (2004). Integrated, collaborative palliative care in heart failure. *Journal of Cardiovascular Nursing, 19* (1), 68–74.

Deaton, C., & Grady, C. L. (2005). State of the science for cardiovascular nursing outcomes. *Journal of Cardiovascular Nursing, 19* (5), 329–338.

Fiatarone Singh, M. A. (2000). *Exercise, nutrition, and the older woman: Wellness for women over fifty.* Boca Raton, FL: CRC Press.

Gehi, A. K., Pinney, S. P., & Gass, A. (2005). Recent diagnostic and therapeutic innovations in heart failure management. *Mount Sinai Journal of Medicine, 72* (3), 176–184.

Ham, R. J., Sloane, P. D., & Warshaw, G. A. (Eds.) (2002). *Primary care geriatrics: A case-based approach* (4th Ed.). St. Louis: Mosby.

Kart, C. S. (1997). *The realities of aging.* Boston: Allyn & Bacon.

Kiyak, H. A. (2004, September). Achieving successful aging: The impact of oral health. *Geriatrics & Gerontology International, 4* (s1), S32–S33.

Manuck, S. B., Jennings, R., Rabin, B. S., & Baum, A. (Eds.). (2000). *Behavior, health, and aging.* Mahwah, NJ: Lawrence Erlbaum Associates, Inc.

Oram, J. J. (1997). *Caring for the fourth age.* London: Armelle.

Phillips, Y. Y., & Hnatiuk, O. W. (1998). Diagnosing and monitoring the clinical course of obstructive pulmonary disease. *Respiratory Care Clinics of North America, 4* (3), 371–389.

Resnikoff, P. M., & Ries, A. L. (1998). Maximizing functional capacity: Pulmonary rehabilitation and adjunctive measures. *Respiratory Care Clinics of North America, 4* (3), 475–492.

Schlenker, E. D. (1998). *Nutrition in aging.* Boston, MA: McGraw-Hill Companies.

Spence, A. D. (1995). *Biology of human aging.* Englewood Cliffs, NJ: Prentice Hall.

Spirduso, W. W., Francis, K. L., & MacRae, P. G. (2005). *Physical dimensions of aging* (2nd Ed.). Champaign, IL: Human Kinetics.

Tyson, S. R. (1999). *Gerontological nursing care.* Philadelphia: Saunders.

Yohannes, A. M., & Hardy, C. C. (2003). Treatment of chronic obstructive pulmonary disease in older patients: A practical guide. *Drugs & Aging, 20* (3), 209–228.

Chapter 5

AGE-RELATED CHANGES WITHIN BIOLOGICAL SYSTEMS: URINARY, REPRODUCTIVE, ENDOCRINE, AND IMMUNE

GARI LESNOFF-CARAVAGLIA

THE URINARY SYSTEM

It has long been held that human beings are born incontinent and die incontinent. Urinary disorders, however, are not a normal aspect of aging and are due to disease states. They are, nonetheless, significant causes of death and morbidity in older persons (Hampton, Craven, & Heitkemper, 1997).

Several body systems are involved in helping to remove waste products or unneeded substances from the body. Through the digestive system cells receive the nutrients they need to function properly and to eliminate waste products following digestion. The respiratory system supplies oxygen to the body for cellular metabolism and eliminates carbon dioxide, a waste product of cellular metabolism. The principal excretory organs of the urinary system are the kidneys. They play a critical role in maintaining the homeostasis of the body. This is done through the regulation of water content within the body and sustaining the balance of additional substances which may either need to be retained in the body or excreted (Chop & Robnett, 1999).

Age-Related Dysfunctions

Urinary incontinence is fairly common among the elderly, especially in women over the age of 65. Cultural stigma and embarrassment have prevented many people from acknowledging and reporting the problem, although it is usually treatable (Spence, 1995). It is about half as frequent among men, but men suffer much more from an opposite problem, involuntary continence. In older males, the prostate gland surrounding the urethra commonly enlarges to constrict the urethra. The prostate gland is also part of the reproductive system.

Urinary tract infections are also quite common in the older population. Urinary tract infections and pneumonia were found to be responsible for more than half of all infections in health care settings. The most commonly associated causes of urinary tract infections include a lack of hand washing between patient contacts by health care professionals, close proximity to others with catheters, poor positioning of drainage bags, and poor catheter insertion techniques (Schulz & Salthouse, 1995).

Urinary tract infections are much more prevalent among women than men and are attributable to such facts as the tendency toward having a short urethra in close proximity to the rectal opening, the absences of prostatic fluid and its bacteriostatic qualities, and urethral compression by an enlarging uterus in pregnancy. Several other factors influence the rate of urinary tract infection including socioeconomic status, personal hygiene practices, and analgesic abuse (Ham, Sloane, & Warshaw, 2002).

Urinary tract infections are usually treated with an antibiotic or antimicrobial treatment therapy in order to insure that the infection will not spread. In addition to drug therapy, increases in fluid intake are recommended to dilute the urine, to increase urine flow, and to prevent dehydration. To prevent urinary tract infections, older persons should be encouraged to stay active and to wear loose-fitting undergarments and clothing. Prevention is difficult due to the fact that many occurrences are caused directly by bacteria.

Frequent urination and extreme urgency to urinate in older persons are results of decreases in bladder size and a delayed micturition reflex. Pressure on the urethra due to obesity increases the need to urinate more frequently (Kart, 1997). These conditions are annoying to the person even if they do not render the person unable to contain the urine.

Such conditions, however, can become embarrassing when the individual cannot reach the toilet in time. The need to urinate can occur at night, and the older person may face interrupted periods of sleep. Physical accidents are more common at night as persons move about the home in the dark to conserve on electricity. Homes can contain additional environmental hazards by way of loose rugs, sharp-edged furniture, and stairwells.

In older women the pelvic diaphragm, a muscular mass that helps maintain the tone of the bladder and contributes to the proper closure of the bladder outlet deteriorates. When women age, the pelvic diaphragm becomes weakened and the bladder does not close completely leading to leakage or stress incontinence. This can be triggered by coughing or sneezing. In many cases this can be corrected by retraining and strengthening the muscles ((Fiatarone Singh, 2000).

URINARY INCONTINENCE: Although urinary incontinence (or involuntary micturition) is a common condition, its exact incidence is difficult to establish as it can occur in varying degrees and, in many cases, the person will not admit to being incontinent. Older persons may try to conceal their urinary incontinence because they assume it is due to the aging process, and there is no hope of recovery. They may also be too ashamed and embarrassed to mention it, or they may fear losing their independence and being forced to accept institutional care.

Urinary incontinence is the involuntary loss of urine in undesirable, inappropriate situations. To be continent one must first identify an acceptable place, secondly be able to get there, and thirdly be able to get there in time. It is both a social and health problem, and its incidence increases with age. Another specific type of incontinence is stress incontinence which involves urine leakage during exercise, coughing, sneezing, or laughing (Viktrup et al., 2005).

Overall, there is a higher rate of incontinence among institutionalized older individuals than those living in the community. Although there is no evidence that normal aging causes incontinence, about 50 percent of older persons in long-term care institutions are incontinent, and approximately 30 percent of all older persons experience some degree of urinary incontinence. This may be, in part, attributable to the fact that persons when they enter long-term care institutions are currently older and sicker. Furthermore, the incontinence may not have been treated as a resolvable problem and has been allowed to continue unchecked. Programs of water intake and regulating the time of toileting may not have been initiated, nor programs of exercise to strengthen the muscles (Lekan-Rutledge, 2004). The incidence of incontinence is about twice as high in women as in men and is often a cause rather than a result of institutionalization.

Physically active individuals are less likely to suffer from incontinence. Underlying diseases which can cause incontinence include certain central nervous system disorders such as stroke, multiple sclerosis, diabetes, and Parkinson's disease. Prostatic hypertrophy in men and senile vaginitis in women are other causes. Psychological factors, including attention seeking, rebellion, regression, and feelings of helplessness and dependency, can also lead to the development of incontinence. Excessive alcohol intake and sedative drugs may be additional contributing factors.

The effects of urinary incontinence on the older person and his or her family are far-reaching. The ability to socialize may be limited, and persons are confined more to their homes. Sooner or later this affects their mental state and morale, and they feel different from or inferior to the rest of society. The home or room can develop an odor, and care of the person can also become an economic burden. Urinary incontinence is, therefore, a common major problem with serious socioeconomic implications.

In many cases, incontinence can be psychologically damaging to the individual, and creates aversion in caregivers. Some institutions will not accept incontinent individuals, indicating a societal reticence in dealing with this problem. Such care, however, can also be quite costly. Incontinence represents a return to an infantile state, returning a previously mature individual to a state of dependency.

Incontinence is not a normal consequence of aging. Many nonphysiological factors are often pertinent to the issue of incontinence. Adequate mental function and motivation must be present for voluntary control of the urinary bladder reflex. The physical ability to move and the skills to do so safely are essential for reaching toilet facilities, particularly in the case of persons suffering from nocturia (Ludgren, 2004).

Incontinence need not be accepted as unchangeable or untreatable. In fact, many older individuals are incontinent in the hospital or long-term care setting, but become continent again in their homes, demonstrating the effect of environment on the problem. A positive correlation exists between urinary incontinence and immobility.

Urinary incontinence is often the precipitating cause for placing an older individual in a nursing home. The inconvenience and the work associated in caring for an incontinent older persons leads to this decision. There are incontinence programs which, if proper community assistance is available, can allow the older persons and the family to maintain the person at home. Assistance by way of confidential laundry service, water ingestion regimens, and timing of when the person will need to void, all are important alternatives to institutionalization based on incontinence.

An environmental inventory of the home and the barriers that may be present in the home that serve as obstacles to reaching the bathroom within the needed time is very helpful. Adequate nighttime lighting, non-slip rugs, and paperless toilets which provide for ease of use, are all important aids in keeping the person continent. Such considerations are particularly important when persons suffer from chronic diseases which lead to frequent urination, such as diabetes (Rembratt, Norgaard, & Andersson, 2002).

Technology in Diagnosis and Treatment

New treatments are available for specific diseases. Measurements of kidney function allow more accurate diagnosis, and certain technical aids can help compensate for the loss of function.

The most dramatic methods that are used to accommodate an individual's need for kidney function during and after renal failure are renal dialysis (the artificial kidney) and kidney transplant. Renal dialysis has been in use long enough to be considered effective in augmenting kidney function. In dialysis, toxic materials are removed as in a normally functioning kidney.

Interventions and Technology

Many technologies are specific to a particular type or types of incontinence and attempt to cure the problem (e.g., artificial sphincters, electric stimulators, drugs, training procedures, and surgery). Diagnostic evaluation is thus critical to the appropriate use of these treatments. Other treatment technologies are nonspecific and palliative rather than curative (bed pads, undergarments, and, in some situations, catheters).

In general, these technologies should be used as a last resort after diagnostic evaluation has excluded treatable conditions.

The various types of technologies for the treatment of urinary incontinence fall into approximately four categories: devices, surgery, drug treatment, and training procedures.

An example of a device includes catheters which collect urine before leakage occurs. A flexible tube is placed directly in the bladder and drains urine into a collecting bag. Catheters can be used continually or intermittently. The use of catheters is recommended when there exists the inability to empty the bladder (urinary retention) which cannot be corrected by surgical or drug treatment. The danger of infection must be carefully controlled.

Devices to prevent or delay urine outflow include the artificial sphincters which consist of an inflatable cuff which is surgically implanted around the urethra and inflated to prevent urine outflow. For females, electrical stimulation through a device inserted into the vagina produces electric impulses that cause contraction of pelvic floor musculature and inhibits bladder contractions. For males, an external penis clamp can be used to prevent urine flow.

Four major types of devices are currently in use: bed pads and undergarments, catheters, electrical stimulation, and artificial sphincters.

Bed pads and undergarments range from those that are completely disposable to those with launderable components. Most acute care hospitals and long-term care institutions use "blue pads" for managing incontinence despite their relatively low absorbency and lack of odor control. More innovative forms, like the Kylie(C) pad that is launderable and draws moisture away from the body, have been marketed widely in the United States only recently. The efficacy of these products in diminishing complications of incontinence such as skin irritation and urinary tract infection has not yet been carefully assessed.

The three types of catheters commonly used are chronic indwelling catheters, intermittent bladder catheterization, and, for men, external catheters. A Foley indwelling catheter is placed in the bladder and attached to plastic tubing that drains urine into an externally worn collection bag. This type of catheter can induce serious complications with urinary tract infection as the most common. It should only be used in patients with urinary retention that cannot be treated surgically, pharmacologically, or by intermittent catheterization, and for patients with skin conditions that are worsened by contact with urine.

External (condom) catheters, used exclusively in men, may reduce infection but require frequent changing, often fall off, and may result in local skin irritation. The National Aeronautics and Space Administration (NASA) has also developed an external female urine-collection device for use of women astronauts. This device may be appropriate for use with some patients.

Devices to Correct Urinary Incontinence

Incontinence is a symptom with many possible causes. As a symptom, it requires full investigation to establish the diagnosis, followed by specific treatment with drugs, physiotherapy, or surgery. External devices should be considered only if these treatments are ineffective. However, many elderly patients with chronic incontinence suffer from a degree of mental impairment limiting their tolerance of certain external devices.

A high percentage of stroke victims and victims of Parkinsonism suffer from some degree of incontinence. Incontinence associated with dementia, a deterioration of intellectual abilities, may be a result of direct involvement of those areas of the brain involved in bladder control, or it may be secondary to the patient's inattention to personal hygiene, inability to communicate needs to the nursing staff, or inability to reach the toilet. Urinary incontinence continues to escalate as a problem in long-term care facilities as the age of admission increases, along with the numbers of persons with multiple severe diseases.

Restoration of urinary control has included application of implantable, indwelling, and external devices. Both electrical and mechanical technologies have been utilized.

Despite severe drawbacks, an indwelling catheter and a diaper or pad are the two most widely employed devices for managing urinary incontinence. Their ease of application and their ability to control leakage in the case of the catheter or to provide storage in the case of the pad, as well as lack of suitable alternative management schemes, have encouraged their widespread use.

The indwelling catheter allows for continuous bladder draining in seriously disabled and totally incontinent patients. It requires less attention than intermittent types of incontinence care and does not require patient capability. The indwelling catheter may be indicated as the method of care for a patient who is senile or bedridden, or who has upper-body disabilities that make self-care impossible.

The drawbacks of the indwelling catheter are several: the patient's mobility is severely limited; the incidence of urinary tract and bladder infection and irritation is extremely high; and the catheter requires changing by professional staff. Bacteria will eventually develop in virtually all cases.

On the other hand, the use of a diaper or pad will allow patient mobility, and can be an aid in the management of incontinence of the bowel, as well as of the bladder. Problems with this type of care include skin irritation, the need for frequent changes to ensure local hygiene, an unpleasant odor, infections of the urinary tract, and the psychological stigma of wearing a diaper. Such garments are available in a variety of sizes, geared to the nature of the urinary problem. Some of these undergarments are treated with absorbent substances that absorb much of the urine, preventing discomfort and skin diseases.

Because of these drawbacks to the use of indwelling catheters and diapers or pads, alternative device treatment modalities, including surgically implanted devices and external patient-applied methods, have been developed.

Environmental controls to offset odors have included automatic room deodorizers and disinfectants. New fibers for use in patient's clothing and bedding that will absorb odors are in the process of development.

THE REPRODUCTIVE SYSTEM

The topic of sexuality and aging has not been, until recently, openly discussed. Historically, sex was not to be introduced as a topic for public discourse. One reason for the emergence of sex and sexual behavior as legitimate areas of human concern is due to the increasing numbers of older persons who, by living beyond the period of childbearing and child rearing, have found sex to be a pleasurable and socially fulfilling activity.

It is no longer sex for procreation, but sex as recreation. Due to their longevity, older persons have linked sex, not to reproduction of the species, but to pleasure. These alterations in sexual attitudes in general are due, in part, to more sophisticated methods of contraception, but also, in part, to the increasing numbers of healthy older persons within the population.

The concept of sex as pleasure and personal fulfillment rose as the aging population increased. Sex linked solely to reproduction became an anachronism (Aiken, 1995). The life expectancy for women has increased, and large numbers of women are living beyond menopause. This means that the years of life experienced by a woman after menopause may be greater than her sexually reproductive years. Alterations in demography which leave more older women than men to experience life to advanced ages, also means that fewer men are available as sexual partners. This older population represents individuals who were married, widowed, divorced, or never-married; all of whom had a decided interest in maintaining continuity in their lives—including sexual continuity.

The reproductive system plays an important role in the lives of older persons. Negative stereotyping of older individuals and a negative attitude towards sexuality in old age has delayed scientific research in this area of human experience. As persons age, the reproductive system does not sustain extensive physiological changes, but those that may occur are felt more on an emotional or psychological level.

Changes in the reproductive system have a significant bearing on personal identity and self concept. Alterations in sexual functioning, more than any other bodily system, may signify to the person that he or she is old. For men, erectile dysfunction can undermine physical and mental well-being. The introduction of the drug Viagra® has helped offset such problems, although its use appears to carry some risk potential (Salonia et al., 2005). One of the major physiological changes in women is menopause with its concomitant hormonal changes which can result in physical and psychological consequences such as mood alterations, irritability, and depression. Not all women experience such changes to the same degree, and some experience menopause with equanimity.

The common changes in the male reproductive system cause some men to become depressed, to experience mood swings, or to become aware of their own finitude. The advent of old age is a precursor of death. The prospect of growing old is viewed with trepidation, alarm, and sometimes fear (Spirduso, Francis, & MacRae, 2005). Psychosocial factors play a large role in attitudes toward self and sexual activity. The first experience of impotence can provoke much self-reflection and anxiety.

Dysfunctions

CANCER: One dysfunction of the reproductive system that becomes more prevalent with age is cancer. Older men frequently experience cancer of the prostate (Freedman, Hahn, & Love, (1996). The incidence of cancer of the ovary, uterus, vagina, cervix, and breast is greater in postmenopausal women.

Breast cancer is a problem for approximately 1 out of every 12 women in the United States. Risk factors for developing breast cancer include factors such as age and family history.

ERECTILE DYSFUNCTION: The term "impotence" has been traditionally used to signify the inability of the male to attain and maintain erection of the penis sufficient to permit satisfactory sexual intercourse. It is recommended that the more precise term "erectile dysfunction" be used instead to signify an inability of the male to achieve an erect penis as part of the overall multifaceted process of male sexual function.

Erectile dysfunction affects millions of men. This condition is not necessarily age-related, but it is progressively more frequent as men grow older. Men who suffer from a variety of physical ailments may be prone to such dysfunctions, particularly diabetics (Godschalk, Sison, & Mulligan, 1997). This is a problem among men who consume large quantities of alcohol, have cardiovascular problems, or are habitual users of drugs for medical reasons or as recreation. Stress and emotional or psychological problems are additional factors that can lead to erectile dysfunction (Aiken, 1995; Kubin, Wagner, & Fugl-Meyer, 2003).

Technology and Sexuality

ASSISTIVE INSEMINATION: Assistive insemination has radically altered the possibilities of reproduction in older women, even after menopause. Although it was always acceptable for older men to marry younger women and to have families at advanced ages, it is now possible for older women, including postmenopausal women, to bear children. This can mean that women, along with men, can now have second and third families. Being able to procreate in old age suggests that women can biologically have the same sexual capabilities as men.

Women in their sixties have borne healthy children, and older women continue to express interest in becoming parents at advanced ages. Some women bear children for other infertile family members or provide children to childless couples. The capability to be able to "rent a womb" extends now to the older female as well.

In assistive insemination, the sperm can be supplied by the husband, and the egg from a donor. The older mother carries the fetus to term and becomes the gestating mother. In some instances, both the sperm and the egg are donated.

Further, women can, at younger ages, freeze and save their own eggs for use in assistive insemination when they are postmenopausal. An older couple, for example, can utilize both the husband's sperm and the wife's egg to form a new family related to their older children who can be several decades apart in age.

Recent developments such as uterus transplants have allowed infertile women to experience the menstrual cycle and thus to become fertile. Uterine transplants are also an alternative for postmenopausal women who wish to create a family in old age. In terms of the reproductive system, age may indeed have become irrelevant.

Some nations have attempted to halt the birth of children to older mothers because there is the fear that she may not live long enough to nurture the child. In cases where the father has been over 70, there has not been a similar outcry.

THE ENDOCRINE SYSTEM

Much like the nervous system, the endocrine system, although poorly understood, is one of the main regulatory systems of the body. It helps regulate body temperature, basal metabolic rate, growth rate, stress responses, and reproductive functions (Masoro & Austad, 2001).

The endocrine system is made up of glands that are closely connected to the nervous system in maintaining internal body balance and stable conditions. The glands control a number of body processes by way of hormones that are directed toward specific organs throughout the body. Endocrine glands include the pituitary or the master gland, the thyroid, the parathyroids, the adrenals, the pancreas, and the gonads (Masoro & Austad, 2001). The hypothalamus region of the brain is also linked to endocrine functions. The hypothalamus is also considered as possibly the site of an "aging clock" that controls the aging process.

The hormones excreted by these glands play very important roles in areas such as sexual identity and activity and the development of secondary sexual characteristics. The hormones are specialized in that they are targeted for specific cells. Hormonal imbalances can induce far-reaching bodily changes, including extremes such as dwarfism and gigantism. The aging process itself may be the result of a programmed deficiency of one or more hormones. This suggests that the aging process could possibly be manipulated through the addition of hormones and hormone-secreting cells (Chadwick & Goode, 2002; Miller, 1996).

The ability of endocrine glands to synthesize hormones does not decrease to a great extent as a person ages. However, the role of the pituitary gland in regulating growth has led to speculation that the maintaining of levels of growth hormone might slow down the rate of aging (Chanson, Epelbaum, Lamberts, & Christen, 2004).

Age-related Dysfunctions

Disorders of the endocrine system are not frequent in old age, and, when they do occur, they are usually the result of pathological changes rather than simply age related. The most common age-related conditions that are often due to endocrine dysfunction are diabetes mellitus, hypothyroidism (goiters), and reactions to stress.

DIABETES MELLITUS: Diabetes mellitus is a condition in which there is an inadequate amount of glucose in tissue cells. The reduction of glucose in the cells may be the result of inefficient secretion of insulin by the pancreas or a lowered sensitivity of target cells to insulin. There are two main forms of diabetes mellitus, type I and type II.

Type II or noninsulin-dependent diabetes mellitus is most prevalent among older persons who are overweight. Type II diabetes can be treated through medications, diet modification, and programs of weight control. Exercise is also recommended. Chronic diabetes can cause skin ulcers, glaucoma, cataracts, frequent urination, and loss of weight. Men may experience problems of erectile dysfunction. Diabetes can also interfere with circulation, especially in the extremities. Such circulatory dysfunction can result in gangrene and subsequent amputation of a total limb or partial amputations of toes or feet.

The long-term complications of diabetes mellitus remain a serious health problem. Diabetes mellitus remains a significant public health problem for the elderly (Haas, 2005). It is a potent risk factor for the development of premature coronary artery disease, visual impairment, renal failure, neuropathy, and peripheral vascular disease.

STRESS RESPONSES: The physiological changes that persons encounter as they age are not very easily accommodated and can lead to stress. A hallmark of aging is the reduced capacity to respond to a variety of stressors (Masoro & Austad, 2001). Stressful events for older persons may include the death of a spouse or friends, physical trauma, infection, intense heat or cold, surgical operations, chronic debilitating diseases, family problems, alteration in living arrangements, incontinence, or sensory losses. Several of these stressful events can occur at one time or as clusters over a short period of time. Some of these problems defy solution. Prolonged stress has been linked to the development of Alzheimer's disease. Stressful situations in the lives of the elderly are frequent and often irreversible. This also probably accounts for the high rates of depression found in older adults (Kart, 1997). It may also provide the roots for suicide in old age.

As far as can be presently determined, the endocrine system in older persons does not materially change with age. Many of the age changes are related to pathological conditions or conditions of lifestyle. Abnormalities of the endocrine system occur long before old age, such as sexual abnormalities or unusual physical characteristics.

Technological Interventions

Older individuals suffer the amputation of toes, feet, or entire limbs. The prognosis for those who refuse such surgical intervention, especially at advanced ages, is extremely poor. Nonetheless, older persons may not consent to amputation. The development of prostheses particularly suited to older amputees is currently being undertaken. New treatment modalities in the rehabilitation of older amputees are being addressed in rehabilitation centers which increasingly serve older clients.

THE IMMUNE SYSTEM

Although poorly understood, the immune system plays a significant role in preventing or counteracting the effects of disease. The immune system is crucial to the maintenance of health, particularly with respect to defense against pathogens (Chandra, 1995). There is a progressive quantitative and qualitative loss in the ability to produce antibodies (Holliday, 1995). Among the numerous physiological defects associated with aging is a generalized decrease in immune function which leads to greater susceptibility to infectious agents, such as bacteria, viruses, fungi, or other foreign substances, as well as to an increase in morbidity and mortality due to infectious disease (Pathy, 1998). This system has received public awareness due to its relationship to the AIDS virus.

The immune system becomes less efficient as people continue to age, and thus they are more susceptible to disease (Masoro & Austad, 2001). It is less effective in protecting the body against various bacterial organisms that attack the various systems. It differentiates less effectively between foreign agents that enter the body and the body's own line of defense. Thus, the likelihood of succumbing to disease is increased.

The progressive weakening of the immune system as people age means that the body has fewer and fewer effective defenses to stave off the inroads of disease. The fact that this system is not well understood; neither as it operates in younger or older people, makes it difficult to develop strategies for prevention or intervention. The greater susceptibility of older persons to disease and the pervasive fragility of the older person lead to its association with the diminished efficiency of the immune system. Improved knowledge of the immune system could probably provide significant information on disease prevention and, as a result, ways to extend the life expectancy (Butcher & Lord, 2004).

Dysfunctions

There are a number of diseases that have direct relationship to the malfunctioning of the immune system. They include AIDS, arthritis, cancer, Alzheimer's disease, cardiovascular disease, and a variety of infectious diseases (Manuck, Jennings, Rabin, & Baum, 2000). Cancer, for which old age is the greatest risk factor, has been linked theoretically to altered immune surveillance, with some experimental validation documented in prostate and skin cancers, but detailed mechanistic information is lacking (Masoro & Austad, 2001). Other age-associated diseases, such as Alzheimer's disease and cardiovascular disease have been better documented.

REFERENCES

Aiken, L. R. (1995). *Aging: An introduction to gerontology.* Thousand Oaks, CA: Sage Publications.

Butcher, S. K., & Lord, J. M. (2004, August). Stress responses and innate immunity: Aging as a contributory factor. *Aging Cell, 3* (4), 151–160.

Chadwick, D. J., & Goode, J. A. (Eds.). (2002). *Endocrine facets of ageing.* New York: J. Wiley.

Chandra, R. (1995). Nutrition and immunity in the elderly: Clinical significance. *Nutrition Review, 53* (4), s80–s85.

Chanson, P., Epelbaum, J., Lamberts, S., & Christen, Y. (Eds.). (2004). *Endocrine aspects of successful aging: Genes, hormones, and lifestyles.* New York: Springer Publishing Company.

Chop, W. C. & Robnett, R. H. (1999). *Gerontology for the health care professional.* Philadelphia: F. A. Davis Company.

Fiatarone Singh, M. A. (2000). *Exercise, nutrition, and the older woman: Wellness for women over fifty.* Boca Raton, FL: CRC Press.

Freedman, A., Hahn, G. & Love, N. (1996). Follow-up after therapy for prostate cancer. *Postgraduate Medicine, 100* (3), 125–134.

Godschalk, M., Sison, A., & Mulligan, T. (1997). Management of erectile dysfunction by the geriatrician. *JAGS, 45* (10), 1240–1246.

Haas, L. (2005). Management of diabetes mellitus medications in the nursing home. *Drugs & Aging, 22* (3), 209–218.

Ham, R. J., Sloane, P. D., & Warshaw, G. A. (Eds.) (2002). *Primary care geriatrics: A case-based approach* (4th Ed.). St. Louis : Mosby.

Hampton, J. K., Craven, R. F., & Heitkemper, M. M. (1997). *The biology of human aging* (2nd Ed.). Dubuque, IA: W. C. Brown.

Holliday, R. (1995). *Understanding aging.* New York: Cambridge University Press.

Kart, C. S. (1997). *The realities of aging.* Boston: Allyn and Bacon.

Kubin, M., Wagner, G., & Fugl-Meyer, A. R. (2003). Epidemiology of erectile dysfunction. *International Journal of Impotence Research, 15* (1), 63–71.

Lekan-Rutledge, D. (2004, August). Urinary incontinence strategies for frail elderly women. *Urologic Nursing, 24* (4), 281–302.

Lundgren, R. (2004, April). Nocturia: A new perspective on an old symptom. *Scandinavian Journal of Urology & Nephrology, 38* (2), 104–108.

Manuck, S. B., Jennings, R., Rabin, B. S., & Baum, A. (Eds.). (2000). *Behavior, health, and aging.* Mahwah, NJ: Lawrence Erlbaum Associates.

Masoro, E. J. & Austad, S. N. (Eds.). (2001). *Handbook of the biology of aging.* San Diego: Academic Press.

Miller, K. (1996). Hormone replacement therapy in the elderly. *Clinical Obstetrics and Gynecology, 39* (4), 912–932.

Pathy, J. (Ed.). (1998). *Principles and practices of geriatric medicine* (3rd ed.). Chichester, England: John Wiley and Sons.

Rembratt, A., Norgaard, J. P., & Andersson, K. E. (2003, November). Nocturia and associated morbidity in a community-dwelling elderly population. *British Journal of Urology International, 92* (7), 726–730.

Salonia, A., Briganti, A., Montorsi, P., Maga, T., Deho, F., Zanni, G. et al. (2005). Safety and tolerability of oral erectile dysfunction treatments in the elderly. *Drugs & Aging, 22* (4), 323–338.

Schulz, R., & Salthouse, T. (Eds.). (1995). *Adult development and aging* (3rd ed.). Upper Saddle River, NJ: Prentice Hall.

Spence, A. D. (1995). *The biology of human aging* (2nd ed.). Englewood Cliffs, NJ: Prentice Hall.

Spirduso, W. W., Francis, K. L., & MacRae, P. G. (2005). *Physical dimensions of aging* (2nd ed.). Champaign, IL: Human Kinetics.

Viktrup, L., Koke, S., Burgio, K. L., & Ouslander, J. G. (2005, January). Stress urinary incontinence in active elderly women. *Southern Medical Journal, 98* (1), 79–89.

Chapter 6

AGE-RELATED CHANGES WITHIN BIOLOGICAL SYSTEMS: THE NERVOUS SYSTEM AND THE SPECIAL SENSES

GARI LESNOFF-CARAVAGLIA

THE NERVOUS SYSTEM

Mental disorders are among the major disorders facing older adults and have a significant effect upon persons who are responsible for their care, both family members and the professional health care community. The interrelationship between psychological and physical well-being has become particularly manifest as the older population continues to expand (Andrews, 1998).

The nervous system is composed of three types of organs: the brain, the spinal cord, and nerves. Internal communication among cells of the body is conducted by two body systems: the nervous system and the endocrine system (Chop & Robnett, 1999).

The nervous system controls body movements through the contraction and relaxation of skeletal muscles and smooth muscles. Sensory information both from outside and inside the body is related to the nervous system, which it then processes and stores (Kart, 1997). Receptors in the nervous system link it to the special sense of vision, hearing, touch, taste, and smell.

The nervous system is also involved in activities that produce conscious remembering, thinking, interpretation, emotions, and personality traits. All of these higher-level functions take place in the brain. Changes in the nervous system due to senescence can slow the processing of information by the system and affect a person's memory and ability to accumulate and apply new information (Spence, 1997).

With age, there is a gradual loss of nerve cells (Ferraro, 1997). Since nerve cells are not replaced, an inevitable reduction in nervous tissue occurs. The effect of such losses varies among individuals and is largely dependent on the site. Since many more nerve cells are present than are necessary for the functioning of the nervous system, such losses may not become problematic until advanced old age.

As the brain ages, it becomes an increasingly finely balanced system. Although the aged brain has a capacity to compensate for damage and to repair itself, the process is limited. The brain has a large reserve capacity through a surplus of neurons and synapses. Depending upon the extent of neuron loss, brain functioning may not be affected. In fact, there is some indication that new nerve cell connections and new synapses may be formed to effectively compensate for those lost and to possibly even create new ones.

The process of learning involves the formation of new synapses. Since learning continues throughout the lifespan, this means that intellectual ability does not necessarily decline with age. In general, highly educated people tend to retain their intellectual abilities longer than do those who are less well educated (Jennings & Darwin, 2003).

The process of consciously remembering information is referred to as memory. Memory is also affected by age. There are at least three broad types of memory: short-term memory that retains information for only several seconds or minutes; intermediate memory that can last for several hours; and long-term memory that requires several hours or days to develop but can last a lifetime (Ferraro, 1997). Long-term memory seems to be less affected by age than short-term memory. In fact, long-term memory seems to appreciably increase in older persons. For instance, persons may have difficulty in remembering what they had for breakfast, but can relate, with great detail, events that occurred in their childhood.

Aging causes a decline in short-term memory in most people, although the rate of decline varies greatly between individuals. This may be due in part to differences in the rate of age changes within the nervous system, but it can be caused by other factors such as differences in general health, diet, presence of particular diseases, habitual levels of mental activity, motivation, economic conditions, psychological well-being, and socialization patterns. Such decline, however, since it is gradual and slow, allows for the development of compensatory strategies (Jennings & Darwin, 2003).

Memory retention does not show appreciable decline among persons endowed with higher intelligence. This also seems to be true of older persons who remain in the workplace or maintain active intellectual interests following retirement. This could be related to the higher earning capabilities of such people and their consequent better standards of living and health care. Also, people who engage in social activities with family, friends, or by volunteering do not seem to suffer from memory deterioration.

Changes in the brain itself as a result of aging occur primarily in the neurons of the hippocampus which is involved in functions such as memory (Baddeley, Wilson, & Watts, 1995). Neurofibrillary tangles and neuritic plaques begin to appear. A neurofibrillary tangle is composed of large groupings of fibrils or microtubules that develop in some neurons. Such clusters or tangles have been found only in the brains of human beings. They increase in number as persons continue to age, and are present in virtually all persons over the age of 80 (Smyer & Qualls, 1999).

The significance of the presence of neuritic plaques and neurofibrillary tangles in aging brains is not well understood. Small numbers have been found in older persons who function well in old age, as well as in the brains of people who suffer from mental health problems. There appears to be a relationship between the number of plaques and tangles and the level of mental impairment. Plaques and tangles are present in significant numbers in brains of persons afflicted with Parkinson's disease, Down syndrome, and Alzheimer's disease (Gatz, Kasl-Godley, & Karel, 1996).

Dysfunctions

PERCEPTION AND COGNITION: One of the reliable findings regarding aging and cognition is a reduction in perceptual speed. This slowness is the result, in part, of a decline in the formational processing rate which results in slower reaction time. Although there is still controversy as to why this change in reaction time occurs, it appears that deficits in the central nervous system probably account for the greatest portion of psychomotor slowness in the elderly.

Reaction time is the time between the onset of a stimulus and the initiation of a response. It is an index of mental processing time as it reflects stimulus identification and response selection. However, much like many other age-related changes, factors other than age influence the magnitude of the change. The nature and familiarity of the task and health status are significant features. Further, older persons put a great premium on accuracy which may result in a slower reaction time. Nonetheless, this age-related slowness in reaction time is of considerable practical importance since it contributes to difficulties in operation of vehicles or equipment.

SLEEP: The aging process appears to affect the length, distribution, and pattern of sleep. Sleep disorders or expressed dissatisfaction with the quality or quantity of sleep are common complaints in old age.

Greater difficulty is experienced in falling asleep. Once asleep, frequent awakenings occur during the night, and, once awakened, it takes longer to return to sleep. Some causative factors for such changes include the presence of pain, indigestion, use of medications, anxiety, or nocturia. It can also be associated with respiratory or circulatory problems. The increase in awakenings is greater in men than in women.

Changes also occur in the type of sleep. Sleep is divided into two principal types: rapid-eye-movement (REM) and nonrapid-eye-movement (NREM). They are designated as such because of the eye movements that occur during each period. During NREM sleep, sleep becomes progressively deeper with brain activity slowing and regularizing. This is followed by REM sleep during which dreaming occurs. REM sleep and NREM sleep alternate during much of the sleep cycle, with periods of REM sleep occurring about every 80 to 100 minutes. During REM sleep, recordings of brain activity resemble those of an alert, awake brain. In contrast, during NREM sleep, brain recordings show lower frequency waves, and the respiratory rate, heart rate, and blood pressure are generally below waking levels. It has been suggested that physiological recuperation occurs during deep NREM sleep.

Although the time spent sleeping changes little with age, significant alteration in sleep patterns often occur. Sleep becomes shallower and is less sound and efficient. For example, the ratio between REM sleep and slow-wave sleep gradually changes with age, resulting in fewer episodes of deep sleep. Older people also complain of problems such as awakening early in the morning and a feeling of fatigue even after a night's sleep. One of the most frequent complaints is the inability to sleep long enough or peacefully enough to feel rested. This problem is referred to as insomnia.

An area of the brain stem known as the reticular activating system is thought to control brain alertness. Changes in sleep patterns with aging may be related in part to alterations in the reticular activating system. If the system maintains the brain in an alert state, a person cannot sleep. Thus, most medications that induce sleep do so by depressing the reticular activating system. Other factors are also thought to contribute to the high incidence of insomnia in the elderly, including frequent daytime naps, anxiety, and depression.

Mental Disorders in the Elderly

Mental disorders are a significant health problem among the elderly. In general, the number and prevalence of mental disorders is similar to those of younger adults, but it is in the relative prevalence of specific disorders that a major difference occurs. Dementias, cognitive impairments based on changes to the brain, are more common in later life. Some of these, such as schizophrenia, typically have an early onset; while others, dementia, for example, usually have a later onset. Others such as depression or alcoholism can begin to affect a person either early or late in life.

DEMENTIA: Dementia is a broad category of diseases which generally presents with a decline in memory and often with major deficits in one or more additional areas of mental functioning. While the number and rate of cases of dementia are increasing, there has been a tendency to overestimate the incidence of dementia among the old and to underestimate that of depression.

Age-related dementia nominally results in the loss of cognitive function, affection, and in particular, the ability to recall events (Hummert & Nussbaum, 2001). Functions that are often reduced include speaking, reading, writing, solving problems, and performing simple voluntary tasks. Dementia can also cause behavioral disturbances, as well as a wide range of changes that indicate mental deterioration.

It has been estimated that approximately one-third of the population over the age of 85 experiences severe dementia. As life expectancy continues to increase, the prevalence of severe dementia will probably rise in the future. Large numbers of nursing home residents currently suffer from some form of dementia.

There are more than 60 different types of dementia. Some forms of dementia are caused by anemia, nutritional deficiencies, medications, and depression. These forms are reversible when appropriate treatment is provided. Atherosclerosis of the blood vessels of the brain or reduced blood supply is largely responsible for the irreversible forms of dementia. The ischemia (deficiency of blood) can be of short duration and not lead necessarily to mental or functional impairment or to brain deterioration. It can, however, be conducive to vertigo, falls, and accidents.

ALZHEIMER'S DISEASE: Dementia caused by Alzheimer's disease is also known as senile dementia of the Alzheimer's type (SDAT). While Alzheimer's disease is very rare in persons under the age of 65, it affects one person in 10 over the age of 85 (Hummert & Nussbaum, 2001). It is found in approximately 15 percent of the 65 to 74-year-old population, and rises to over 45 percent in the 85+ population. Alzheimer's disease is the most frequent cause of institutionalization for long-term care and accounts for an estimated 30–60 percent of those in nursing homes (Zarit & Zarit, 1998).

Alzheimer's disease is an organic brain disease that causes progressive loss of mental functions over a period of years. Its clinical progression is usually divided into several stages, with increasing debility as the stages advance.

It is important to recognize that moderate declines in intellectual competence of otherwise well-functioning individuals may simply result from disuse. There is a substantial body of evidence to show that noteworthy decline in intellectual abilities is not characteristic of all persons as they age. Individual differences in adulthood are maximized by differential lifestyles that can markedly affect the maintenance or decline of cognitive functions. Until the early '80s, decrement remains quite small on the average. It is only for the very old that substantial decline in intellectual competence begins to become a normative experience and may be linked to disease states. Diminishment in intellectual functioning can become apparent prior to death and is known as "terminal drop."

There is some suggestion that unfavorable environments and maladaptive lifestyles may be at the root of both increased risk for cardiovascular disease and for intellectual decline. The lack of stimulating environments, disengaged lifestyles, inflexible attitudes, and the absence of supportive interpersonal networks may all be causal factors in the experience of intellectual decline. It appears, thus, that the intellectual competence of the elderly can be increased by suitable training and alteration of the environment. Individual differences in maintenance or decline of intellectual competence are associated with health status, active or inactive lifestyles, presence or lack of supportive family settings, and flexible or rigid personalities.

Declines can be reversed in many persons. Prescriptive programs of educational intervention have been successful in reversing well-documented decline for substantial proportions of individuals and have provided for the enhancement and reduction of generational differences in performance for many other older persons who have not declined. Chemical and physical changes in the brain can also account for some of the memory deficits in Alzheimer's disease and for benign forgetfulness of the aged.

NON-ALZHEIMER DEMENTIAS: In some cases of dementia, the cognitive and behavioral changes resemble Alzheimer's disease in general but differ in that they may not be progressive. Rather, the changes may appear suddenly, but not become worse with time. In other cases, new memory retention may decrease while brain functions remain relatively normal.

MULTI-INFARCTION DEMENTIA: Dementia caused by circulatory disease is often called multi-infarct dementia. Atherosclerosis of blood vessels leading to the brain may cause periods of decreased blood flow alternating with periods of adequate blood flow resulting in repeated mini-strokes referred to as transient ischemic attacks (TIAs). The mini-strokes may cause damage to such small regions of the brain that the person is not aware of the strokes. However, cells in the affected regions of the brain do die, producing deteriorated areas called infarcts. If the mini-strokes continue, the person may begin to show symptoms similar to those of Alzheimer's disease, including memory loss. Approximately 20 percent to 30 percent of dementia cases are of this type. Absent-mindedness can be an early symptom of brain damage.

PARKINSON'S DISEASE: Parkinson's disease refers to a clinical condition characterized by muscular rigidity and a rhythmic tremor. It is a leading disease of the nervous system among older persons. It is chronic with symptoms slowly progressing over an extended period of time that can reach 15 to 20 years. Symptoms are usually noted at approximately age 50. The highest rate of incidence occurs at approximately the age of 75. This condition is more commonly found in men than in women. While symptoms increase in severity over the years, the person may continue to be mentally sound and alert.

Parkinson's disease has essentially three basic components: rigidity, tremors, and diminished spontaneous movements. Spontaneous movements, such as swinging of the arms when walking, changing positions and crossing legs while sitting down, are diminished or absent. Akinesia and rigidity are probably responsible for mask-like faces, monotonous speech, and slowness of movement. The useless contractions of skeletal muscles cause not only muscle rigidity but tremors. The tremors, which are present at rest, become less when movement is initiated. They are absent during periods of sleep.

Persons with Parkinson's disease have a characteristic gait. The general posture is that of flexion: the knees are slightly flexed, the trunk appears flexed and bent forward, and the elbows and wrists are flexed. They may take short shuffling steps and tend to lean forward. Although the initiation of the first few steps is slow, the person appears as if glued to the floor, then starts to walk faster and faster. If suddenly asked to stop and to turn around, the person may be unable to do so. Persons with Parkinson's disease are particularly at risk of falling. They cannot take avoiding actions to stop the fall or at least to reduce its impact.

Muscle contractions for swallowing and breathing are also weakened and slower. Declining muscle control and muscle activity may cause drooling. Handwriting deteriorates, and there is often loss of facial expression. Severe disability can be delayed for many years.

CEREBROVASCULAR ACCIDENT: Cerebrovascular accident (CVA) or stroke originates as a disease of the cardiovascular system. Strokes are the third leading cause of death among people over the age of 65. The death rates from strokes and heart disease have steadily declined due to better prevention of atherosclerosis and better diagnosis and treatment of strokes and heart disease.

A stroke occurs when blood flow to and through the brain is disrupted. Because of the sudden and devastating effects on the brain, the victim appears to have been struck with a heavy blow, and thus the term "stroke" was adopted. Since strokes affect the brain and are usually caused by abnormalities in the blood vessels, such as a buildup of fatty deposits and blood clots, or abnormalities in the heart, they are also referred to as cerebrovascular accidents (CVAs).

Many people who suffer a stroke survive. The neurological effects of a stroke may vary, depending upon the side and extent of brain damage.

Large strokes may cause paralysis or dementia. The death rates due to stroke increase substantially in individuals over the age of 65. Many survivors loose the capacity to walk, to speak, and to read. Many experience confused mental states affecting memory and the capability to think clearly. Severe depression is a common aftermath (AHCPR, 1999).

Physical symptoms produced by a stroke generally appear on the opposite side of the body from the side of the brain in which the lesion occurred. This is caused by the fact that most of the nerve tracts connecting the brain and spinal cord cross. Those who survive are often left with serious lifelong disabilities.

Strokes occur more frequently in men than in women. This incidence is significantly higher in the African American population than in the Caucasian population. This is the case in both sexes. Lifestyle factors are often contributing factors.

Substance Abuse

Although older persons are less likely to misuse illegal narcotics than younger adults, alcohol and substance abuse is a significant problem. Alcohol abuse is among the most common mental health problems found in older men. Rates of alcohol abuse are also higher among persons suffering from psychiatric disorders. Problems regarding alcohol consumption are also common in retirement facilities (Bucholz, Sheline, & Helzer, 1995). Due to the fact that older persons are prescribed more drugs and purchase large quantities of over-the-counter medications, prescription drug abuse is an additional growing concern.

Suicide

Although the elderly make up approximately 12 percent of the population, they represent 20 percent of all suicides. In all ages, men commit suicide at higher rates than do women. Stressful life events often lead to thoughts of suicide. Isolation, loneliness, and the fear of becoming a family burden are also prominent factors (Moscicki, 1995).

Since many of the problems faced by the elderly are linked to the provision of health and social services, efforts to reduce the incidence of suicide among the elderly would need to include many environmental considerations such as housing, communication services, and transportation. Health services that focus on psychological well-being and psychiatric services, as well as physiological problems, would need to be extended.

Treatment Modalities

MICROSURGERY AND NEW NERVE PATHWAYS: Microsurgery, which is used primarily in reconstructive surgery, has been utilized to develop new pathways for severed nerves. It functions very much like a coronary by-pass in that once the ordinary pathway is no longer usable, a new one is initiated to continue nerve function. Just as it has become possible to attach severed limbs and to have them function, it is now possible to mend severed nerves and to allow them to function once again. Spinal cord lesions can be repaired through the introduction of such new pathways to allow paraplegics and persons with nerve damage to recover their mobility. The peripheral nervous system is utilized in resolving spinal cord dysfunctions, with the brain adapting to this new pattern. The nervous system "by-pass" also created new cerebral circuits which activate leg muscle movements. For older individuals nerve damage can thus be repaired, and limb functions can be improved. In addition, new methods for the boosting and manipulation of brain functions are under study ("Ethics of Boosting," 2004; Farah & Wolpe, 2004).

REHABILITATION OF DEMENTIA PATIENTS: Patients with severe brain damage can be retrained so that impaired cognitive processes are reacquired through different routes, using healthy brain tissue. Electronic television games have a compelling, almost addictive, attraction for many people. It appears likely that this would apply to elderly people suffering from dementia. Participation in games can help develop alertness and lengthen attention span.

THE SPECIAL SENSES

Information concerning the external environment is received through special sensory receptors for vision, hearing, equilibrium and balance, taste, and smell. The receptors for vision are located in the eyes; those for hearing, equilibrium, and balance are located in the ears; the receptors for taste are in the mouth and throat; and the receptors for smell are located in the nose. Touch receptors, as part of the integumentary system, are located throughout the body. These receptors monitor the environment by transforming light waves, sound waves, fluid movement, or chemical stimuli into nerve impulses that are transmitted to the brain over sensory pathways. The cerebral cortex processes the sensory information, and the stimuli are perceived as objects, sounds, body position and movements, tastes, or smells.

The functional capabilities of these special senses may be altered with aging, and, thus, older people are often unable to detect as much sensory information from their environments as can younger people. Generally, these losses accelerate at particular ages: vision, age 50; hearing, age 40; touch, age 55; taste, ages 55-59; and smell after age 70. Such changes continue to accelerate with each decade after 65. Consequently, by the late '70s or early '80s, the sensory deterioration may become quite serious.

Approximately one-half of the persons who are legally blind in the United States are over the age of 65. An additional one million are severely impaired. There are up to two million profoundly deaf Americans and more than seven million who suffer significant bilateral hearing impairment. Reliable statistics on the prevalence of severe hearing loss by age are not available, but it is very likely that auditory impairment is one of the most prevalent forms of sensory disability among the elderly (Desai et al., 2001).

A majority of the 3.5 million American diabetics affected by peripheral neuropathy have a disorder that impairs sensation in the distal extremities. Most of the complications of the "diabetic foot" are the indirect consequence of neuropathy and are identical in nature to complications seen in nondiabetic insensitive feet.

Sensory changes do not begin in everyone at the same age; there are persons who suffer slight or no losses into advanced ages while there are others who suffer from multiple sensory losses. Sensory changes occur over a period of time, and persons learn to compensate for such losses in numerous ways.

VISION

Without adequate vision, individuals are isolated from the environment and are almost completely dependent upon others to provide them with mental stimulation. Persons with poor vision often lose interest in the environment, become withdrawn, and depressed. This is particularly true as vision deteriorates late in life, and when some older persons are unable to learn new skills such as reading Braille. They are often unable to compensate for their disability.

The eye is a very complex organ, and it is composed of a number of elements within the eye that work together to unite it as a unit. One of these essential elements is the liquid in the eye. This moisture serves several functions. The tear ducts, or lacrimal glands, supply the moisture that washes the eye and keeps it moist, thus preventing the accumulation of foreign particles such as dust or insects. It provides a smooth surface for the muscles of the eye to operate easily, and, through the blinking of the eye, the fluid is spread across the eye.

The drying of this liquid in the eye is an age-related problem that can cause pain and irritation. To offset the malfunctioning of the lacrimal glands, substitute tears and liquids to provide moisture and to cleanse the eye are frequently prescribed. The drying of the eye can also result from various disease states, such as fevers.

With age, the cornea of the eye also becomes less of a sphere and becomes a little flatter. There is a yellowing of the lens as well, and not as much light reaches the retina. The pupil does not dilate as openly or fully causing approximately one-third of the light to not reach photoreceptors in the back of the eye, resulting in decreased input to the brain. This causes older persons to require more light than do younger persons to read or to carry out activities effectively. The yellowing of the lens also affects color perception of such hues as blues and greens. Such changes can also lead to faulty color perception, such as the mismatching of colors in clothing.

Failure of vision with age results from changes in the eye itself–the surrounding muscles and the central nervous system (Ferraro, 1997). Two major changes in the eye begin to occur in the mid-50s. The lens of the eye becomes increasingly rigid, opaque, and gradually yellows; the surrounding eye muscles begin to weaken and to become more lax.

As a result of these physical changes, several problems occur–a decrease in visual acuity, or the ability to see objects clearly; a decrease in the ability to focus on objects at different distances; a decrease in the ability to discern certain color intensities; and a decrease in the ability to judge distances. The occurrence of presbyopia (farsightedness) is generally considered to be a facet of normal aging.

Dysfunctions

GLAUCOMA: The most serious eye disease in old age is glaucoma which is caused by an elevated pressure within the eye. Symptoms of the disease include blurred vision, the experience of pain, and watering of the eye. Additional symptoms may include severe headache, dizziness, and nausea. A gradual loss of peripheral vision, usually affecting both eyes simultaneously, is usually the first sign. The visual field may eventually become so restricted that persons only see objects that are in their direct line of vision. They are left with what is known as tunnel vision. Untreated, the condition gradually worsens, and total blindness is the result.

CATARACTS: Cataracts are the most common disability of the aged eye. Cataracts seem to be a consequence of aging; their incidence increases progressively after age 50 and approaches 95 percent of the population 85 years or older. In the United States, cataracts account for more than half of the hospitalizations caused by eye disorders, and the cataract operation is the single most common surgical procedure done in this country.

AGE-RELATED MACULAR DEGENERATION: Age-related macular degeneration is the leading cause of legal blindness among older adults, especially women. There are also indications that it may be genetic. It is a disease in which the eye's macula, a remarkably sensitive structure in the middle of the retina, gradually loses its ability to distinguish shapes and colors. While not a fatal disorder, it can be extremely debilitating. Although the macula (named after the Latin word for spot) is no wider than a pencil, it is a hundred times more sensitive to small-scale features than the rest of the retina. Without a healthy macula, people cannot read a newspaper, recognize a friend, thread a needle, watch TV, safely negotiate stairs, or see much of anything at all.

Until now, physicians have been able to offer only palliative care to patients with macular degeneration: more powerful eyeglasses; visual aids, such as machines that enlarge print; and, for a minority of cases, laser therapy that sometimes slows down the disease, at least for a time.

People with macular degeneration do not become completely blind; peripheral vision, which is handled by other areas of the retina, remains unaffected by the disease. However, as damage to the macula builds up, central vision fades making it difficult to distinguish fine detail of the objects viewed. The external world dissolves into an indistinct blur.

Leading ophthalmologists have recently begun exploring the possibility of replacing the dysfunctional RPE cells with healthy fetal cells. The transplanted cells proliferate, forming minute projections that stretch toward the diseased macula. Fetal RPE cells can divide and thus increase in number.

Unfortunately, most cases of age-related macular degeneration do not respond to medical or surgical treatment. The use of magnifying devices–either hand-held or incorporated into eyeglass lenses–has proved beneficial in overcoming some of the loss of visual acuity. Because only the macular region of the retina is affected, this condition does not cause the person to become completely blind.

Vision and Technology

Many people maintain their vision into advanced old age. The presence of new interventions in terms of surgical procedures (laser surgery), new types of glasses, contact lenses, industrial safety, and better understanding of preventive measures have all led to improved vision in old age. The maintenance of general good health, particularly the cardiovascular system, improves the conditions and functioning of the visual apparatus in old age.

One of the most innovative devices is the development of the robot-dog that takes the place of the guide dog. In appearance, it resembles a large vacuum cleaner with a long handle. The long handle keeps the user in contact with the mechanism as it moves through space avoiding obstacles. Derived from a model used in industry, this mechanism can be equipped with lights for nighttime use, sound elements, and attachments to suit individual needs.

HEARING

Impaired hearing is common among older individuals. Some loss is due to age-related physiological change in the auditory system, and some is due to disease and superimposed environmental insults. There is great variability in the decline of hearing (Hull, 1995).

The ear is made up of three sections: the external, the middle, and the inner ear. The external ear collects the sound waves which travel through the middle ear to the inner ear in which the sound is then interpreted by the brain. The inner ear contains the cochlea which is the organ of hearing and the temporal bone which is frequently the site for cochlear implants used to offset hearing problems. Sounds are the result of vibrations that travel over the fluid that is present in the inner ear.

Hearing loss is often gradual and occurs at about middle age, and is more common among males than females. It is not clear why men experience hearing loss earlier, but it could be due to environmental factors such as industrial noise or listening to certain forms of music.

Dysfunctions

Even the partial loss of hearing that is often associated with aging can limit independence and negatively affect quality of life for the elderly (Cox & Alexander, 1995). Hearing loss restricts the individual's ability to interact with others and to give, receive, and interpret information (Hummert & Nussbaum, 2001). Sound is important for self-protection and identification of hazards in the environment. Ultimately, hearing loss can affect mental and physical health, decreasing the ability of some individuals to function independently and increasing the need for formal and informal long-term care services. Hearing impairment rises sharply with age. The hearing loss that develops as a function of advancing age is known as presbycusis.

TINNITUS: Tinnitus is the perception of background noise generated in the ears or head. It can be present in one or both ears and can be intermittent or constant. This is commonly referred to as ringing of the ears, but the sound may also be described as buzzing, whirring, humming, or other annoying sounds.

The development of devices which are inserted in the ear and produce a sound similar to the crackling of frying bacon help to offset the constant noise produced by tinnitus. There is no known cure for tinnitus due to nerve degeneration. Tinnitus may become quite severe; there are anecdotal reports of suicide because of this condition.

DIZZINESS AND VERTIGO: Older persons are more likely to experience dizziness or vertigo, and it is a common complaint. These conditions can be caused by an inflammation within the inner ear which is related to balance and equilibrium or of an inflammation of the nerve fibers of the vestibulocochlear nerve. Vertigo is usually a symptom of inner ear disease.

PRESBYCUSIS: With aging comes a gradual, progressive hearing loss which is known as presbycusis ("old hearing"). It is a sensorineural or permanent hearing loss resulting in degeneration of the sensory hair cells in the inner ear (Ferraro, 1997). It usually occurs in both ears, but the rate of loss may be different in each ear. Some researchers believe that presbycusis is associated with normal aging, while others believe it results primarily from disease conditions. Not all elderly individuals experience presbycusis, and some people in their 90s retain acute hearing.

Although presbycusis is a progressive loss of hearing, the symptoms are not readily apparent until the person is over age 65. The loss is complicated by other factors such as illnesses, substance abuse, and noise. Men are affected more than women, and urban dwellers suffer greater losses than those living in rural areas. The degree of loss is more severe for high-frequency sounds than for low-frequency sounds. The selective loss of high-frequency hearing makes it difficult for older persons to hear consonants. Such changes also cause speech to sound muffled.

INTERVENTION STRATEGIES: Although a certain amount of hearing loss might be inevitable and attributed to the aging process, there are many approaches to intervention that can be noted. Medical and surgical advances report impact on the elimination of hearing loss, or the reduction of the extent of loss. Examples are the 'miracle drugs' effects upon mastoid infections and the perfection of microsurgery in the treatment of otosclerosis. Legal intervention, such as the Occupational Safety and Health Administration (OSHA) regulations on reasonable constraints on noise in the workplace, represents an attempt to meet the problem at its source in order to prevent damage.

The hearing-aid industry places great importance on its research-and-development programs in the attempt to produce hearing aids that give greater fidelity to the sound and that extend the range of the frequency response. Hearing aids are amplification devices designed to compensate for partial hearing loss (Bridges & Bentler, 1998).

Continued research in the area of cochlear implants may lead to improvements for the profoundly deaf or hard-of-hearing population. Intervention also is found in the increase in the availability of assistive listening devices other than hearing aids. Such intervention includes the FM broadcasting by a teacher or minister in a classroom or a church that is transmitted to a receiving mechanism worn by the hard-of-hearing listener. Many theaters now have special infrared amplification systems in which the actors' voices are picked up at the stage level and broadcast into the auditorium, where the sound can be received by a special listening device worn by the person who is hard-of-hearing. These, and other assistive listening devices, are designed to overcome problems that are present in certain communication situations where a conventional hearing aid does not prove to be adequate to the task (Carmen, 1999; Tyler & Schum, 1995).

TASTE

Taste is a chemical sense, and its loss is a common complaint among older persons. Such losses can be attributed to the atrophy of the taste buds which comes with age, or by lesions of the facial nerve and the brain.

Changes in taste perception can affect the quality and quantity of the foods that people consume. Receptors for taste or taste buds are found on the tongue, the inside of the cheeks, in the throat, and on the roof of the mouth.

Diseases in these areas, such as cancers, can result in taste alterations. Oral health is important in preserving the sense of taste. Lifestyle factors such as abuse of alcohol, other drugs (including medications), and tobacco can all change taste perception (Pathy, 1998). The sense of taste accounts for only four of the sensations that many people call flavors; all other flavors are due to the sense of smell. These four primary taste sensations include: salty, sour, sweet, and bitter. Aging seems to cause slight decreases only in the ability to detect salty and bitter substances. The amount of change is highly variable among individuals, and the ability to detect salt declines the most. The degree of taste impairment seems to vary from taste to taste, being less pronounced for sweet and most profound for salt (Walter & Soliah, 1995).

Other contributing factors to alterations in taste include decreases in the amount of saliva in the oral cavity and changes in the surface texture of the tongue. In addition, medication and lifestyle factors such as abuse of alcohol or years of addiction to cigarette smoking can also alter the taste of food.

In order to compensate for this loss, taste perception can be enhanced through oral sprays that provide moisture to the mouth. They also help in the dissolving of food. The addition of various herbs to food preparations can also make food more palatable to older persons.

SMELL

Much like taste, there are variations in the ability of older persons to smell particular odors. A decline in the sense of smell (hyposmia) can, however bear serious consequences (Pathy, 1998). With age, there is a loss in the ability to distinguish individual odors in a mixture. Such losses in the sense of smell seem to have a greater effect upon men than women.

As individuals age, there is a decrease in the number of sensory neurons for smell. These neurons are called olfactory neurons and are located in the upper portion of the nasal cavities (Pathy, 1998). Since much of what is commonly referred to as flavor is actually aroma, age changes in the sense of smell tend to reduce the pleasure derived from eating and can contribute to malnutrition. The sense of smell is of particular importance in older persons because of its close relationship with the sense of taste. Persons with a long history of cigarette smoking are more prone to alterations in smell perception.

Reduced olfaction also means a reduced ability to detect harmful aromas such as toxic fumes and dangerous gases (Pathy, 1998). The protective measures provided by the sense of smell are considerable. Environmental cues such as the presence of gas or burning substances can be overlooked.

TOUCH

Touch receptors and pressure receptors in the skin decrease in number and become structurally distorted as a person ages. Such changes can lead to a decreased ability to notice that something is touching the person or the ability to recognize an object by touch (Spirduso, Francis, & MacRae, 2005). Decreases in the ability to detect, locate, and identify objects touching or pressing on the skin result in decreases in the ability to respond to those objects and can lead to accidents.

Pain perception and pain reaction thresholds are somewhat reduced. Reactions to hot or cold objects appear to be delayed, resulting in unintentional injuries such as burns. In general, the ability to sense danger tactilely and to respond accordingly is reduced. Reductions in sensation from the skin seem to result from a weakening in the conduction of impulses to the cortical nervous system.

Telecommunications Systems

HEARING: One of the most common and frequent problems for hearing impaired older individuals is the inability to use the telephone. This problem is compounded for those who experience visual as well as hearing losses. For older persons, particularly for the great numbers who live alone, the telephone is a link to the outside world; inability to use the telephone can compromise safety and interfere with independent functioning.

Hearing over the telephone is difficult even for those with mild hearing loss because telephone signal transmission omit very low- and high-frequency sounds that are important for understanding speech. Line noises and other sound distortions also interfere with the quality of sound transmission.

Devices to assist hearing impaired individuals to use the telephone include amplifiers that can be built into the telephone handset or attached to the side of the telephone. In addition, telecoils are also helpful. Telecoils are built into hearing aids to pick up electronic signals directly from the telephone receiver and bypass the hearing aid microphone.

The development of effective computerized speech recognition systems could also greatly simplify telephone use for the hearing impaired. These systems convert spoken words into printed output that is then displayed on a screen attached to the telephone. Currently, available speech recognition systems still have major limitations.

SIGNALING AND ALARM SYSTEMS: Signaling and alarm systems that convert sound to visual or tactile signals are important for the safety and independence of hearing impaired persons. Flashing lights and vibrating devices that signal the ringing of a fire alarm, smoke alarm, telephone, doorbell, or alarm clock substitute for sounds the person cannot hear. Tactile paging devices use radio signals to generate vibrations in a portable receiver carried by the hearing impaired individual.

ENVIRONMENTAL DESIGN: Building design characteristics affect the behavior of sound and the relative ease or difficulty of hearing. For example, hard-surfaced walls and floor reflect sound, creating reverberations that interfere with hearing, while sound-absorbent wall covering materials decrease reverberations.

While much is known about design characteristics that affect hearing, this information is seldom applied in buildings used by the elderly. Reduction of reverberations and background noise in these facilities could considerably ameliorate some of the problems of those with hearing loss.

ASSISTIVE DEVICES: In general, hearing impairment in old age is often mild to moderate and is often progressive. Hearing impairment in the elderly often coexists with other health problems that complicate treatment and limit the effectiveness of available assistive devices.

Denial of hearing impairment on the part of the older person is a continuing obstacle to treatment. The most effective method of treatment available at present is the use of devices and techniques that compensate for hearing loss. An assortment of signaling devices exist to provide either tactile or visual cues to phone rings, doorbells, clock alarms, smoke alarms, door knocks, or cries of an infant. Strobe-type fire alarms, flashing phone ringers, and doorbell flashers are inexpensive and have been available for some time. There are, however, few distributors for many such devices, and those who could possibly benefit from these devices rarely know about what the devices do and how one acquires them. Marketing typically concentrates on advertisement through specialized journals, which are unfamiliar to the average hearing-disabled older person.

VISION: Low vision may be functionally defined as loss of visual acuity or visual field severe enough to prevent performance of a desired task. Most of the severely vision-impaired older populations have residual vision that may be optimized by comprehensive low-vision services. Such services are typically provided through clinics specializing in low vision.

Problems posed by blindness and by low vision have prompted the development of new technology. One example is the Kurzweil Reading Machine which can read aloud a book or magazine. Another example is Optacon (Telesensory Systems, Inc.) which allows people to learn to read text by converting print to a vibrating tactile pattern on the fingertip. In addition, a long cane is still relatively inexpensive, and with proper training, it affords a good deal of independent mobility. Other products available include talking books, radio, and the new flood of literature recorded on standard audiocassettes (designed for general consumption). All of these products provide some solutions to loss of reading ability.

TACTILE IMPAIRMENT AND TECHNOLOGY: There are a few technologies that may be employed to the benefit of those who are "touch-blind." Special gloves that indicate excessive cumulative pressure by color change generated when dye-containing microcapsules rupture may be worn during repetitive tasks. A few simple experimental systems, designed for measuring cumulative pressures at points in the sole, provide audible alerts once a certain critical threshold is passed.

Attempts to design systems that provide a form of artificial skin sensation have been unsuccessful to date. Sensory substitution (or, rather, sensory transfer) technology could allow development of an unobtrusive appliance, built into footwear or gloves, that transmits relevant haptic information electrically to transducers placed on areas of sensitive skin.

FUTURE TECHNOLOGICAL DEVELOPMENTS: The sense of touch begins to assume major importance when other sensory channels are less efficient. Regardless of how advanced cochlear prostheses become, it remains likely that there will always be a population for whom a tactile hearing substitution system is required or preferred for acoustic reception.

Future development of high-resolution tactile systems may provide a substitute for vision. Very little is known about how age-related changes might influence information transmission through the skin, and even less is known about how pathological changes in skin or nerve affect functional sensation, orientation, and movement.

Age-related changes broaden the range of ergonomic variables that must be considered in developing new devices and appliances for use by older persons. If such design included the attributes of populations with the most common visual, hearing, tactile, and motor limitations, substantially expanded markets might emerge. These products would be of great benefit for home use and in health care settings. Such developments could effectively alter health care environments, treatment modalities, and living arrangements. Greater emphasis upon visual displays, acoustic signals and alarms, audibility levels, and tactile discrimination in home appliances, along with more effective communication systems and flexible transportation systems, could effectively prevent many of the barriers that transform impairment into disability.

REFERENCES

AHCPR. (1999). Depression in primary care: Treatment of major depression, clinical practice guideline, 2(5), AHCPR Publication Number 93-0551.

Andrews, G. R. (Ed). (1998). Ageing beyond 2000: One world one future. *Australian Journal on Aging, 17* (1), Supplement.

Baddeley, A. D., Wilson, B. A., & Watts, F. N. (Eds.). (1995). *Handbook of memory disorders.* Chichester, England: John Wiley & Sons Ltd.

Bridges, J. A., & Bentler, R. A. (1998). Related hearing aid use to well-being among older adults. *The Hearing Journal, 51* (7), 39–51.

Bucholz, K. K., Sheline, Y. I., & Helzer, J. E. (1995). The epidemiology of alcohol use, problems and dependence in elders: A review. In T. Beresford & E. Gomberg (Eds.), *Alcohol and aging* (pp. 19–41). New York: Oxford University Press.

Carmen, R. (1999). Sensorineural Insights. Part 1: Aging: It may never be too late. *Hearing Health, 15* (1), 21–24.

Chop, W. C., & Robnett, R. H. (1999). *Gerontology for the health care professional.* Philadelphia: F.A. Davis.

Cox, R. & Alexander, G. (1995). The abbreviated profile of hearing aid benefit. *Ear & Hearing, 16* (2), 176–183.

Desai, M., Pratt, L. A., Lentzner, H., & Robinson, K. N. (2001, March). Trends in vision and hearing among older adults. *Centers for Disease Control and Prevention, National Center for Health Statistics,* pp. 1–8.

Ethics of boosting brainpower debated by researchers (2004, May 28). *Drug Week,* pp. 412.

Farah, M. J., & Wolpe, P. R. (2004, May–June). Monitoring and manipulating brain function: new neuroscience technologies and their ethical implications. *Hastings Center Report,* pp. 35–45.

Ferraro, K. F. (Ed.). (1997). *Gerontology: Perspectives and issues* (2nd ed.). New York: Springer Publishing Company.

Gatz, M., Kasl-Godley, J. E., & Karel, M. J. (1996). Aging and mental disorders. In J. E. Birren, & K. W. Schaie (Eds.). *Handbook of the psychology of aging* (4th ed.) (pp. 365–382). San Diego: Academic Press.

Hull, R. H. (1995). *Hearing in aging.* San Diego: Singular Publishing Group, Inc.

Hummert, M. L., & Nussbaum, J. F. (Eds.). (2001). *Aging, communication, and health: Linking research and practice for successful aging.* Mahwah, NJ: Lawrence Erlbaum Associates.

Jennings, J. M., & Darwin, A. L. (2003). Efficacy beliefs, everyday behavior, and memory performance among older elderly adults. *Educational Gerontology, 29,* 71–91.

Kart, C. S. (1997). *The realities of aging.* Boston: Allyn & Bacon.

Moscicki, E. K. (1995). North American perspectives: Epidemiology of suicide. *International Pyscogeriatrics, 6,* 355–361.

Pathy, J. (Ed.). (1998). *Principles and practices of geriatric medicine* (3rd ed.). Chichester, England: John Wiley and Sons.

Smyer, M. A., & Qualls, S. H. (1999). *Aging and mental health.* Malden, MA: Blackwell Publishers.

Spence, A. (1997). *Biology of aging* (2nd ed.). Englewood Cliffs, NJ: Prentice Hall.

Spirduso, W. W., Francis, K. L., & MacRae, P. G. (2005). *Physical dimensions of aging* (2nd ed.). Champaign, IL: Human Kinetics.

Tyler, R. S., & Schum, D. J. (Eds.). (1995). *Assistive devices for person with hearing impairment.* Boston: Allyn and Bacon.

Walter, J., & Soliah, L. (1995). Sweetener preference among non-institutionalized older adults. *Journal of Nutrition for the Elderly, 14,* 1–13.

Zarit, S. H., & Zarit, J. M. (1998). *Mental disorders in older adults.* New York: The Guilford Press.

PART III

Chapter 7

GERONTECHNOLOGY AND VISION

Cynthia Stuen and Michael Fischer

BACKGROUND AND DEMOGRAPHICS OF AGE-RELATED VISION LOSS

Vision impairment affects approximately 17 percent of people age 45 and older in the U.S. according to self-reported data of a population-based survey conducted by Lou Harris and Associates on behalf of Lighthouse International. The prevalence of vision loss significantly increases with age, affecting approximately 15 percent of people ages 55 to 64, 17 percent of the 65 to 74-year olds, and 27 percent of people age 75 and older (The Lighthouse Inc., 1995). In this same study, 94 percent of the adults with self-reported vision loss indicated that they did not receive any type of vision rehabilitation service which would have exposed them to high and low technology that might be helpful to maximize their independence (The Lighthouse Inc., 1995).

There are normal changes in one's vision with age and it is important to understand and differentiate them from age-related eye disorders. In one's forties or fifties, the most common vision change that occurs is presbyopia. The lens of the eye becomes denser, more yellow and less elastic making it harder to focus for near tasks such as reading. This is correctable with reading glasses or glasses with bifocal, trifocal or progressive lenses. The pupil of the eye tends to become smaller thus permitting less light to enter the eye. Older persons require more light than younger people to perform tasks. Older persons take longer to adjust to changing light levels and have some loss of contrast sensitivity and col-

115

ors tend to appear less vivid. There is often more sensitivity to glare. While visual acuity remains quite well preserved in the normal aging eye, it is important to note that visual function requires much more than visual acuity.

The World Health Organization (WHO) in the ninth edition of the *International Classification of Diseases* officially abandoned the dichotomy of vision versus blindness and recognized the continuum that exists between normal vision and blindness. Low vision or partial sight is experienced by the vast majority (over 90%) of older adults who experience vision loss.

In 2004, the World Health Organization presented new estimates of global blindness. They estimated that there are now 37 million blind people and 124 million people with low vision (Resnikoff et al., 2004). In the United States, older people who become visually impaired do so typically as a result of one or more common, age-related eye disorders such as cataract, macular degeneration, glaucoma, and/or diabetic retinopathy. With increasing numbers of people living into their eighties and nineties, vision loss will continue to affect a growing number of older people. By 2010, it is estimated that 20 million people nationwide will report some form of vision impairment.

Common Eye Diseases and Their Impact on Function

The most common age-related eye disorders affect vision differently and, therefore, require different rehabilitation interventions and technology to compensate for the type of vision loss. Conceptually, one can think of vision loss affecting one's central field, one's peripheral field, overall blur or splotchy vision.

Age-related macular degeneration (AMD) is the leading cause of vision loss among older adults in the U.S. Numerous risk factors have been identified, including race and eye color (for example, Caucasians and people with light-colored eyes have increased risk). The disease results in the loss of the central field of vision making reading and doing any fine detail work difficult. The most frequent complaint of persons with AMD is the difficulty or inability to read; parts of letters appear missing and lines are wavy (see Figure 7.1D).

Peripheral field loss is most commonly caused by glaucoma in older adults. It usually has a very gradual onset, and a person may not recognize the loss of peripheral vision until it is quite advanced. In addition

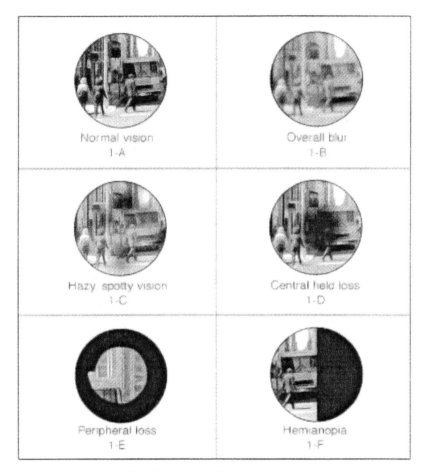

Figure 7.1. Simulations of different types of vision loss.

to age, risk factors include African ancestry, a family history, diabetes, and nearsightedness. While reading usually remains intact (at least until the late stages of the disease), mobility can become a major difficulty for persons with advanced glaucoma. Bumping into things, and the inability to detect obstacles in one's peripheral field of view, create safety hazards for people with glaucoma (see Figure 7.1E, Peripheral Vision Loss Simulation).

Having diabetes will eventually lead to diabetic retinopathy whereby the blood vessels of the retina break down and leak blood or fluid into the eye causing blurred or splotchy vision and/or blind spots. At times one's vision may fluctuate based on the time of day and can vary from almost normal to very impaired. People of African, Native American, and Hispanic ancestry have higher prevalence rates of diabetes and hence have higher rates of diabetic retinopathy (see Figure 7.1B & C, Overall Blur/Splotchy Vision Simulation).

Hemianopia is often a concomitant of a cerebral vascular accident. The most common presentation is the homonymous hemianopia, which results in loss of corresponding halves of one's field of view; it could be the left or right when related to strokes, upper, or lower half of the field of view when associated with other disease processes. Hemianopia may, at times, go undetected in the post-stroke or head trauma patient (see Figure 7.1F, Simulation of Hemianopia).

Impaired vision later in life can be both psychologically and functionally devastating. There is strong evidence from a number of studies demonstrating that the experience of chronic vision impairment is linked to depression and poorer perceived life quality (e.g., Carabellese et al., 1993; Horowitz & Reinhardt, 1996a). In fact, several studies suggest that approximately one-third of older adults who are visually impaired experience clinically significant depressive symptomatology (Horowitz, Reinhardt, & Kennedy, 2005). Consistent relationships have been documented between age-related vision loss and lower morale, social isolation problems, affective disorders, and reduced feelings of self worth (e.g., Bazargan & Hamm-Baugh, 1995; Wahl & Oswald, 2000). The literature certainly documents the importance of recognizing and addressing the psychosocial factors for persons with impaired vision in order for any rehabilitation or use of technology to be successful (Stuen, 2006). Furthermore, vision loss is often feared more than other age-related physical impairments because it tends to be associated with a state of complete dependency and helplessness (Brennan & Silverstone, 2000). Vision loss also affects a person's ability to perform valued activities (Rovner & Casten, 2002).

Addressing the Problem through Vision Rehabilitation

Vision rehabilitation can help restore independent function for persons with vision loss. There is a cadre of vision rehabilitation professionals on the multi-disciplinary team to help the older adult restore and/or maintain the functional activities of daily living, work, and leisure pursuits. The team members include low vision specialists, low vision therapists, vision rehabilitation therapists, occupational therapists, orientation and mobility specialists, vocational counselors, adaptive technology specialists, and social workers.

Most vision rehabilitation will begin with a functional vision assessment conducted by a low vision specialist, an ophthalmologist or optometrist with specialized training (Fischer & Cole, 2000). As part of the exam, the low vision eye doctor will obtain a detailed functional history to understand the patient's difficulties. Then a series of tests are performed, including visual acuity, central and peripheral visual field, and contrast sensitivity, to obtain a complete picture of how the patient is functioning. Once this is completed, the doctor will determine what optical and adaptive technologies, or other vision rehabilitation services, may be helpful to the individual based on the type and severity of the vision loss. Recommendations and prescriptive devices are often task specific, as it is unlikely that a single device or service will address all the patient's needs.

There are literally hundreds of different devices that the low vision doctor may consider when trying to address a specific patient's problems. While the focus of this chapter is geared toward "high tech" solutions, it is important to note that many problems are addressed successfully using lower tech optical low vision devices or other simple adaptive items. In fact, it is not uncommon to have a geriatric patient who is "technophobic" and prefers the use of a magnifier or a pair of low vision glasses to address specific problems.

As such, it is useful to have an understanding of the staples of low vision care, the optical devices that are routinely prescribed:

1. *Microscopic spectacles:* high-powered glasses that provide increased magnification and a better field of view than most hand-held magnifiers. An advantage of spectacles is that they allow the user's hands to be free (i.e., one hand is not occupied as when using a magnifier). A disadvantage of these glasses is that they require the user to hold materials very close, and the stronger the glasses, the closer the working distance. It is sometimes difficult for the geriatric patient to maintain the close-working distance for an extended period of time, as the muscles in the person's arms tend to relax, taking the material beyond the focal range of the glasses.

2. *Hand magnifiers:* these devices are often prescribed for near, short-term (spotting) tasks, such as reading price tags, labels, and appliance dials. Some patients prefer them for text reading as well. While it is

common to find low-powered hand magnifiers sold in many commercial outlets, the ones prescribed by low vision doctors are often much higher power, and may require the person to receive training to insure success with the device.

3. *Stand magnifiers:* these are magnifiers that are placed directly on the reading material. Because the focal distance is pre-set, it eliminates the problem some people have of maintaining the proper distance with a hand magnifier; this can be a particular issue for some geriatric patients who may have a hand tremor. Both hand and stand magnifiers come in a variety of styles. In recent years, LEDs (light emitting diodes) have become more popular as light sources for illuminated magnifiers. Since the bulbs almost never need replacing and LEDs have lower power consumption, the batteries last longer.

4. *Telescopes:* for the person who needs magnification to see distant objects, telescopic devices are frequently prescribed. They come in different styles and powers. Hand-held telescopes are generally used for quick spotting tasks, such as seeing street signs, traffic lights, bus numbers, or faces or objects at a distance. A spectacle mounted telescope will be considered if the patient needs the telescope for more extended viewing tasks, such as classroom or work-related activities, theatre, or sporting events, where using a hand-held scope would be impractical. From a technology standpoint, auto-focusing telescopes have been developed that may be of benefit for the patient who has difficulty manually focusing a scope, or who needs to quickly shift between targets at different distances.

These 4 categories—microscopic spectacles, hand magnifiers, stand magnifiers, and telescopes—are the most commonly prescribed optical low vision devices. Simple adaptive devices, such as check writing guides, signature guides, talking clocks and watches, felt-tipped pens, and large number phones, also are frequently recommended to address specific needs. There are times when more sophisticated technology is the answer.

Technology in Vision Rehabilitation

Many of the latest developments have been in the area of "high tech" devices, which include electronic magnification systems and computer assistive technology. Such devices are often a better solution for the patient with very reduced acuity, poor contrast sensitivity, or large central scotomas that necessitate extreme eccentric viewing.

The first high tech device used in low vision was introduced over 35 years ago, the closed circuit television, or CCTV. CCTVs are electronic magnification systems that allow the user to present printed materials and objects enlarged on a television monitor. The person can adjust magnification and contrast as needed, based on visual function.

Since their introduction, numerous improvements have been made to CCTVs. Where they once were simple black and white systems that provided basic magnification and required manual focusing, current desktop CCTVs have many enhanced features, including flat screen monitors, autofocus capability, and the ability to accept speech commands (Figure 7.2). One recent system provides the ability to perform electronic text manipulation: the text is captured via optical character recognition (as with a computer scanner), and allows the user to view the text in a variety of modes (presented like a teleprompter, or as text scrolling across the screen, as examples).

The trend over the past decade has been to develop electronic magnification devices that are more portable or more affordable (and sometimes both). Some examples include:

- Hand-held cameras that interface with standard TV sets or other portable devices, such as headborne video displays or flat panel displays. These tend to be some of the more affordable devices, compared with desktop CCTVs, but they are still several hundred dollars. Some recent portable systems have large flat panel displays with cameras that can be flipped up for distance viewing and down for near tasks; these systems cost as much as desktop systems (Figure 7.3).
- Head-mounted systems, where the camera and LCD displays are combined into a headset (Figure 7.4).
- Self-contained portable units, where the camera and screen are in a single unit. Initial units, while portable, still weighed several pounds. The newer units, miniature LCD magnifiers, are very small and lightweight, so that they can be carried in a pocket or handbag (Figure 7.5). The small screen dimension, however, makes it more difficult to use these devices for more than spot-reading tasks.

Computers are extremely important and valuable tools that provide people with vision impairments access to a wealth of information. Accessibility can be achieved using screen magnification, speech out-

Figure 7.2. A collapsible CCTV with a flat panel display.

put, or a combination of the two. Numerous programs exist that have a variety of options for how the contents of the screen are magnified, and speech engines used for voice output are sounding closer to normal human speech than ever before. These programs all work with standard browsers and email systems, so accessing information on the Internet and corresponding with friends, family and others can be achieved more easily.

Typewritten material is also more easily accessible through the use of computer scanners, which take printed text and through optical character recognition, allow the user to access the material using speech or screen enlargement. For those who do not use computers, there are stand-alone units that look like a photocopier, and with the touch of a

Figure 7.3. A portable CCTV system with flip-up camera.

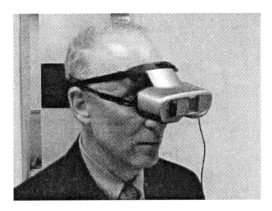

Figure 7.4. A head-mounted system.

button, will convert typewritten text to speech and read the document back in a synthesized voice.

With the baby boomers approaching retirement age, it seems appropriate that the most recent efforts in terms of technology in low vision have been directed toward interfacing computers and electronic video

Figure 7.5. A miniature LCD magnifier set for reverse contrast.

magnifiers. Many manufacturers of video magnifiers (especially the hand-held cameras) are now producing systems with VGA output, to allow the user to see the video image on a computer screen.

Promises for the Future:

Independent travel is, of course, highly valued by older persons, but those with impaired vision are at a particular disadvantage. Signs that once pointed one in the correct direction may now not be readable. In the area of orientation and mobility, there are some exciting possibilities with global positioning system (GPS) technology. Signals from GPS satellites which are available anywhere in the world can be accessed to plan a route and then accompany individuals as they navigate the unknown route.

However, the GPS devices available at local electronics stores are not designed for use by people with visual impairment. These devices require modification to be accessible. According to May (2005), such a modification can be achieved by plugging the GPS into a portable unit with speech output that will announce the information provided by the GPS map system. Larger units have full-size keyboards or Braille keyboards, and are typical used by people with no usable vision. The price range for a combined GPS and voice output system ranges from $2800–$4,000. More recently, personal digital assistants (PDAs) have also been adapted to provide voice output in combination with GPS

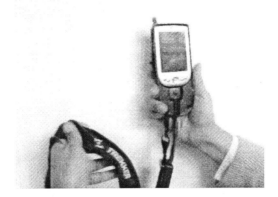

Figure 7.6. A PDA with GPS technology and speech output.

technology (Figure 7.6). While not easily in the reach of many older persons, it certainly holds promise for independent travel for people with impaired or no usable vision.

SUMMARY

While technology is one important aspect of vision rehabilitation, it is only one aspect and it will not solve everything; it should be kept in perspective as an aid to maximize function and participation. While technology can be an enabler, much technology is inaccessible or difficult to access for people with impaired vision.

Many older persons often have co-morbidities that must also be taken into consideration, such as poor mobility or poor cognition. There is a need to educate designers and manufacturers of appliances and technologies of the common age-related chronic and disabling conditions so that at the design phase these needs are addressed rather than constantly increasing retrofits to make them accessible. Gill (2005) points out that it currently can take a number of years from the research and design outcomes to benefit persons who are blind or have partial sight advocates for inclusive design of mainstream products out the outset. He also recognizes that RFID (radio frequency identification) tags hold promise for visually impaired users. The conventional barcode used by many stores, can provide audible access to important product information for the user with vision impairment. This could also be very helpful for prescription and over-the-counter drugs.

Smart Home technology needs to incorporate needs of people with normal age-related vision changes and those with vision loss in design of these environments. The built environment provides many opportunities for inclusive design for people with vision and other chronic and disabling conditions.

Smart Card technology that was first developed in Europe also holds promise for ease of accessibility for people with disabling conditions. The preferred means for communication, for example, could be programmed into the smart card. Having a consistent user interface is possible with smart card technology and as Gill (2005) notes, that is a very important feature for persons with impaired vision. Private industry must realize that designing for an aging population is a good investment and good business.

Recognizing that future cohorts of older persons, especially the baby boomers and the Gen X and Gen Y cohorts will have much more ease with technology solutions than the majority of current cohorts of older persons is important. Since, older persons are one of the fastest growing age groups to get online (next to the teens), this phenomenon may be changing quite quickly. Recognition and accommodation for the normal age-related vision changes and common age-related vision disorders in development of technology solutions for the aging population will be imperative for those in the gerontechnology field.

REFERENCES

Bazargan, M., & Hamm-Baugh, V. P. (1995). The relationship between chronic illness and depression in a community of urban black elderly persons. *Journal of Gerontology: Social Sciences, 50B* (2), S119–S127.

Brennan, M., & Silverstone, B. (2000). Developmental perspectives on aging and vision loss. In B. Silverstone, M. A. Lang, B. P. Rosenthal, & E. F. Faye (Eds.), *The Lighthouse handbook on vision impairment and vision rehabilitation* (pp. 409–429). New York: Oxford University Press.

Carabellese, C., Appollonio, I., Rozzinin, R., Bianchetti, A., Frisoni, G. B., Frattola, L., & Trabucchi, M. (1993). Sensory impairment and quality of life in a community elderly population. *Journal of the American Geriatrics Society, 41,* 401–407.

Fischer M. L., & Cole, R. G. (2000). Functional assessment of the adult: Optometric and ophthalmologic evaluations. In B. Silverstone, M. A. Lang, B. P. Rosenthal, & E. F. Faye (Eds.),

The Lighthouse handbook on vision impairment and vision rehabilitation (pp. 833–854). New York: Oxford University Press.

Gill, J. (2005). Priorities for Technological Research for Visually Impaired People. *Visual Impairment Research, 7,* 59–61.

Horowitz, A., & Reinhardt, J. P. (1996a, December). *Prevalence and predictors of depression among low vision elders.* Paper presented at the Annual Meeting of the American Academy of Optometry, Orlando, FL.

Horowitz, A., Reinhardt, J. P., & Kennedy, G. (2005). Major and subthreshold depression among older adults seeking vision rehabilitation services. *American Journal of Geriatric Psychiatry, 13* (3), 180–187.

The Lighthouse Inc. (1995). *The Lighthouse National Survey on Vision Loss: The experience, attitudes, and knowledge of middle-aged and older Americans.* New York: The Lighthouse Inc. (Data applied to population estimates from the US Census Bureau, Census 2000).

May, M. (2005). Using new technology to improve wayfinding for older adults with visual impairment. *Maximizing Human Potential,* Newsletter of the American Society on Aging, 13, 1, 3–4.

Resnikoff, S., Pascolini, D., Etya'ale, D., Kocur, I., Pararajasegaram, R., Pokharel, G. P., & Mariotti, S.P. Global data on visual impairment in the year 2002, Bulletin WH0, 2004;82: 844–851.

Rovner, B. W., & Casten, R. J. (2002). Activity loss and depression in age-related macular degeneration. *American Journal of Geriatric Psychiatry, 10,* 305–310.

Stuen, C. (2006). Older adults with age-related sensory loss. In B. Berkman, (Ed.) *Handbook of Social Work in Health and Aging.* New York: Oxford University Press.

Wahl, H. W., & Oswald, F. (2000). The person-environment perspective of vision impairment. In B. Silverstone, M. A. Lang, B. Rosenthal, & E. Faye (Eds.), *The Lighthouse handbooks on vision impairment and vision rehabilitation* (pp. 1069–1088). New York: Oxford University Press.

Chapter 8

GERONTECHNOLOGY AND HEARING

Eric W. Sargent and Rodney Diaz

BASIC ACOUSTICS

Sound is the condensation and rarefaction of a pressure wave conducted through a gas or fluid medium. For terrestrial animals, propagation of the vibration through air stimulates the auditory systems. The pressure wave can be characterized by its frequency (wavelength) and sound pressure. The speed of sound through air is approximately 350 m/sec, but varies with temperature, density, and humidity of the air. Humans can perceive sound frequencies between 20Hz and 15,000–20,000Hz, although clinically, hearing is typically measured between 125 and 8000Hz.

The human auditory system has a dynamic range of 1012–that is, the greatest intensity of perceivable sound pressure is 1012 greater than the smallest intensity. For this reason, sound intensity is measured on a logarithmic scale named in honor of Alexander Graham Bell. A sound pressure (P1) can be expressed as decibels measured against a reference pressure (P2) of 20 µPa (found in experiments in the 1930s to be the smallest amount of pressure for a young adult to detect the presence of a 1000- to 4000Hz sinusoid) according to the equation:

$$\text{Decibel (dB)} = 10\log(P1/P2)$$

The result of this is a *sound pressure level* or SPL.

Human hearing perception is non-linear with respect to sound pressure: peak hearing sensitivity is found between ~250 – ~10,000Hz. Below and above these frequencies, hearing sensitivity falls dramatical-

128

ly. Because of this nonlinearity, clinical hearing is not measured according to sound pressure level. Instead of using absolute SPL, *hearing level* (HL) is used where 0dB is the softest sound perceivable by normal hearing adults at each frequency tested.

So far the testing for hearing sensitivity using *pure tones* has been described. However, along with pure-tone threshold testing, clinical audiometry includes testing of word recognition and speech reception thresholds. Word recognition represents more complicated processing of sound by the inner ear and higher centers. In fact, for most elderly individuals complaining of hearing impairment it is the effect of hearing loss on word recognition, with its effects on social interaction, which is most bothersome.

Basic Auditory Physiology

As terrestrial animals evolved from water-dwelling animals, the problem of the transfer of sound from air to the fluid-filled inner ear required the development of an *impedance-matching* or *transformer* system. This requirement stems from the reflection of sound energy at the air-fluid interface from the acoustic impedances of the two media. At the boundary of an expanse of air and water, only 0.001% of the sound energy enters the water. The ossicular chain, thought to have evolved from the jaw structures of fish, is the transformer system of the middle ear.

The external ear and external auditory canal, by virtue of their resonant frequencies, start the process of impedance matching. More important are the functions of the eardrum and ossicular chain. The area of the tympanic membrane is 20 times larger than the area of the oval window (where the stapes contacts the inner ear). This *area ratio* is responsible for the largest part of the transformer function. The length of the long process of the malleus, compared to the long process of the incus, is a ratio of 1.3:1. This *lever* ratio further serves the transformer function of the middle ear. While these ratios assume an "ideal transformer" function, in reality the physical properties of the eardrum and ossicular chain deviate from the ideal situation. For example, the eardrum does not vibrate uniformly at all frequencies and the ossicular chain has mechanical limitations. Nonetheless, the eardrum and ossicular chain work well in the absence of disease and the combined effect of the area ratio of the tympanic membrane: oval window and the lever ratio of the malleus: incus augments transmission of sound pressure in air to the fluid inner ear by ~20dB.

Problems of the tympanic membrane and ossicular chain lead to *conductive* hearing losses. Common problems include perforations of the eardrum, fluid in the middle ear, or fixation of or damage to one or more of the ossicles. Fixation of the stapes is common in *otosclerosis.* Depending on the cause and degree of a conductive hearing loss, the impairment may be corrected by surgery. Alternatively, a conventional hearing aid may be used.

Once the transfer of sound energy from air to the fluid-filled inner ear has occurred, the auditory system converts sound vibrations in fluid to a neural signal. Four rows of hair cells organized along the basilar membrane, three outer rows and one inner row, respond to deflection of their tips with a flow of ions that leads to depolarization of the cell and synaptic transmission to the associated nerve fiber. Tips of the hair cell stereocilia are linked with proteins that can be broken with noise exposure. The cochlea is arranged *tonotopically,* i.e., in order of frequency. Thus, high frequencies are encoded by hair cells near the round window. Low frequencies are encoded by hair cells near the cochlear apex. A volley of impulses along the VIIIth nerve generated by the hair cells is then transmitted to centers in the brainstem and then to the auditory cortex.

The function of the outer and inner hair cells is quite distinct: while the inner hair cells contact the afferent fibers of the VIIIth nerve, the outer hair cells contact VIIIth nerve efferent fibers. It has been found that the function of the outer hair cells is to tune the response of the basilar membrane through myosin-mediated contraction. Interestingly, most hearing loss caused by hair cell pathology–by far the most common cause of hearing loss–is due to outer hair cell damage and loss.

Within the cochlea, there exists a standing current represented as the endocochlear potential, which is the main driving force for hair cell transduction (Davis, 1957). Maintenance of this endocochlear potential is imperative to establish the high efficiency and exquisite sensitivity of hair cell function (Pickles, 1982). This standing current is generated within cells lining the outer wall of the membranous cochlea, the stria vascularis (Offner, Dallos, & Cheatham, 1987; Salt, A.N., Melichar, & Thalmann, 1987). Each of these structures within the cochlea is vital to hearing, and damage or injury to any component can lead to sensorineural hearing loss. Medical intervention to prevent or reverse sensorineural hearing loss has historically been limited to temporary or incomplete rescue of hearing with anti-inflammatory or circulatory-modulating medications such as corticosteroids, vasodilating agents, and lidocaine and other anesthetics (Borri, 1957; Taillens, 1968; Naftalin, 1975; Shaia & Sheehy, 1976). However, this approach has been neither specific, comprehensive, nor consistent (Wilkins, Mattox Jr., & Lyles, 1987; Kanzaki, Taiji, & Ogawa, 1988; Chen, Halpin, & Rauch, 2003).

Disease of the outer hair cells leads to a loss of the tuning capability of the ear. This, in turn leads to loss of word recognition as sound becomes "smeary" and noise intolerance (known as *recruitment*), in addition to the simple impairment of the ability to hear pure tones, occurs.

Epidemiology of Age-Related Hearing Loss

Hearing loss is a common disorder of aging and is, after arthritis and hypertension, the 3rd most reported health problem in the elderly (Havlik, 1986). About one in three of persons aged 65–75 and half of patients older than 75 have hearing impairment to a degree that subjectively impairs communication. Age-related hearing loss is so common, in fact, that hearing impairment is popularly considered a normal part of the aging process, although for many individuals it should not be.

Age-related hearing loss is, in fact, becoming more common: surveys in 1971 and 1991 revealed a 53 percent increase in the number of American adults who experienced hearing difficulty. From 1971–1991, the prevalence of hearing impairment increased by 25 percent. When controlled for changes in age structure of the population for the period, the survey revealed a 14 percent increase in hearing problems.

Impaired hearing affects individuals with identical hearing thresholds differently, making assessment of "disability" difficult to quantify. In fact, there is no commonly accepted threshold at which hearing loss is considered a disability. To some degree, this reflects different personality types, expectations of communication and other factors such as depression, anxiety, or dementia that may complicate the picture. However, in some cases the different ways in which individuals may process the raw auditory signal *(central auditory processing)* may play a large role in determining how a given person deals with hearing loss. For example, when individuals with identical, normal hearing in one ear and

deafness in the other are tested for speech understanding in noise conditions that approximate "real world" situations, variance in speech
understanding between individuals is large, presumably reflecting differences in central auditory processing (Sargent, Herrmann, Hollenbeak, & Bankaitis, 2001). The understanding of behavioral aspects of
central auditory processing is in its relative infancy as is treatment of
disordered or ineffective processing.

Causes of Age-related Hearing Loss

It is difficult to separate individual possible causes of age-related
hearing loss. Many persons with hearing loss in older age will have
acquired (i.e., not inherited) hearing loss. Of all causes, noise exposure is
the chief culprit. Precise prevalence data are not available; however, in
a study from a Swiss clinic, approximately 18 percent of patients with
hearing loss were considered to have noise-induced hearing loss
(NIHL) (Spillmann, & Dillier, 1983). Extrapolating from this data, at
least four million Americans have NIHL causing communication difficulties. Other causes with clear links to hearing loss, such as meningitis,
autoimmune inner ear disease, and otologic conditions such as
Ménière's syndrome are, by comparison, relatively rare.

Effects of Noise on the Ear

While short-term noise exposure induces reversible injury of the tip-
links of hair cell stereocilia, corresponding to the phenomenon of *temporary threshold shift* (temporary hearing loss), extreme acoustic trauma
causes irreversible membrane damage and degeneration of hair cells
(Cotanche, Saunders, & Tilney, 1987; Barrenas, 1997; Patuzzi, 2002;
Chen, Liu, Cheng, Yeh, Lee, & Hsu, 2003). Experimental animals
exposed to chronic noise or explosive sounds show hair cell loss consistent with both necrosis and apoptosis (programmed cell death).

In necrosis, cells–damaged by injury–swell and lose membrane
integrity in an unregulated process. In apoptosis, cells die as a result of
a regulated process characterized by, among other things, cell shrinkage, preservation of membrane integrity, and activation of specific
enzymes. Apoptosis is the process that, for example, allows the development of individual fingers from a limb bud in an embryo.

In noise-induced hearing loss, apoptosis is caused by release of a family of cysteinyl aspartate-specific proteases *(caspase)* that signal and play a role in programmed cell death (Hu, Henderson, & Nicotera, 2002). Other protein kinases, such as mitogen-activated protein kinases (MAPKs) and c-jun N-terminal kinases (JNKs), play a role in cochlear damage. Interestingly, treatment with a JNK activation inhibitor demonstrated reduction in hair cell death and attenuation of hearing threshold shift in experimental animals (Pirvola, Xing-Qun, Virkkala, et al., 2000).

Presbyacusis

Hearing-impaired elderly individuals who have no obvious cause of hearing impairment are said to have *presbyacusis*. However, studies of populations with suspected presbyacusis have not eliminated unrecognized, but suspected causes of hearing loss, such as diabetes or hypertension. Also, while most studies of presbyacusis eliminate patients with hearing loss due to occupational noise exposure, they do not consider nonoccupational noise exposure (termed *socioacusis* by Glorig and Nixon, 1962). Thus, the true incidence of pure age-related hearing loss is unknown. In fact, it is thought that the 14 percent increase in hearing loss noted on epidemiologic studies from 1971–1991 is largely due to socioacusis and environmental noise.

Although epidemiologic studies showing actual increase in the incidence of age-related hearing loss (probably due to socioacusis) argue against it, the greatest technical advance in age-related hearing loss may be in its prevention through industrial hearing conservation measures. Industrial and military hearing conservation programs (HCPs) began sporadically in the 1950s and 1960s (Dobie, 1993). Lack of consensus about harmful levels of noise hampered early efforts. National regulation of industrial noise exposure began in 1971. Although the main motivation for compliance with HCPs has chiefly been threat of litigation and not government penalty, and while some industries are exempt from regulation, the noise environment of many industrial jobs that formerly were almost universally associated with hearing loss is now carefully monitored and controlled. Depending on the work environment, many industrial workers now have hearing protection on the job and their hearing is regularly tested.

Unfortunately, improvements in hearing conservation on the job may have been offset by noise exposure in recreational activities which lead to socioacusis. For reference, the sound pressure of normal conversation is about 60dB SPL, a humming refrigerator is about 40dB SPL. In contrast, personal stereo systems are capable of generating 105–120dB SPL at maximum volume. Some children's toys are quite loud, and in one Canadian study some toys exceeded 100dB SPL. A 357-magnum pistol, producing 165dB SPL for 2msec, is equivalent to 40 hours in a noisy workplace in terms of damage to the auditory system. The start of a NASCAR race generates >130dB SPL to fans in the stands, many of whom find the overwhelming roar part of the sport's appeal. Noise levels in sports stadiums frequently exceed 110dB SPL. In 1976, the rock band *The Who,* notorious at the time as "the world's loudest rock band," was measured 50 meters from the sound system at 120dB SPL. Depending on a number of factors, at 120dB (e.g., an ambulance siren, or *The Who* in 1976), hearing loss may begin after nine seconds of exposure; at 110dB (leaf blower), hearing loss may begin after 1.5 minutes of continuous exposure; at 100dB (snowmobile), hearing loss may begin after 15 minutes; and, at 90dB (stadium football game), hearing loss may begin after 2.5 hours. Sound pressures above 140dB can cause instantaneous hearing loss.

Genetic (or familial) hearing impairment is both common and multifaceted, affecting both children, where its effects are more obvious, as well as adults. While children are thought of as typical patients with familial hearing loss, discovery of genetic causes of hearing loss in children has sparked growing knowledge of the effects that genetic errors also play a role in age-related hearing loss. The explosion of knowledge of the human genome and the insights gained in the molecular basis of hearing promises the most dramatic future benefits for the hearing impaired and, for this reason, congenital hearing loss will be discussed.

Approximately one in 1,000 children are born with profound hearing loss, one in 300 with congenital hearing loss of a lesser extent, and one in 1,000 will develop profound deafness before adulthood (Mason, & Herrmann, 1998; Parving, 1999). It is estimated that 75 percent of congenital and prelingual (i.e., hearing loss that develops before speech develops) sensorineural hearing loss has a hereditary or genetic base, the remaining 25 percent attributable to environmental factors such as infection, ototoxicity, trauma, and prematurity (Schrijver, 2004). Of the genetic causes of hearing loss, approximately one-third are syndromic (i.e., a condition that has a recognizable pattern of abnormalities), while a full two-thirds are nonsyndromic (i.e., hearing loss alone), unrelated to other congenital defects or anomalies (Li & Friedman, 2002). Over 120 individual genes associated with hereditary hearing loss have been identified to date, 80 for syndromic forms and over 40 for nonsyndromic forms (Finsterer & Fellinger, 2005).

Of the hereditary nonsyndromic forms of hearing loss, the most common genetic locus involves the mutation of the GJB2 gene (Lefebvre & Van De Water, 2000; Snoeckx, Huygen, Feldmann et al., 2005). This gene codes for the connexin 26 protein, a component of gap junctions–proteins pores that allow passage of intercellular messengers between adjacent cells–found within the basilar membrane, spiral ligament, and stria vascularis of the inner ear (Kikuchi, Kimura, Paul, & Adams, 1995; Kikuchi, Kimura, Paul, Takasaka, & Adams, 2000). Gap junctions are implicated in the critical role of potassium recycling and homeostasis within the endolymphatic and perilymphatic compartments of the cochlea.

Genetic mutation of genes encoding these gap junction proteins leads to pore dysfunction, deregulation of potassium activity within the endolymph, loss of endocochlear potential, and obliteration of the normal structure of the stria vascularis and scala media. In addition, local potassium concentration builds up within the confines of the basilar membrane and organ of Corti and leads to cytotoxicity and widespread hair cell loss (Lefebvre, Weber, Rigo, Delree, Leprince, & Moonen, 1990; Jun, McGuirt, Hinojosa, Green, Fischel-Ghodsian, & Smith, 2000).

Genetic testing is available for mutations of GJB2/connexin-26 and other hereditary forms of hearing loss to aid in genetic counseling, but currently no site-specific therapeutic interventions are available. Identification of the offending genes affords the potential for future gene therapy to correct such errors.

Effects of Age-Related Hearing Loss

Hearing impairment is stressful for individuals accustomed to good hearing for most of their lives and may lead to social isolation and contribute to depression. Hearing loss is often associated with tinnitus. Tinnitus, a phantom auditory perception of sound in the absence of an external source, is usually an annoyance but capable of causing serious psychological distress. Fifteen to twenty percent of adults report spontaneous tinnitus lasting more than 5 minutes. Fourteen percent of adults with tinnitus note that the tinnitus is extremely bothersome; it interferes with daily activity in 4–6 percent of these adults with tinnitus.

Historical Treatment of Hearing Loss

Commercially available electric hearing aids have only been in use since the early 1900s. Prior to the introduction of electric aids, mechanical devices were used. In fact, the first published scientific reports of hearing instruments were of large hearing and speaking trumpets used in ship-to-shore oral communication. Hearing trumpets were speaking trumpets applied to the ear. Only later did it become clear that these sound collectors would be useful in hearing-impaired persons.

The first mention of an ear trumpet was in 1657. In 1670, Sir Samuel Moreland (England) invented a large speaking trumpet. Throughout the eighteenth and nineteenth centuries, trumpets came into wide use and a number of companies were formed to make them. Mälzel (Germany), for example, was the maker of several trumpets for Ludwig von Beethoven. Trumpets of a variety of designs and material were available. Trumpets were commonly made of thin metal or tortoise shell, although economy models of cardboard and other cheap materials were available. Smaller collectors, called *ear cornets* were also available, as were collectors hidden in hats and beards.

Fascinating and elaborate variations of sound collectors have been contrived. In 1819, King John of Portugal had an *acoustic throne* made. Open-mouthed carved lion's heads at the front of the throne led to hollowed armrests. The tubes of the armrests connected to a resonant box located in the seat of the throne. A hearing tube led from the cavity and to the ear of the king. A number of variations in chairs designed for this purpose were available, including some made for portable use.

Before operations for causes of conductive hearing loss were developed or perfected or electric hearing aids were available, a variety of bone conduction devices (hearing aids that bypass a dysfunctional eardrum and middle ear) were made. One, called the *Fonifer* (1876), was a rod with a semicircular end that rested against the throat of the speaker and a small cup-shaped end that rested against the listener's teeth, forehead, or mastoid, thus transmitting the speaker's voice via bone vibration. The *Rhodes Audiophone* (1879) was a fan-like device consisting of a thin piece of pliable material, the upper edge of which the listener held against or in the teeth. A system of cords permitted adjustment of the tension on the fan, allowing for adjustment in response. A large number of imitators soon followed and the idea served its purpose for mild-to-moderate conductive hearing losses.

The first electric hearing aid was probably shown in 1898 or 1899. The *Akoulallion* consisted of a tabletop instrument with a carbon microphone and up to three pairs of earphones. The Akoulallion, invented by Miller Reese Hutchison (also the inventor of the klaxon horn) of the Akouphone Company (Alabama), was not powerful and helped only those with mild to moderate hearing losses.

Highlight of the historical development of hearing aids are shown in Table 8.1.

Available Products

Conventional Hearing Aids

Conventional hearing aids, from their inception at the dawn of the twentieth century, basically consist of a microphone–amplifier–speaker system. Predictably, advances in miniaturization, more efficient amplifiers, signal processing and batteries have lead to a cleaner output and more flexibility in fitting the aid to the individual's hearing loss while allowing a smaller and more cosmetically acceptable device.

More than 80 percent of hearing aids now sold in the United States are digital aids–i.e., utilizing digital signal processing. Companies offer aids with remote controls that allow the wearer to change the hearing aid program to emphasize different frequencies depending on the listening situation or background noise environment. Many hearing aids now have adaptive circuits that can automatically adjust the shape of the frequency response depending on the noise environment.

Hearing aids come in a variety of physical shapes, from behind-the-ear (BTE) aids (where the microphone and amplifier are situated behind the ear and the output is channeled to a mold in the ear), to in-the-ear (ITE) aids (where the microphone, amplifier and speaker are situated in the bowl of the external ear), to completely-in-the-canal (CIC) aids (which place the microphone, amplifier and speaker much more deeply and less conspicuously in the ear canal itself. Increasingly pop-

TABLE 8.1

1551 Description of a bone conduction device (metal shaft or spear)
1657 Description of Spanish ear trumpets
1757 Rediscovery of the bone conduction rod as hearing aid
1800 Alessandro Volta: electrical current created auditory sensation
1836 First known British patent for hearing aid
1855 First US patent for hearing aid
1876 Telephone invented by Bell
1887 US patent for ear trumpet with diaphragm
1892 First US patent for electric hearing aid
1898 Commercial US production of electric hearing aid (Akoulallion)
1912 First volume control for hearing aid
1920 First vacuum tube hearing aid patented
1923 Vacuum tube aids made by Marconi (England) and Western-Electric (US)
1923 First in-ear electric hearing aid patent (Germany)
1926 Patent for custom earmold
1936 First AGC in hearing aid (London)
1936 First hearing aid with telephone pick-up (telecoil)
1936 First wearable hearing aids in England (1937: US)
1938 First audiometer built to hearing threshold (Maico)
1947 Transistor invented (Bell Labs)
1952 First hearing aid that employed transistor (vacuum tube/transistor hybrid)
1953 First all-transistor aid
1955 First at-ear hearing aid
1957 First 'cochlear implant' experiment (France)
1960 ANSI standard for measurement of hearing aid characteristics published
1963 US experiments with VIIIth nerve stimulation reported
1964 First hearing aid with an integrated circuit
1969 First directional microphone in a hearing aid
1972 First commercially available single-channel cochlear implant
1984 First commercially available multiple channel cochlear implant

ular are open-mold devices that selectively amplify the high frequencies (for patients with purely high frequency hearing loss) through a small unit hidden behind the ear. The output is fed into the ear canal by a thin, inconspicuous tube, leaving the ear canal open for low- and mid-frequencies. One benefit of the open mold devices is the reduction of the occlusion effect–the complaint of many hearing aid wearers (particularly new ones) that their voices sound funny or that they are talking in a barrel, as well as the blockage of a conventional hearing aid.

Whatever their design, conventional hearing aids are prone to feedback. For this reason, BTE aids remain the most commonly fitted hearing aids for severe hearing loss since the BTE separates the microphone (typically situated near the top of the ear) from the output source (in the ear canal) more widely than the other designs. Here, too, hearing aids have benefited from digital signal processing which can allow feedback cancellation.

Implantable/Semi-implantable Hearing Aids

While appealing for a number of reasons, especially in the potential for reduced feedback and elimination of the occlusion effect, development of totally and partially implanted hearing aids has been problematic. All current implantable hearing aids require an external component to drive the implanted portion, thus none are fully implantable. Several ways of transmitting acoustic energy directly to the ossicular chain have been developed. One U.S. FDA–approved device (the Symphonix Soundbridge®) has a tiny coil (described by the company as a "floating mass transducer") that is clipped to the incus in the middle ear. The coil vibrates with an applied current, in turn vibrating the ossicular chain. Others are similar, either clipping a magnetic transducer that is driven by a magnetic field applied by a hearing aid-shaped part placed in the ear canal to an ossicle or putting a part fixed to the mastoid with a vibrating part in contact with the ossicular chain.

The semi-implantable devices that have been developed have not met with wide acceptance for a number of reasons: Surgical implantation is costly, involves some risk, and may not be reimbursed by insurance companies; furthermore, gains in hearing obtained with these devices are typically modest. Nonetheless, the device described above has potential utility in patients with chronic inflammation and infection of the ear canal.

The Osseo-Integrated Bone Conduction Implant (Bone Anchored Hearing Aid)

Patients who have either undergone ear surgery that has resulted in a mastoid cavity, particularly if the cavity is "wet" (i.e., drains mucus) or who have congenital aural atresia (which causes a maximal conductive hearing loss because of an absent or malformed eardrum or ossicular chain), may have limited opportunities for aural rehabilitation. Patients without an ear canal cannot wear a conventional hearing aid and patients with a "wet" mastoid cavity cannot wear a conventional hearing aid without getting infections of the trapped secretions.

For patients with conductive hearing loss who cannot wear a conventional hearing aid, bone conduction aids offer the best hope and have been used in various forms for centuries. Basic modern bone-conduction aids have a vibrating sound transducer that is pressed to the skin-covered mastoid prominence or skull with a firm metal or elastic headband. This is the typical hearing aid fitted to a child with congenital aural atresia until surgical correction can be attempted.

An outgrowth of the study of biomechanical applications of osseointegration is the Bone-Anchored Hearing Aid (or *BAHA*). Like artificial joints and dental implants, the BAHA relies on the incorporation of a metallic titanium implant. The fixture (a 3 or 4mm screw) for the BAHA is placed in the skull behind the ear requiring amplification and after a three month (adults) or six month (children) healing period, a removable external sound processor is clipped to the implanted fixture. The battery-powered sound processor—a hearing aid modified with its output channeled through the implanted fixture, transmits sound via bone conduction. In addition to its use in conductive hearing loss, it is also approved in patients with profound unilateral hearing loss who have normal hearing in the opposite ear. The most powerful BAHA can be applied to patients with a sensorineural hearing loss component of up to 60 dB HL.

Cochlear Implants

Before the 1970s, profoundly hearing-impaired individuals who had little or no use of conventional hearing aids were limited in their communication options to visual (e.g., written or signed language) and tactile (e.g., vibrotactile devices).

The first description of hearing generated by electrical stimulation was that of Allesandro Volta who in 1800 connected batteries to his temples and described the sound he experienced as "a boom within the head" followed by a sound of boiling thick soup (Volta, 1982). Subsequently, crude applications of electrical energy to the ear for a variety of reasons were described by a variety of authors in Europe through the nineteenth century. However, the optimism that electrical stimulation could cure deafness fostered by these initial reports was quickly followed by skepticism.

Informal reports from European centers in the 1930s and 40s suggested that battery-powered current could stimulate auditory perception through the auditory nerve. In 1957, Djourno and Eyries described the results of direct stimulation of the auditory nerve in deafness. A wire was temporarily implanted on the auditory nerve through the cochlea in a deafened patient. With the application of current to the wire, the patient reported sounds like a "cricket" or "roulette wheel." In time, the patient developed limited recognition of common words and improved speech reading ability.

In 1961, two U.S. patients were temporarily implanted in Los Angeles through the scala tympani. The patients noted that increasing voltage corresponded to increasing loudness perception while increasing stimulation rate corresponded to increasing pitch. Neither patient tolerated the implanted hardware and it was removed (Doyle, J., Doyle, D., & House, 1963).

The first commercially marketed cochlear implant was the House 3M device. This device had a single electrode placed in the basal turn of the cochlea. More than 1,000 were implanted between 1972 into the mid-1980s. In 1980, the age limit for the device was lowered from 18 years to 2 years and by the mid-1980s, several hundred children had been implanted. However, single-channel implants were limited in their ability to code spectral properties of sound because they stimulated narrow areas of the cochlea. In 1984, the first multiple channel devices were implanted and quickly replaced the single channel device. Reports demonstrated enhanced speech recognition ability and better spectral perception (Gantz, Tyler, Knutson et al., 1988).

Current implants include features such as: a pre-curved electrode that hugs the modiolus of the cochlea, thus placing the current source closer to the auditory nerve, reducing current spread; faster rates of stimulation; 16–22 electrodes; neural response telemetry (electrically monitoring auditory nerve fiber response to the cochlear implant stimulus).

Illustrations of Device Evolution

A partially implanted device that is marketed in Europe and the U.S. for high frequency loss uses a titanium tube passed percutaneously from behind the ear and terminating in the ear canal. The output of a small microphone-amplifier-speaker device attached to the tube behind the ear is channeled into the ear canal. The device is cosmetically appealing since it is hidden in the shadow of the pinna and works well for individuals with limited high frequency loss. The problem with the device is that a nonimplanted competitor has been developed to serve the same market. The open-mold hearing aids, described above, serve the same purpose as the implanted device but are less expensive and do not require surgical implantation.

BAHA vs Audient. Although no longer marketed, the Audient™ bone conductor (termed a *temporal bone stimulator* by the company) was a device approved by the U.S. Food and Drug Administration (FDA) that consisted of an external processor that used transcutaneous inductive electromagnetic energy to cause vibration of an implanted titanium magnet screwed into the temporal bone. Compared to the BAHA, the Audient may have been less vulnerable to infection since there is no skin penetrating implant. However, the relatively wide distance between the implanted magnet of the Audient and the driving coil resulted in limited power to vibrate the skull, limiting the role for the device. The Audient is no longer made.

Current Research Directions

There are, as of this writing, no treatments for sensorineural hearing loss that restores the function of damaged hair cells. Repair and regeneration of the neural structures of the human cochlea has, until recently, been an elusive goal. However, recent advances in molecular biology and genetics, built on a foundation of increased understanding of cell cycle regulation and differentiation, neuronal regeneration in nonmammalian vertebrates, and apoptosis, are bringing this target tantalizingly close.

Advances in genetics and cell biology have made cell therapy and stem cell transplantation potential options in this regard. Multiple types of stem cell transplantation into the inner ear have been described: those involving neural stem cells (NSCs), embryonic stem cells (ESCs), and fetal otocyst cells (FOCs).

Motivated by the potential for retinal cell restoration by neural stem cells in experimental rats, transplantation of NSCs (typically harvested from the hippocampus) into the inner ear has been attempted (Nishida, Takahashi, Tanihara et al., 2000). Hippocampal-derived NSCs implanted into the mouse inner ear have demonstrated survival as well as differentiation into neural and glial cells. In some cases, grafted cells have integrated into sensory epithelia and expressed neurotrophic factors and hair cell markers (Ito, Kojima, & Kawaguchi, 2001; Iguchi, Naka-gawa, Tateya et al., 2003; Tateya, Nakagawa, Iguchi et al., 2003). How-ever, functional recovery of the inner ear following NSC grafting has not been observed.

Embryonic stem cells confer the advantage of pluripotency, but direct ESC transplantation into damaged or immature inner ears undergo differentiation only as far as epithelial cells, without hair cell differentiation (Sakamoto, Nakagawa, Endo et al., 2004). Stepwise induction of ESCs to otic progenitor cells can be demonstrated *in vivo,* and such cells can then undergo terminal differentiation to hair cells and integrate into the sensory epithelium when transplanted at this stage (Li, Roblin, Liu, & Heller, 2003).

Transplanted fetal otocyst cells migrate to the sensory epithelium and differentiate into supporting cells (Kojima, Murata, Nishio, Kawaguchi, & Ito, 2002). While current availability of FOCs is a problem, recent studies suggest that *otic progenitor cells* from adult inner ears exhibit stem cell behavior in vitro. If otic progenitor cells could be harvested, this may lead to a more accessible source of otic stem cells (Malgrange, Belachew, Thiry et al., 2002; Li, Liu, & Heller, 2003).

A characteristic feature of mammalian sensory hair cells is that, like other highly differentiated, specialized cells, they are held in mitotic arrest and cannot undergo further cell division following embryonic terminal mitosis (Taylor & Forge, 2005). In contrast, it was first demon-strated in the 1980s that avian species, and later amphibians, readily regenerate sensory hair cells following lethal external insults such as severe acoustic trauma and aminoglycoside toxicity (Cruz, Lambert, & Rubel, 1987; Corwin & Cotanche, 1988; Ryals & Rubel, 1988; Jones & Corwin, 1996; Taylor & Forge, 2005).

Cell lines within the organ of Corti develop from a common otic epithelial progenitor cell, which may remain bi-potential until its final mitotic division and terminal differentiation into hair cells and support-ing cells (Fekete, Muthukumar, & Karagogeos, 1998). It was thus hypothesized that a potential source population for regenerated hair cells in the avian model were these supporting cells (Girod, Duckert, & Rubel, 1989). Further studies demonstrated that regenerated hair cells were being generated from existing supporting cells which had survived the initial insult and reentered mitosis, producing new hair cells and renewing themselves, often through multiple mitotic cycles (Raphael,

1992; Raphael, 1993; Stone & Cotanche, 1994; Stone, Choi, Woolley, Yamashita, & Rubel, 1999).

In addition to cell cycle re-entry as a means for hair cell regeneration, some avian supporting cells change their cell type from supporting cell directly to sensory hair cell without mitosis, a process termed *phenotypic conversion* or *direct transdifferentiation* (Beresford, 1990). This mode of hair cell repopulation is believed to occur in the initial reparative phase following ototoxic insult, as direct transdifferentiation occurs much more quickly than cell-cycle mediated replenishment and can provide early recovery of hearing function while the remaining cochlea regenerates through mitosis (Adler, Komeda, & Raphael, 1997; Li & Forge, 1997; Baird, Burton, Fashena, & Naeger, 2000; Roberson, Alosi, & Cotanche, 2004).

How then to convince mammalian supporting cells to do the same thing? Numerous growth factors–including fibroblast growth factor (FGF) as well as insulin growth factor (IGF), brain derived neurotrophic factor (BDNF), epidermal growth factor (EGF), and transforming growth factor alpha (TGF-alpha)–have been infused *in vivo,* individually and in cocktails, in experimental animals in an attempt to promote hair cell regeneration, with modest results (Bermingham-McDonogh & Rubel, 2003). *In vivo* infusion of TGF-alpha plus insulin seems to stimulate growth activity within the sensory epithelium. However, only a small subset of supporting cells appeared to be stimulated (Oesterle, Cunningham, Westrum, & Rubel, 2003).

A more promising avenue of investigation appears to be in influencing the cell cycle directly. Forskolin, which has gained recent popularity in western culture as an Ayurvedic medicinal, induces cell proliferation in cochlear supporting cells *in vitro* (Navaratnam, Su, Scott, & Oberholtzer, 1996; Montcouquiol & Corwin, 2001; Kim, Nakagawa, Lee et al., 2004).

Two proteins central to cell cycle regulation seem to be crucial mediators of mitotic arrest in hair cells, and modulating their expression may play a role in eventual clinical hair cell regeneration.

Cyclin-dependent kinase inhibitors hold terminally differentiated cells in mitotic arrest, preventing them from re-entering the cell cycle (Parker, Eichele, Zhang et al., 1995). In the supporting cells of adult mouse cochlea, the cyclin-dependent kinase inhibitor p27 (Kip1) is selectively expressed at high levels. A mouse bred without a functioning gene for p27 (Kip1) has continued post-natal mitosis and proliferation of supporting cells, well beyond the expected onset of quiescence. These "knockout mice" exhibit supernumerary hair cells and supporting cells (Chen & Segil, 1999; Lowenheim, Furness, Kil et al., 1999).

The retinoblastoma protein pRb, encoded by the retinoblastoma tumor suppressor gene *Rb1* also functions in cell cycle regulation as well, inhibiting expression of genes necessary for cell cycle entry (Lipinski & Jacks, 1999; Frolov & Dyson, 2004). Mice genetically engineered to have a nonfunctioning *Rb1* gene localized to the inner ear grow supernumerary hair cells and inner and outer hair cell rows (Sage, Huang, Karimi et al., 2005). These hair cells appear to be functional, although they organized randomly along the sensory epithelia and grossly outnumbered supporting cell production.

While mice genetically engineered to lack p27 (Kip1) or pRb show possible treatment avenues, they do not yet suggest specific approaches to hair cell regeneration. Despite their proliferation of otic progenitor cells, p27 (Kip1) knockout mice are profoundly deaf. Mice engineered to not have pRb in their cochleae are embryonic lethal, despite the overproduction of electrically functional hair cells. Methods of regulated, tissue-directed inactivation of these target proteins will need to be devised.

Direct transdifferentiation of existing supporting cells into new viable hair cells has recently been demonstrated. The Math1 gene encodes a transcription factor necessary for terminal differentiation of otic epithelial progenitor cells into hair cells (Bermingham, Hassan, Price et al., 1999; Chen, Johnson, Zoghbi, & Segil, 2002). When stimulated by overexpression of the Math1 gene (copies of which were carried on bits of genetic material called *plasmids*), nonsensory epithelial cells transdifferentiated into hair cells *in vitro* (Zheng & Gao, 2000). When Math1 (as well as the human version of the gene, Hath1) was experimentally inserted into cells *in vivo* using a genetically engineered adenovirus conversion of nonsensory cells to hair cells was seen (Kawamoto, Ishimoto, Minoda, Brough, & Raphael, 2003). More incredibly, spiral ganglion projections extended to some of these nascent hair cells, suggesting some semblance of function (Shou, Zheng, & Gao, 2003).

Most recently, the first demonstration of gene therapy mediated recovery of hearing loss was reported (Izumikawa, Minoda, Kawamoto et al., 2005). In this experiment normal adult guinea pigs were deafened and then inoculated with adenovirus carrying Math1 into one ear, with the opposite ear serving as the control. Hearing function was restored in the treated ears eight and 10 weeks following inoculation and initiation of gene therapy, matching the timing of the appearance of new hair cells seen in sacrificed animals studied histologically after treatment.

CONCLUSION

Dramatic changes in auditory rehabilitation have occurred over a relatively short period. From the hearing horns used centuries ago to the explosion in hearing technology over the last 100 years–development of the first, awkward electronic hearing aids at the advent of the twentieth century to the cochlear implant (the first neural implant) in the latter twentieth century to the promise of biotechnologic solutions to hair cell loss at the turn of the twenty-first century–the pattern of technologic advances in hearing rehabilitation is a model for rehabilitation of many other disabilities common to aging. For example, the development of deep brain stimulation for treatment of movement disorders (e.g., Huntington's Chorea and Parkinson's Disease) was foreshadowed and spurred by the cochlear and (not discussed in this chapter) auditory brainstem implants.

REFERENCES

Adler, H. J., Komeda, M., & Raphael, Y. (1997). Further evidence for supporting cell conversion in the damaged avian basilar papilla. *International Journal of Developmental Neuroscience, 15,* 375–385.

Baird, R. A., Burton, M. D., Fashena, D. S., & Naeger, R. A. (2000). Hair cell recovery in mitotically blocked cultures of the bullfrog saccule. *Proceeding of the National Academy of Sciences U S A, 97,* 11722–11729.

Barrenas, M. L. (1997). Hair cell loss from acoustic trauma in chloroquine-treated red, black and albino guinea pigs. *Audiology, 36,* 187–201.

Beresford, W. A. (1990). Direct transdifferentiation: Can cells change their phenotype without dividing? *Cell Differentiation and Development, 29,* 81–93.

Bermingham-McDonogh, O., & Rubel, E. W. (2003). Hair cell regeneration: Winging our way towards a sound future. *Current Opinion in Neurobiology, 13,* 119–126.

Bermingham, N. A., Hassan, B. A., Price, S. D., et al. (1999). Math1: An essential gene for the generation of inner ear hair cells. *Science, 284,* 1837–1841.

Borri, G. (1957). Preliminary report on the use of prednisone in therapy of some neuro-labyrinthine syndromes. *Arch Ital Otol Rinol Laringol, 68,* 821–824.

Chen, C. Y., Halpin, C., & Rauch, S. D. (2003). Oral steroid treatment of sudden sensorineural hearing loss: A ten year retrospective analysis. *Otol Neurotol, 24,* 728–733.

Chen, P., Johnson, J. E., Zoghbi, H. Y., & Segil, N. (2002). The role of Math1 in inner ear development: Uncoupling the establishment of the sensory primordium from hair cell fate determination. *Development, 129,* 2495–2505.

Chen, P., & Segil, N. (1999). p27(Kip1) links cell proliferation to morphogenesis in the developing organ of Corti. *Development, 126,* 1581–1590.

Chen, Y. S., Liu, T. C., Cheng, C. H., Yeh, T. H., Lee, S. Y., & Hsu, C. J. (2003). Changes of hair cell stereocilia and threshold shift after acoustic trauma in guinea pigs: Comparison between inner and outer hair cells. *Journal for Oto-rhino-laryngology and Its Related Specialties, 65,* 266-274.

Corwin, J. T., & Cotanche, D. A. (1988). Regeneration of sensory hair cells after acoustic trauma. *Science, 240,* 772–1774.

Cotanche, D. A., Saunders, J. C., & Tilney, L. G. (1987). Hair cell damage produced by acoustic trauma in the chick cochlea. *Hearing Research, 25,* 267–286.

Cruz, R. M., Lambert, P. R., & Rubel, E. W. (1987). Light microscopic evidence of hair cell regeneration after gentamicin toxicity in chick cochlea. *Archives of Otolaryngology Head and Neck Surgery, 113,* 1058–1062.

Davis, H. (1957). Biophysics and physiology of the inner ear. *Physiological Reviews, 37,* 1–49.

Djourno, A., & Eyries, C. (1957). Prosthèse auditive par excitation électrique à distance du nerf sensoriel à l'aid d'un bobinage inclus á demeure. [Auditory prosthesis by means of a distant electrical stimulation of the sensory nerve with the use of an indwelling coil.] *Presse Med, 65,* 1417.

Dobie, R. (1993). *Medical–legal evaluation of hearing loss.* (pp. 1). New York:Van Nostrand Reinhold.

Doyle, J., Doyle, D., & House, W. (1963). Electrical stimulation of the nerve deafness. *Bulletin of the Los Angeles Neurological Society, 28,* 148–150.

Fekete, D. M., Muthukumar, S., & Karagogeos, D. (1998). Hair cells and supporting cells share a common progenitor in the avian inner ear. *Journal of Neuroscience, 18,* 7811–7821.

Finsterer, J., & Fellinger, J. (2005). Nuclear and mitochondrial genes mutated in nonsyndromic impaired hearing. *International Journal of Pediatric Otorhinolaryngology, 69,* 621–647.

Frolov, M. V., & Dyson, N. J. (2004). Molecular mechanisms of E2F-dependent activation and pRB-mediated repression. *Journal of Cell Science, 117,* 2173–2181.

Gantz, B. J., Tyler, R. S., Knutson, J. F., et al. (1988). Evaluation of five different cochlear implant designs: Audiologic assessment and predictors of performance. *Laryngoscope, 10,* 1100–6.

Girod, D. A., Duckert, L. G., & Rubel, E. W. (1989). Possible precursors of regenerated hair cells in the avian cochlea following acoustic trauma. *Hearing Research, 42,* 175–194.

Glorig, A, & Nixon, J. (1962). Hearing loss as a function of age. *Laryngoscope, 72,* 596–1610.

Havlik, R. (1986). Aging in the eighties: Impaired senses for sound and light in persons age 65 years and over. Preliminary data from the supplement on aging to the National Health Interview Survey: United States, January–June 1984. Advance data from vital and health statistics. DHHS (PHS) publication no.125. Hyattsville, MD: National Center for Health Statisitics, 86-1250.

Hu, B. H., Henderson, D., & Nicotera, T. M. (2002). Involvement of apoptosis in progression of cochlear lesion following exposure to intense noise. *Hearing Research, 166,* 62–71.

Iguchi, F., Nakagawa, T., Tateya, I., et al. (2003). Trophic support of mouse inner ear by neural stem cell transplantation. *Neuroreport, 14,* 77–80.

Ito, J., Kojima, K., & Kawaguchi, S. (2001). Survival of neural stem cells in the cochlea. *Acta Oto-Laryngologica, 121,* 140–142.

Izumikawa, M., Minoda, R., Kawamoto, K., et al. (2005). Auditory hair cell replacement and hearing improvement by Atoh1 gene therapy in deaf mammals. *Nature Medicine, 11,* 271–276.

Jones, J. E., & Corwin, J. T. (1996). Regeneration of sensory cells after laser ablation in the lateral line system: Hair cell lineage and macrophage behavior revealed by time-lapse video microscopy. *Journal of Neuroscience, 16,* 649–662.

Jun, A. I., McGuirt, W. T., Hinojosa, R., Green, G. E., Fischel-Ghodsian, N., & Smith, R. J. (2000). Temporal bone histopathology in connexin 26-related hearing loss. *Laryngoscope, 110,* 269–275.

Kanzaki, J., Taiji, H., & Ogawa, K. (1988). Evaluation of hearing recovery and efficacy of steroid treatment in sudden deafness. *Acta Otolaryngol Suppl, 456,* 31–36.

Kawamoto, K., Ishimoto, S., Minoda, R., Brough, D. E., & Raphael, Y. (2003). Math1 gene transfer generates new cochlear hair cells in mature guinea pigs in vivo. *Journal of Neuroscience, 23,* 4395–4400.

Kikuchi, T., Kimura, R. S., Paul, D. L., & Adams, J. C. (1995). Gap junctions in the rat cochlea: Immunohistochemical and ultrastructural analysis. *Anat Embryol (Berl), 191,* 101–118.

Kikuchi, T., Kimura, R. S., Paul, D. L., Takasaka, T., & Adams, J. C. (2000). Gap junction systems in the mammalian cochlea. *Brain Res Brain Res Rev, 32,* 163–166.

Kim, T. S., Nakagawa, T., Lee, J. E., et al. (2004). Induction of cell proliferation and beta-catenin expression in rat utricles in vitro. *Acta Otolaryngology Supplementum,* 22–25.

Kojima, K., Murata, M., Nishio, T., Kawaguchi, S., & Ito, J. (2002). Survival of fetal rat otocyst cells grafted into the damaged inner ear. *Acta Otolaryngology Supplement,* 53–55.

Lefebvre, P. P., & Van De Water, T. R. (2000). Connexins, hearing and deafness: Clinical aspects of mutations in the connexin 26 gene. *Brain Res Brain Res Rev, 32,* 59–162.

Lefebvre, P. P., Weber, T., Rigo, J. M., Delree, P., Leprince, P., & Moonen, G. (1990). Potassium-induced release of an endogenous toxic activity for outer hair cells and auditory neurons in the cochlea: A new pathophysiological mechanism in Meniere's disease? *Hearing Research, 47,* 83–93.

Li, H., Liu, H., & Heller, S. (2003). Pluripotent stem cells from the adult mouse inner ear. *Nature Medicine, 9,* 1293–1299.

Li, H., Roblin, G., Liu, H., & Heller, S. (2003). Generation of hair cells by stepwise differentiation of embryonic stem cells. *Proceedings of the National Academy of Sciences U S A, 100,* 13495–13500.

Li, L., & Forge, A. (1997). Morphological evidence for supporting cell to hair cell conversion in the mammalian utricular macula. *International Journal of Developmental Neuroscience, 15,* 433–446.

Li, X. C., & Friedman, R. A. (2002). Nonsyndromic hereditary hearing loss. *Otolaryngology Clinics of North America, 35,* 275–285.

Lipinski, M. M., & Jacks, T. (1999). The retinoblastoma gene family in differentiation and development. *Oncogene, 18,* 7873–7882.

Lowenheim, H., Furness, D. N., Kil, J., et al. (1999). Gene disruption of p27(Kip1) allows cell proliferation in the postnatal and adult organ of corti. *Proceedings of the National Academy of Sciences U S A, 96,* 4084–4088.

Malgrange, B., Belachew, S., Thiry, M., et al. (2002). Proliferative generation of mammalian auditory hair cells in culture. *Mechanisms of Development, 112,* 79–88.

Mason, J. A., & Herrmann, K. R. (1998). Universal infant hearing screening by automated auditory brainstem response measurement. *Pediatrics, 101,* 221–228.

Montcouquiol, M., & Corwin, J. T. (2001). Brief treatments with forskolin enhance s-phase entry in balance epithelia from the ears of rats. *Journal of Neuroscience, 21,* 974–982.

Naftalin, L. (1975). The medical treatment of fluctuant hearing loss. *Otolaryngology Clinics of North America, 8,* 475–482.

Navaratnam, D. S., Su, H. S., Scott, S. P., & Oberholtzer, J. C. (1996). Proliferation in the auditory receptor epithelium mediated by a cyclic AMP-dependent signaling pathway. *Nature Medicine, 2,* 1136–1139.

Nishida, A., Takahashi, M., Tanihara, H., et al. (2000). Incorporation and differentiation of hippocampus-derived neural stem cells transplanted in injured adult rat retina. *Investigative Ophthalmology & Visual Science, 41,* 4268–4274.

Oesterle, E. C., Cunningham, D. E., Westrum, L. E., & Rubel, E. W. (2003). Ultrastructural analysis of [3H]thymidine-labeled cells in the rat utricular macula. *Journal of Comparative Neurology, 463,* 177–195.

Offner, F. F., Dallos, P., & Cheatham, M. A. (1987). Positive endocochlear potential: Mechanism of production by marginal cells of stria vascularis. *Hearing Research, 29,* 117–124.

Parker, S. B., Eichele, G., Zhang, P., et al. (1995). p53-independent expression of p21Cip1 in muscle and other terminally differentiating cells. *Science, 267,* 1024–1027.

Parving, A. (1999). The need for universal neonatal hearing screening–Some aspects of epidemiology and identification. *Acta Paediatrica Supplementum, 88,* 69–72.

Patuzzi, R. (2002). Non-linear aspects of outer hair cell transduction and the temporary threshold shifts after acoustic trauma. *Journal of Audiology and Neurootology, 7,* 17–20.

Pickles, J. O. (1982). *An introduction to the physiology of hearing* (4th Ed.). New York: Academic Press, p. 341.

Pirvola, U., Xing-Qun, L., Virkkala, J. et al. (2000). Rescue of hearing, auditory hair cells, and neurons by CEP-1347/KT7515, an inhibitor of c-Jun N-terminal kinase activation. *Journal of Neuroscience, 20,* 43–50.

Raphael, Y. (1992). Evidence for supporting cell mitosis in response to acoustic trauma in the avian inner ear. *Journal of Neurocytology, 21,* 663–671.

Raphael, Y. (1993). Reorganization of the chick basilar papilla after acoustic trauma. *Journal of Neurocytology, 330,* 521–532.

Roberson, D. W., Alosi, J. A., & Cotanche, D. A. (2004). Direct transdifferentiation gives rise to the earliest new hair cells in regenerating avian auditory epithelium. *Journal of Neuroscience of Research, 78,* 461–471.

Ryals, B. M., & Rubel, E. W. (1988). Hair cell regeneration after acoustic trauma in adult Coturnix quail. *Science, 240,* 1774–1776.

Sage, C., Huang, M., Karimi, K., et al. (2005). Proliferation of functional hair cells in vivo in the absence of the retinoblastoma protein. *Science, 307,* 1114–1118.

Sakamoto, T., Nakagawa, T., Endo, T., et al. (2004). Fates of mouse embryonic stem cells transplanted into the inner ears of adult mice and embryonic chickens. *Acta Acta Otolaryngology Supplement,* 48–52.

Salt, A. N., Melichar, I., & Thalmann, R. (1987). Mechanisms of endocochlear potential generation by stria vascularis. *Laryngoscope, 97,* 984–991.

Sargent, E. W., Herrmann, B., Hollenbeak, C. S., & Bankaitis, A. E. (2001). The minimum speech test battery in profound unilateral hearing loss. *Otology & Neurotology, 22,* 480–486.

Schrijver, I. (2004). Hereditary non-syndromic sensorineural hearing loss: transforming silence to sound. *Journal of Molecular Diagnostics, 6,* 275–284.

Shaia, F. T., & Sheehy, J. L. (1976). Sudden sensori-neural hearing impairment: A report of 1,220 cases. *Laryngoscope, 86,* 389–398.

Shou, J., Zheng, J. L., & Gao, W. Q. (2003). Robust generation of new hair cells in the mature mammalian inner ear by adenoviral expression of Hath1. *Molecular and Cellular Neuroscience, 23,* 169–179.

Snoeckx, R. L., Huygen, P. L., Feldmann, D., et al. (2005). GJB2 mutations and degree of hearing loss: A multicenter study. *American Journal of Human Genetics, 77,* 945–957.

Spillmann, T., & Dillier, N. (1983). Der internationale klassierungscode (ICD) in der audiologie. VIII. Audiosymposium, Rexton, Zurich: 147–159.

Stone, J. S., Choi, Y. S., Woolley, S. M., Yamashita, H., & Rubel, E. W. (1999). Progenitor cell cycling during hair cell regeneration in the vestibular and auditory epithelia of the chick. *Journal of Neurocytology, 28,* 863–876.

Stone, J. S., & Cotanche, D. A. (1994). Identification of the timing of S phase and the patterns of cell proliferation during hair cell regeneration in the chick cochlea. *Journal of Comparative Neurology, 341,* 50–67.

Taillens, J. P. (1968). Cortisone in clinical otorhinolaryngology. Its action mechanisms; its indications; its contraindications. *Fortschr Hals Nasen Ohrenheilkd,* 32–63.

Tateya, I, Nakagawa, T., Iguchi, F., et al. (2003). Fate of neural stem cells grafted into injured inner ears of mice. *Neuroreport, 14,* 1677–1681.

Taylor, R., & Forge, A. (2005). Developmental biology. Life after deaf for hair cells? *Science, 307,* 1056–1058.

Taylor, R. R., & Forge, A. (2005). Hair cell regeneration in sensory epithelia from the inner ear of a urodele amphibian. *Journal of Comparative Neurology, 484,* 105–120.

Volta, A. (1982). Historical records documenting the first galvanic battery, "The Volta Column." Circa 1800. *Asimov's biographical Encyclopedia or Science and Technology.* Garden City, New York: Doubleday & Company.

Wilkins, S. A., Mattox Jr., D. E., & Lyles, A. (1987). Evaluation of a "shotgun" regimen for sudden hearing loss. *Otolaryngology Head and Neck Surgery, 97,* 474–480.

Zheng, J. L, & Gao, W. Q. (2000). Overexpression of Math1 induces robust production of extra hair cells in postnatal rat inner ears. *Nature Neuroscience, 3,* 580–586.

PART IV

Chapter 9

ERGONOMIC DESIGN FOR OLDER ADULTS

Arunkumar Pennathur

ERGONOMICS DEFINED

Ergonomics, also known as human factors engineering, is broadly defined as *fitting the task to the human*. Implied in this definition is the idea that designers of products, built environments, and all systems including work systems, must not attempt to fit the human to products, environments and work systems. The science of ergonomics is hence concerned with designing and engineering the interaction of humans with products, daily living environments and other systems such as work systems (hereafter in this chapter we will use the word *systems* to include products, built environments and work systems).

Broadly, the goal of ergonomics is to enhance the human-systems interaction at every design and engineering opportunity so that humans are comfortable, safe, productive, and effective in their activities. To enhance human-systems interaction, human factors engineers quantify and model human limitations and capabilities and compare these to use requirements of products, environments and systems. If use requirements of a system are more than what the human can handle, then the system may be poorly designed and engineered. At the same time, if system use requirements and design capitalize on capabilities of the human, overall system performance may be enhanced.

How can ergonomics possibly conceive of all variables that can influence system design? A common generic framework used for capturing important ergonomic variables during design is the TOME framework.

153

T in the framework stands for task variables; O is for operator-related variables; M relates to machine variables; and E is for variables in the environment. Task variables could include task duration (for how long does the human have to perform the task), task frequency (how many times must the task be performed in a given period of time), task sequencing and criticality, task demands, and provision of user discretion for the task. Operator-related variables could include user age, gender, previous experience, knowledge, skills and prior training, physical traits, cognitive capacities, learning styles, and personality traits. Machine or device-related variables could include speeds, accuracies, ease of use and maintenance, and other designed capabilities. Environmental variables could include both micro-level variables such as heating, lighting, ventilation, and noise factors, as well as macro-level variables such as policies and procedures. Tables 9.1, 9.2, and 9.3 provide examples of generic criteria for task variables, operator variables, and macro-environmental variables. Detailed methods for identifying and quantifying task, operator, machine, and environmental variables are available in the ergonomics literature.

Two key distinctions made by scientists in the ergonomics and human factors profession must be taken into account before considering age-related design and engineering variables. These are the differences between physical ergonomics and cognitive ergonomics, and between human performance and human behavior. Physical ergonomics, in general, deals with physical measures such as physical size, shape, aerobic capacity, muscular strength, tolerance to heat stress, tolerance to noise, and physical work fatigue to name a few measures. Cognitive ergonomics, on the other hand, deals more with information processing and sensory functions of the brain, mental workload, memory, psychomotor functions such as reaction time, and speech intelligibility. There is also the view that physical ergonomics enables measurement of human performance, whereas cognitive ergonomics enables modeling human behavior. Human performance may be externally manifest in measures such as speed (of task completion), accuracy (in task completion), muscular strength exerted, etc. Human behavior may be more difficult to quantify and model, for example, in judgment and decision-making tasks.

Regardless of these distinctions, the science and practice of ergonomics have evolved significantly over the last 40 years. Methods and measures have been developed to more than adequately address human

TABLE 9.1.
Common task criteria and variables.

Goals	What are the important goals and supporting tasks?
Intrinsics of the task	What is the task?
	What are the inputs and outputs for the task?
	What is the transformation process (inputs to outputs)?
	What are the operational procedures?
	What are the operational patterns?
	What are the decision points?
	What problems need solving?
	What planning is needed?
	What is the terminology used for task specification?
	What is the equipment used?
Task dependency and criticality	What are the dependency relationships between the current task and other tasks and systems?
	What are the concurrently occurring effects?
	What is the criticality of the task?
Current user problems	What are the current user problems in performing this task?
Task performance criteria	What is the speed?
	What is the accuracy?
	What is the quality?
Task criteria	What is the sequence of actions?
	What is the frequency of actions?
	What is the importance of actions?
	What are the functional relationships between actions?
	What is the availability of functions?
	What is the flexibility of operations
User discretion in task	Can the user control or determine pace?
	Can the user control or determine priority?
	Can the user control or determine procedure?
Task demands	What are the physical demands?
	What are the perceptual demands?
	What are the cognitive demands?
	What are the environmental demands?
	What are the health and safety requirements?

limitations and capabilities in design of systems. The main focus of this
chapter will be on physical ergonomics of the older adult.

AGING AND ERGONOMIC DESIGN VARIABLES

The age of an individual is an important *operator-related variable* that
needs to be taken into account when designing products and systems.

TABLE 9.2.
Common operator (user) related criteria.

Data about users	What is the target user group?
	What proportion of users are male and what proportion are female?
	What is the average age/age range of users?
	What are the cultural characteristics of users?
Data about job	What is the role of the user?
	What are the main activities in the job?
	What are the main responsibilities of the user?
	What is the reporting structure for the user?
	What is the reward structure for the user?
	What are the user schedules?
	What is the quality of output from the user?
	What is the turnover rate of the user?
Data about user background	What is the education/knowledge/experience of the user?
	What are the relevant skills possessed by user?
	What relevant training have users undergone?
Data about usage constraints	Is the current equipment use by users voluntary or mandatory?
	What are the motivators and demotivators for use?
Data about user personal preferences and traits	What is the learning style of the user?
	What is the interaction style of the user?
	What are the aesthetic preferences of the user?
	What are the personality traits of the user?
	What are the physical traits of the user?

TABLE 9.3.
Common environmental variables and criteria.

	What are the likely situations that could arise during system use and how will these affect use of the system?
Equipment	Does equipment fall short of target performance?
	Does equipment fall short of specification?
	Does equipment fail?
Availability	Is data missing?
	Are materials missing?
	Are personnel missing?
	Is support missing?
Overloads	Of people/machines
	Of data, information, materials, etc.
Interruptions	Does the process breakdown?
	Is a complete restart of process required?
Environment	Changes in physical or social environment
Policy changes	Changes in laws, rules, standards and guidelines

The changes that occur with aging may be physical, such as changes in body shape, size, and strength. Sensory functions such as vision and hearing may change with age. Age could also influence cognitive and psychomotor functions in individuals. While the biological bases for these age-related changes are discussed in depth in other chapters in this book, accommodating these age-related changes in the design of products, built-environments, and work systems is vital for effective use of these systems by older adults.

The most important physical changes of interest to designers and engineers are changes in anthropometry, ranges of motion of various joints, and strength and dexterity changes. Aerobic capacity changes also interest designers of work systems if the work involves heavy physical components (although aerobic capacity has become less important in recent years due to mechanization and use of technology and automation for the performance of tasks which previously required use of human muscle power). Cognitive abilities that interest designers include general cognitive functioning including perception, memory and learning, and psychomotor abilities including reaction and movement time when responding to stimuli. Physical, cognitive, and psychomotor changes with aging are briefly reviewed in the following sections. Sensory changes including changes in vision and hearing, and cognitive changes are discussed in detail in other chapters in this book, and, therefore, not presented in any great detail in this chapter.

Physical Changes

Physical changes in individuals that most interest designers and engineers include are changes in anthropometry, ranges of motion of joints and dexterity, and strength.

Anthropometry

Anthropometry, a branch of anthropology, and derived from the words *anthropos* meaning human, and *metrikos* meaning pertaining to measuring, is defined as the science of measurement and the art of application that establishes the physical geometry, mass properties, and strength capabilities of the human body (Anthropology Research Project Staff, 1978a, 1978b, 1978c; Roebuck, 1995; Roebuck, Kroemer, & Thomson, 1975). Anthropometry can be static or functional anthropometry.

Static anthropometry, in general, is the measurement of body dimensions when the body is held in standard, static postures. Static anthropometry is most commonly used to assure that designs will physically fit the older adult. Static anthropometric measurements include heights, breadths, depths, circumferences, and arcs (Anthropology Research Project Staff, 1978a, 1978b, 1978c).

For example, heights, such as a sitting height (vertical distance from a specified body point to sitting surface or footrest surface); breadths such as torso breadth (horizontal distance measured from a specified point on right side of body to the same point on left side); depths such as torso depth (horizontal measurement in a sagittal plane from front to rear of body); circumferences such as hand circumference (circumference of hand measured around its knuckles); and arcs such as sagittal arc (distance over top of head from glabella to nuchale at base of the skull) are static anthropometric measures. The NASA Anthropometric Sourcebook (Anthropology Research Project Staff, 1978a, 1978b, 1978c) list, many other static anthropometric dimensions.

Functional anthropometry is the measurement of movement limits of the human body. For example, distances that can be reached overhead, in front of, or lateral (right or left side) to the body, are functional anthropometric measures. Functional anthropometry is most commonly used to ensure that designs are easy to access and to operate by the older adult.

Changes in stature (height) are perhaps the most commonly studied and cataloged information (Fozard, Vercruyssen, Reynolds, & Hancock, 1990; Stoudt, 1981). Borkan, Hults, and Glynn (1983), Damon and Stoudt, (1963), Damon, Seltzer, Stoudt, and Bell (1972), and Friedlaender et al. (1977) have shown that the stature of adult individuals declines with age. In measuring stature, most existing data are from cross-sectional research studies. These studies (Ayoub et al., 1984; Bailey, Carter, & Mirwald, 1982; Damon et al., 1972; Engel, Murphy, Maurer, & Collins, 1978; Martin et al., 1975; Parris & McConville, 1983; Stoudt, Damon, McFarland, & Roberts, 1965; Stoudt, Damon, & McFarland, 1960) use the 20–29-year-old group of cohorts as the reference group with which to compare older age groups. According to Roche (1990) this comparison is appropriate as growth in stature is complete in almost 90 percent of the population by age 23.5 in men and 21.1 years in women. Therefore, the decline in stature is visible after these ages for the population. Most cross-sectional investigations on stature have shown a gradual decline in stature beginning at age 40. By age 80, there is a 5 to 6 cm average decline in stature (Annis, Case, Clauser, & Bradtmiller, 1991). Available data on the Canadian population (Bailey et al., 1982) show an average of 3 cm loss in stature from the 20–29 years age bracket to the 60 and older age bracket for Caucasian women, and a 3.4 cm loss in stature in men. Annis et al. (1991) conclude from a review of other cross-sectional studies on stature that the overall net loss in stature is no more than 6 cm on an average. Ten-year longitudinal studies on stature show the greatest loss of stature in the oldest age group in the study (75–84 years of age), with an average loss of 7 cm across ages over a 10-year period (Shock, 1972). Borkan et al. (1983) also observed a 3 cm total change in stature from the youngest to the oldest cohorts. Data from the longitudinal study by Hertzog, Garn, and Hempy (1969) show stature losses in women ranging from 0.24 cm/decade for 34-45 year old cohorts to about 2.4 cm/decade for 55-65 year old cohorts.

In the Boston Normative Study of Aging Veterans, Damon et al. (1972) found significant decreases in the biacromial, bideltoid, and chest torso breadths, across cohorts from 20–29 to 70 years and older. Bi-iliac, foot, hand, head and ear breadths did not show any appreciable decrease. Depth of chest and abdomen increased linearly with age with an average 13 percent increase in abdominal depth in the waist. Circumferences also increased at the chest and abdomen (at the waist) by nearly 1.5 cm and 6 cm respectively over the 50-year range of the sample. Waist circumference increased linearly at the rate of 1cm/decade; chest circumferences followed an inverted U-shape curve with peaks occurring at 40–49 years of age. For Boston Veterans, fifth-year remeasurements did not produce any appreciable differences in breadths and depths (Friedlander et al., 1977).

Shoulder span was the only data for which 10-year follow-up data are available for the Boston Veterans (Borkan et al., 1983). The largest changes in shoulder span occurred between seventh and eighth decades. Other cross-sectional surveys such as the HES (Stoudt et al., 1965) and HANES (Engel et al., 1978) show similar trends for body circumferences. Girths (except waist circumferences) follow an inverted U-shape curve with age, with peaks occurring between the ages of 50 and 60. Annis et al. (1991) conclude that, in general, age does not seem to have a profound influence on circumferences in bony areas of the body such as the wrist, hand, and foot, even though, from a purely design perspective, these dimensions are important to measure and catalog. Body circumferences, in general, after the middle-age spread, decline by a small margin in the seventh decade.

Dimensions related to workspaces and work environments are also measured in anthropometric surveys. The HES (Stoudt et al., 1965), for example, measured, in addition to stature, 10 other workspace dimensions including sitting height (erect), biacromial diameter, knee height, popliteal height, elbow rest height, thigh clearance height, buttock-knee length, buttock-popliteal length, elbow-to-elbow breadth, and seat breadth. Important findings from the HES included a loss in stature for both males and females, a decrease in sitting height, and a gradual decline in other workspace-related dimensions as well, explained perhaps by age-related changes in skeletal structure in some cases, and muscle and fat losses in some others.

It is very important to note that data related to workspace anthropometry obtained and interpreted from cross-sectional research studies tend to agree with interpretation of research findings from longitudinal research designs. Based on task analyses, Clark, Czaja, and Weber (1990) identified different human-machine interactions that are essential in task initiation, performance and completion, for common activities of daily living for the elderly, based on body postures and types of actions and grips employed in task performance. Other data sources such as Kroemer, Kroemer, and Kroemer-Elbert (1990), include dimensions such as eye height, shoulder height, elbow and knuckle height, forward functional reach, hip breadth, head circumference, etc., for males and females 20 to 60 years old, to serve as reference for changes in anthropometric characteristics of elderly from U.S. adult civilian population. Wright, Govindaraju, & Mital (1997a, 1997b) in their cross-sectional study on reach profiles in elderly, found decreases in vertical fingertip and vertical grip reach measurements for men 85 to 89 years of age.

Ethnicity of an individual can have a profound effect on anthropometric characteristics. An ethnic group, is in general, defined as a population of individuals who inhabit a specified geographical distribution and who have certain common physical characteristics, which serve to distinguish them from other groups of people (Pheasant, 1996; Pheasant & Haslegrave, 2006). Ethnic groups may or may not be co-extensive with national, linguistic, or other boundaries. Ethnic differences between groups of individuals can manifest in the form of differences in overall size (measured by stature and weight), or in other bodily proportions. For example, black Africans (considered by anthropologists as the

Negroid division of humankind) have been found to have proportionally longer lower limbs than Europeans (considered as the Caucasoid division of humankind) (Pheasant, 1996); Far Eastern populations (considered by anthropologists as a part of the Mongoloid division of humankind) have proportionally shorter lower limbs, the difference being the most marked in Japanese, less in the Chinese and Koreans, and least in the Thai. Ethnic differences in body size and proportion seem to have evolutionary significance as identified by Roberts (1973) in an extensive survey of anthropometric literature on indigenous populations of the world. The survey showed that body weight was negatively correlated with mean annual temperatures. Further, the linearity of body forms showed a strong positive correlation with mean annual temperatures. The overall conclusion from Roberts' study is that ethnic groups inhabiting hot climates will tend to have a large ratio of surface area to body mass for promoting heat loss. According to Pheasant (1996), several studies (Boas, 1912; Kaplan, 1954; Koblianski & Arensburg, 1977; Shapiro, 1939) of migrant samples have shown significant differences in growth patterns and adult dimensions between individuals born in new environments and equivalent samples in the old country.

Range of Motion of Joints

The range of motion of joints is typically measured as angles of extension, flexion, rotation, bending (lateral), abduction, adduction, and deviation, depending upon the part of the body measured. The most commonly measured joints are range of motion of the head, the shoulder, elbow joint, the wrist joint, and finger for upper extremities, and the hip, knee, ankle and foot for the lower extremities. It is generally known that the range of motion of joints declines with age. Further, in general, women tend to have a greater range of joint movement than men. The decline in the range of motion of joints may be different for different joints of the body—for example, the knee joint in older adults may exhibit pronounced decline compared to the neck joint or the wrist joint.

Strength and Dexterity

Human body strength is considered an important measure of an individual's capability to exert force or to sustain some form of external loading without inflicting personal injury. Strength can be static or dynamic. Absence of body segment, object and muscle movement during maximal voluntary contraction is the major difference between static and dynamic strengths. Static strength does not account for effect of inertial forces. Several factors can affect an individual's dynamic strength exertion capabilities. Factors that have been studied extensively in the ergonomics literature (Mital and Kumar, 2000) include posture, reach distance (as a measure of mechanical advantage/disadvantage that people have when exerting strength), arm orientation, speed of exertion, and the frequency and duration of strength exertion.

The types of strength assessed include arm strength, shoulder strength, composite (leg strength), back (torso) strength, isokinetic strength including dynamic lift strength, dynamic back extension strength, and dynamic elbow flexion strength. Isoinertial and psychophysical strengths are also commonly measured in industrial work settings.

Strength, in general, declines with age. If male strength at age 24 is taken to be 100 percent, proportionally, at age 24, women have about 62 percent of the strength exertion capability of men. A 50-year-old man is expected to have 83 percent strength of that a 24-year-old man. A 50-year-old woman is expected to have 46 percent of the strength of a 50-year-old man. A 65-year-old man's strength is roughly 71 percent of the 24-year-old man. A 65-year-old woman's strength is only 38 percent of the 65-year-old man.

Grip strength and pinch strength are also assessed in older adults to determine functional capacities of the upper extremities. Grip strength has been found to be significantly related to upper extremity posture in older adults (Contreras, Pennathur, Ahmed, & Premkumar, 2004). Studies on grip strength have also compared the grip span, grip type, and the dominance of the hand. Pinch strength, especially in tasks requiring manipulation of small objects, is related to the separation distance of the digits of the fingers and wrist posture. An extensive review of strength databases and guidelines for practitioners and designers and the scientific bases for the strength databases can be found in Mital & Kumar (2000).

Manual dexterity is another measure that can be used to measure manipulation of objects using upper extremities. Dexterity can be quantified based on gross movements of the hands, fingers and arms, and fine finger dexterity (ability to integrate speed and precision with finely controlled discrete movements of the finger). The ability to move two arms in a simultaneous and coordinated manner can also be used as one indicator of dexterity (for example in tasks requiring operation and control or driving and operating). Another dexterity measure used in ergonomics is the dexterity of participants when using common hand tools. Pennathur, Contreras, Arcaute, and Dowling (2003) have studied manual dexterity of older adults using a Purdue pegboard test, a two-arm coordination test and a hand-tool dexterity test. Comparison between dexterity of older adults and young adults indicates significant differences in Purdue pegboard tasks using the preferred hand, the non-preferred hand, both hands and an assembly task. Older adults took significantly longer times and made significantly more errors in the two-arm coordination test compared to young adults. In the hand-tool dexterity test, older adults took significantly longer times to complete the task compared to young adults. Other studies using Purdue pegboard tasks (Desrosiers, Herbert, Bravo, & Dutil, 1995; Desrosiers, Herbert, Bravo, & Rochette, 1999; Haward & Griffin, 2002) also suggest similar findings among older adults.

Aerobic Work Capacity

The basal metabolic rate of individuals declines with age. In general, the aerobic capacity (maximum oxygen uptake) is peak between the ages of 18 and 21, and there is up to a 2 percent decline per year after 25 years (Astrand, Rodahl, Dahl, & Stromme, 2003; Saltin, 1990). Further, at age 65, the average aerobic capacity is roughly 70 percent of the aerobic capacity at age 25. After age 50, individual variations in aerobic capacity are more pronounced among men than women (Illmarinen, 2000).

Physical training, or a lack thereof, is strongly associated with nearly one-fifth to one-quarter decline in adults 45 to 60 years old. The fraction of oxygen consumption during work measured relative to the maximum aerobic capacity is taken as the aerobic strain on the individual. Normally, it is recommended that aerobic strain not exceed 33 percent.

Provision of adequate rest breaks and design of the work-rest allowances and schedules (Konz, 2000) is also essential during the working day (typically an 8-hour shift). Physical activity is especially important for maintaining physical work capacity reserves for recovery from work stress caused by physically demanding work. Additionally, gender differences in aerobic capacity have to be taken into account when designing work. During physically demanding work, care has to be exercised not to exceed acceptable levels of heart rate. Even though aerobic capacity measures are still used for setting work design limits for physically demanding tasks, with automation and technological advances, tasks have become more cognitive than physical, especially tasks performed by older adults after retirement.

Cognitive and Psychomotor Changes

The cognitive processes that determine how an individual responds to external stimuli broadly include, at a minimum, perception of stimuli, memory functions, and learning (and forgetting) effects. In considering the overall effects of aging on cognitive processes, studies show that by age 67, there is some cognitive decrement, and that this decline is substantial (although not linear) by age 80 (Schaie, 1989, 1990, 1994; Schaie & Willis, 1986). Studies show that recovery, and even an increase in cognitive function may be possible with suitable intervention (Schaie & Willis, 1986; Willis, 1990). Psychomotor functions are typically a measure of an individual's ability to react to stimuli and to take controlling action. Researchers have concluded that most psychomotor functions decline with age (Birren, Woods, & Williams, 1980; Fozard et al., 1990; Lahtela, Niemi, & Kuusela, 1985; Salthouse, 1985; Stelmach & Nahom, 1992). There are several products of daily use that require cognitive and psychomotor capacities with different sensing mediums, such as design of traffic lights, consumer electrical products such as televisions and cooking appliances, telephones, automated teller machines, etc. Unless the cognitive and psychomotor capacities of older adults are considered in design of these products, the net effect is likely to be an unusable and even an unsafe product for the older adult. Memory and reaction time measures are useful in designing products and systems for older adults and are briefly reviewed further in this chapter.

Memory

Several types of memory are of interest to human factors engineers among which the most important are working (also known as short-term) memory, and long-term memory. Researchers conclude that the capacity of the short-term memory to store information does not decline with age, but the efficiency with which information in the short-term memory is processed declines with age (Craik, 1994; Howard & Howard, 1997; Salthouse, 1994). Long-term memory could be specific to episodes in a person's life (also known as episodic memory), be related to factual knowledge (also called semantic memory), or be related to recall of procedures for actions. Age declines in episodic memory have been reported (Baddeley & Hitch, 1994; Howard & Howard, 1997). Decline in semantic memory, however, is not as pronounced (Bowles, 1993; Light, 1992). Learning of skills including motor skills and cognitive skills, in general, have been shown to improve in older adults with practice (Charmess & Bosman, 1992; Kausler, 1994).

Reaction Time

Several studies of reaction times in older adults indicate in general that there is a slowing of psychomotor processes with age. Simple reaction time (i.e., there is only one choice for one stimulus presented), an adult 60 years of age has only one-fifth the reaction time of a 20-year-old (Houtkamp & van Beijsterveldt, 1998; Small, 1987). Choice reaction times (when there is a choice in action in responding to stimuli), expectedly, are greater than simple reaction times for older adults. The type of stimuli may also slow choice reaction times, with older adults responding faster to visual stimuli than for auditory stimuli (Houtkamp & van Beijsterveldt, 1998). As a component of reaction time, human factors researchers have also studied movement time. The overall finding is that movement time also increases with age for visual and auditory stimuli and for simple and choice reaction tasks (Houtkamp & van Beijsterveldt, 1998).

SYSTEM DESIGN AND ENGINEERING
CONSIDERATIONS

This section presents the human centered design approach for system design and discusses various design scenarios and rules when human physical variation is to be included in system designs. Examples relating to functional anthropometry of older adults and product design are presented to illustrate the process of design accommodation.

Human Centered Design Approach

Traditionally, system designers have accounted for human limitations and capabilities by considering the user as an information processor having sensory and motor limitations and capabilities. User interaction with systems has been mediated through displays and controls through a two-way exchange of information.

Figure 9.1 illustrates the human-centered design approach to system design. In this approach, human attributes in the system are put ahead of system goals. The entire system is built around the human user of the system. This approach has also been called the user-centered design approach [see Mital and Pennathur (2000) for a detailed discussion of different system design approaches].

The first step in this approach is information collection. Information about user needs, user cognitive and mental models, information on existing products and interfaces, requirements of the design, etc. are collected. Requirements and constraints of the design may include costs, engineering constraints, legal and regulatory controls, and hazard analyses data. This information serves as ergonomics input to the design process. New concept designs are then created. At this stage, input from ergonomics can include safety criteria, human capability data, and other ergonomics guidelines. After detailed designs are prepared, designs are evaluated. Prototype development and testing of the prototype are then performed just as in any other design process. During evaluation and testing stages, users are included and feedback from users is incorporated into the design. Use of the human-centered approach to design should result in products that are usable and safe.

Data Use in Design and Design Rules

In the preceding sections in this chapter are highlighted some of the ergonomic design variables that can help achieve successful designs. Also, briefly reviewed were the effects of aging on these ergonomic design variables. In this section, an important aspect of aging–individual differences, their influence on design, and common approaches available for designers to account for individual differences are considered.

Simply put, people vary. People vary in size, shape, muscular strength, and in cognitive and psychomotor functioning. Hence, the challenge for designers and engineers is to determine the extent of vari-

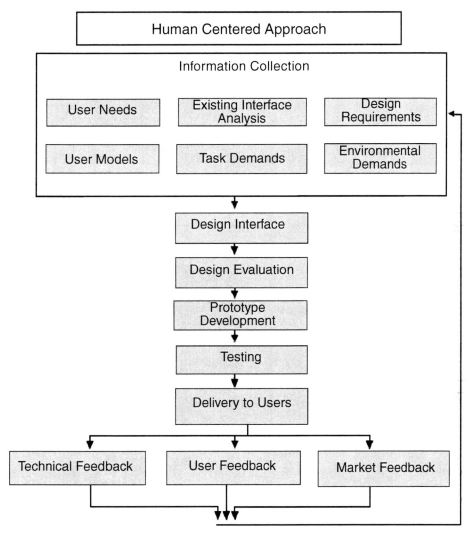

Figure 9.1. Human centered approach to design.

ation in the target (for the design) population, and to quantify the extent of accommodation and/or exclusion for a certain system design for the ergonomic design variables specified in the design. Based on quantification of the extent of accommodation and/or exclusion in design, one can conceive the following design rules:

1. *Custom design for a specific individual:* In this design rule, an individual is accommodated 100% and excluded 0% from the design.

Often, custom designs are expensive and if the individual can afford a custom design, then this may be the best way to design; hence, the extent of accommodation and/or exclusion in design can also be viewed as a design costing problem;

2. *Design for the average:* In this design rule, the system is designed for the average individual; designing for the average person works in some instances and does not work in others. For example, in designing work systems, industrial work standards and wages and incentives are commonly set based on performance of a "normal" worker (someone who is not a superhuman or a complete slacker). In this instance, some workers may be below the normal worker and others may be above the normal worker. If a doorway is designed, however, for the average person, only half the population can pass through the doorway. In this instance, the design for average rule fails;

3. *Designing for specific percentiles and ranges of population:* This is the most commonly used design rule. One example of such a design is to accommodate the middle 90% or 95% and to exclude the smallest and the largest 5% or 2.5%.

4. *Transgenerational and universal design ideas:* Recognizing the differences between different ages and genders in body size and proportions, this design approach consists in designing products across generations (i.e., to fit the old and the young), or to design across genders (example, to fit the tallest man and the shortest woman); usually, a combination of percentiles from different generations or different genders or otherwise different populations are used in generating the designs. For older adults, health status indicators and culture can also play major roles in the design of products and living environments.

Since measurements of humans are time-consuming, labor-intensive, and expensive, it is difficult to measure everyone in the population to use in designs. Therefore, the usual approach is to measure a random sample of people representing the target group for design. Depending upon the sampling methods employed in a research experiment (for example, convenience samples versus stratified random samples), the accuracy of the sample data in predicting the population can be specified using inferential statistical methods.

Since most human body measurements are normally distributed (except body weight which is generally positively skewed), principles of the normal distribution can be used to predict the limits of the range of variability, or to compute a range of values of the normal random variable within which a specified percentage of the people will fall. When reporting human body dimensions, some common statistics reported in studies include the sample size, the mean, the minimum and maximum values (can be used to compute ranges), and the standard deviation (or standard error) of the measurement. Based on the mean and the standard deviation values, for a normal random variate, other percentiles can be calculated from the standard normal distribution. The reader is referred to any book on basic statistics for calculation of standard normal percentiles. Often, data sets from samples are combined to accommodate a range of individuals. The percentile in the combined distribution is obtained as a weighted (by sample size) proportion of the original percentiles.

When applying physical ergonomics data, there could be several design goals (HFES 300 Committee, 2004; Kroemer, 2006; Robinette, 1998; Smith, Norris, & Peebles, 2000). The most common among these design goals are:

1. *Design to assure user-system fit and match:* Some examples are automobile seat dimensions, work surface heights, etc. When designing to fit, designs must accommodate a maximum range of the target population (5th to the 95th percentile of the population for instance). Maximum and minimum values of the dimensions would determine critical values of the design.

2. *Design to ensure reach and access:* Some examples are shelf heights in supermarkets, design of kitchen cabinets, etc. When designing for accessibility and reach, designs must accommodate the smallest of the population (the 5th percentile female for instance). Minimum values of the dimensions would determine critical values of the design.

3. *Design considering strength:* Strength considerations in design will ensure easy operability of the device or system. Some examples are prescription medicine containers, jar lids, bottle tops, etc. When designing for strength, designs must accommodate the smallest of the population (the 5th percentile female for instance). Minimum values of the dimensions would determine critical values of the design.

4. *Design to avoid entrapment:* The goal is to avoid having body parts or the whole body getting trapped in devices. Some examples

could be scissor holes, railings, machines without safety guards etc. With this design goal, the largest in the population have to be accommodated (for example, the 95th percentile). Maximum values of the dimensions would determine critical values of the design.

5. *Design for posture:* The goal in this design scenario is to design so that the user is able to adopt a comfortable and safe posture to operate the device or complete a task. Some examples could be work surface heights in maintenance and repair tasks, automobile seat dimensions in relation to rear view mirrors, etc. The design must accommodate the maximum possible range of the population (5th to the 95th percentile for instance). Maximum and minimum values of the dimensions would determine design extremes.

6. *Design for clearance:* Clearance is provided in the design to allow for adequate accessibility and maneuverability especially when using the device or system. Some examples are legroom in an airplane, size of keys on a computer keyboard, hand clearance to unscrew a part for maintenance or repair from a copy machine, etc. When designing for clearance, the largest of the population should be accommodated (the 95th percentile for instance). Maximum value of clearance would determine the design limit.

7. *Design to exclude users:* The goal of this design is to exclude users from accessing or operating certain devices or systems; for example, guards, railings, etc. Normally, designs should accommodate the maximum range of a population (5th to the 95th percentile, for instance). Maximum and minimum values of dimensions would determine design limits.

Sometimes designs may involve safety considerations to prevent accidents when using systems. In such cases, designs should include additional tolerances to the design limits to be safe and effective in preventing accidents for *any and all* users. Some other design considerations may include clothing (for example, gloves add thickness to hands and need additional clearance spaces for accommodation), and the strength and posture when measurements are made.

To further highlight the process of using ergonomic data in designing for older adults, the rest of this section covers two specific examples of analyses of living environments, one for a bathtub and shower, and the other a kitchen workspace. Both these cases were motivated by self-reports of difficulty among older adults in using these environments in daily living.

Using the bathtub, shower, and the kitchen are considered daily living tasks that demand significant reaching abilities for task initiation, task performance, and successful task completion. Hence, these built-environments need to be designed or redesigned considering convenient reach zones of older adults. Functional reach abilities became important to measure and assess. An anthropometric survey of older men and women (these men and women were of Mexican origin due to study location) was conducted to assess stature, vertical fingertip reach, vertical grip reach, vertical reach angle, horizontal fingertip reach at 90 degrees, horizontal fingertip reach at 0 degrees, horizontal lateral fingertip reach, horizontal lateral reach angle, horizontal grip reach at 90 degrees, horizontal grip reach at 0 degrees, horizontal lateral grip reach, sitting height, maximum grip diameter, finger angle, and maximum step height (ascending). Older adults were recruited from several senior recreation centers in the city. Participants lived independently, were of sound health, and reported no major medical problems. They did not use walkers, wheelchairs, or canes for improved mobility.

Anthropometric and reach dimensions were measured with Swiss-made GPM anthropometer #101 and the Lafayette Instrument Company's #J00200 goniometers. All measuring instruments were portable and were carried to the senior centers for data collection. Sitting height and all horizontal reach measurements were taken with participants in a seated position. Participants were seated in a chair with a flat seat pan positioned 40 cm from the floor level and backrest positioned 17 cm vertically from the seat pan. The backrest was 40 cm in height. No adjustments were made to chair dimensions during the study. A radial scale with different radial degree markings in increments of 10 degrees (much like a large protractor) was constructed out of cardboard to be used a reference scale when making horizontal reach measurements. A plumb bob attached to the end of a small chain as described by Asfour, Ayoub, Mital, and Bethea (1978) was used to align the arm to the radial scale. Anthropometric reach measurements made in the case (too lengthy to describe in greater detail in this chapter) were based on identical valid protocols as outlined in detail in Pennathur and Dowling (2003). For further details of different protocols, readers are referred to chapter sources. Participants were provided adequate rest periods between measurements to minimize the effect of static fatigue.

TABLE 9.4.
Summary statistics for older males (all reaches in cm and angles in degrees)
(Adapted from Pennathur and Dowling, 2003).

Dimension	Mean	SD	Minimum	Maximum
Stature	166.43 (n=40)	7.90	152.65	178.69
Vert. fingertip reach	193.10 (n=40)	24.08	98.17	221.25
Vert. grip reach	180.91 (n=16)	24.23	134.35	210.0
Vert. reach angle	136.25 (n=40)	26.33	19.0	172.5
Sitting height	80.09 (n=16)	3.33	72.65	86.1
Horiz. Fingertip reach at 90 deg.	69.91 (n=40)	4.58	58.6	78.7
Horiz. Fingertip reach at 0 deg.	70.95 (n=40)	4.45	60.05	78.23
Horiz. Lateral fingertip reach	70.36 (n=40)	4.41	61.0	79.63
Horiz. Lateral reach angle	23.3 (n=40)	9.11	7.0	47.5
Horiz. Grip reach at 90 deg.	57.28 (n=16)	4.35	48.25	64.25
Horiz. Grip reach at 0 deg.	58.57 (n=16)	3.85	51.55	64.2
Horiz. Lateral grip reach	58.87 (n=16)	4.13	50.8	65.7
Max. grip dia.	4.156 (n=16)	5.08	3.30	5.15
Finger angle	80.31 (n=16)	12.54	55.0	110.0
Max. step ht. (ascending)	36.24 (n=16)	8.54	21.5	57.65

The baseline data collected from this sample of older men and women are presented in Tables 9.4 and 9.5 respectively. Figure 9.2 is a depiction of the top view of the current design of the shower/bathtub with distances. An initial step in problem clarification was to understand the operational sequence of use based on observation and brainstorming. Dark arrows in Figure 9.2 represent the sequence of use of the bathtub/shower. Older adults (and even younger adults for that matter) would enter the bathtub/shower, and hold on to the grab bar. They would then open the tap (adjust water level and test heat level of water). In cases where a detachable showerhead was included they would grab the showerhead. They would then hold on to the grab bar, take a shower, and then close the water tap and exit from the bathtub/shower. The critical ergonomic variables in this case would be the stature, vertical fingertip reach, vertical reach angle, and the maximum step height (ascending). Figure 9.3 shows the bathtub/shower from the side, and also depicts the critical ergonomic variables for older adults and corresponding measurements for young adults.

TABLE 9.5.
Summary statistics for older females (all reaches in cm and angles in degrees)
(Adapted from Pennathur and Dowling, 2003).

Dimension	Mean	SD	Minimum	Maximum
Stature	152.57 (n=106)	9.89	82.93	178.9
Vert. fingertip reach	180.69 (n=106)	15.16	110.62	201.68
Vert. grip reach	167.41 (n=42)	20.39	84.9	191.0
Vert. reach angle	142.79 (n=106)	21.54	90.5	180.5
Sitting height	75.66 (n=42)	3.88	66.4	84.65
Horiz. Fingertip reach at 90 deg.	64.04	3.53	54.99	72.52
Horiz. Fingertip reach at 0 deg.	65.74 (n=106)	7.82	56.52	136.91
Horiz. Lateral fingertip reach	64.96 (n=106)	4.99	53.21	97.79
Horiz. Lateral reach angle	27.93 (n=106)	16.27	4.0	109.5
Horiz. Grip reach at 90 deg.	53.05 (n=42)	4.01	46.2	62.0
Horiz. Grip reach at 0 deg.	54.03 (n=42)	4.09	46.25	64.2
Horiz. Lateral grip reach	54.39 (n=42)	3.72	47.8	63.15
Max. grip dia.	3.972 (n=42)	5.96	3.05	7.08
Finger angle	77.21 (n=42)	12.67	56.5	109.0
Max. step ht. (ascending)	28.15 (n=42)	8.12	3.8	45.0

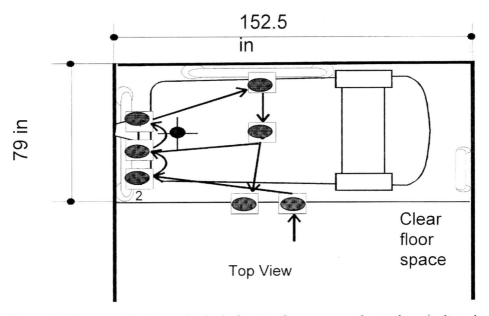

Figure 9.2. Top view of a shower/bathtub showing the sequence of typical use (indicated by the dark arrows).

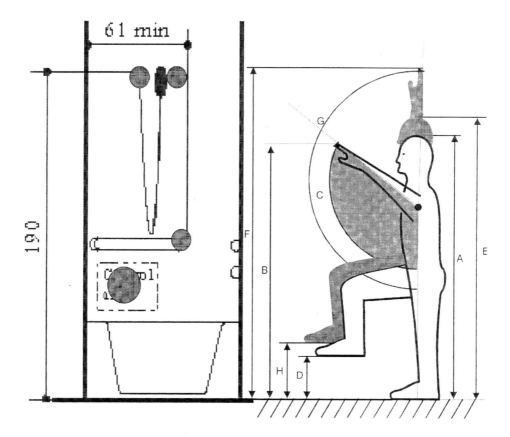

Figure 9.3. Critical reach dimensions in relation to bathtub/shower design.
A is stature, B is vertical fingertip reach, C is vertical reach angle, and D is step height all
for older adults. This study also measured younger adults for the same dimensions–these
are represented as E, F, G and H respectively for young adults.

Based on matching the current bathtub/shower design requirements
and reach capabilities of the older adult group (determined from sample data), it was determined that only 55 percent of males and 95 percent of females could enter the shower (based on maximum step height
dimension). For the requirement of reaching horizontally to hold the
support grab bar, the current design covered 80 percent of the males
and 85 percent of the females. Similarly, in adjusting the showerhead
by exerting a vertical grip reach, with the position of the shower head
in the current design, only 50 percent of the males and 45 percent of the
females could perform the task.

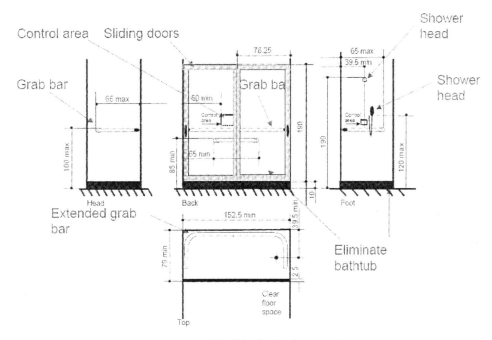

Figure 9.4. Modified bathtub/shower design.

Based on engineering analyses, the new proposed design of the bathtub and shower is depicted in Figure 9.4. The designers decided to eliminate the bathtub (redesign based on the maximum step height of the population). With the modified design, the knobs, grab bars and showerhead were positioned to accommodate a greater percentage of older adults than the current design. The new design accommodated 100 percent of the older adults with respect to entering the shower. Ninety-five percent of males and 95 percent of females could use the grab bars, the knobs and the showerhead in the new design.

A similar design process was followed for the kitchen workspace design. Surveying 83 older adults revealed that reaching top and bottom cabinets to retrieve items was a problem among a majority of older adults. A mannequin was created with a stature of 56.3 inches (according to the 5th percentile older female stature) and superimposed on the current kitchen workspace design. This is illustrated in Figure 9.5. The current kitchen design was difficult for the mannequin to access and to

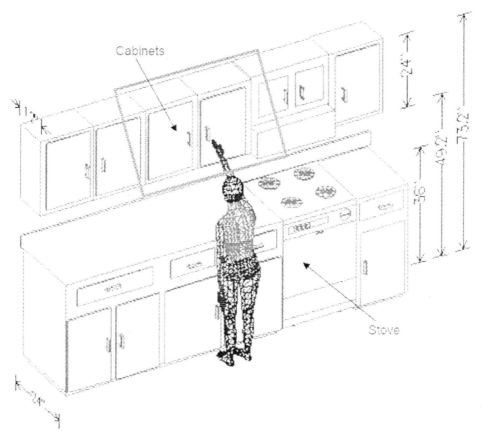

Figure 9.5. Current kitchen cabinet workspace design.

effectively use the cabinets. Only 46 percent of males and 50 percent of females were accommodated in a task requiring opening a cabinet and grabbing an item from the cabinet (assessment based on vertical grip reach dimension). The redesigned cabinets are shown in Figure 9.6a and 9.6b. With the new design, nearly 98 percent of the older adult males and 95 percent of older adult females were accommodated.

As these cases illustrate, understanding and modeling the influence of design variables (in daily living and product use environments) in the disablement process faced by older adults, will help prevent and circumvent problems and provide for graceful and successful aging.

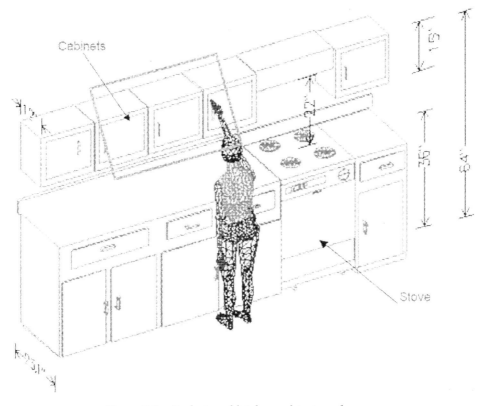

Figure 9.6a. Redesigned kitchen cabinet workspace.

Conclusions

At a minimum, accommodating age-related changes in functional abilities when designing products and systems is vital for increasing functional independence of older adults. The difficulties older adults face when using products and systems of daily use may be mediated not only by various physical impairments, and psychological and social factors specific to the aging process, but also by the external built-environment. *Accommodation* in design is still only a reactive idea. Universal design principles for designing products and systems right the first time, and user-centered design approaches, will enable *all* users to profit from the designs. Outlined above are some of the important design variables to consider when designing systems for older adults.

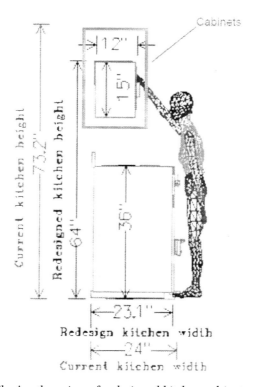

Figure 9.6b. Another view of redesigned kitchen cabinet workspace.

REFERENCES

Annis, J. F., Case, H. W., Clauser, C. E., & Bradtmiller, B. (1991). Anthropometry of an aging work force. *Experimental Aging Research, 17* (3), 157–176.

Anthropology Research Project Staff. (1978a). *Anthropometric sourcebook. Vol I: Anthropometry for designers.* Yellow Springs, OH: NASA.

Anthropology Research Project Staff. (1978b). *Anthropometric sourcebook. Vol II: A handbook of anthropometric data.* Yellow Springs, OH: NASA.

Anthropology Research Project Staff. (1978c). *Anthropometric sourcebook. Vol III: Annotated bibliography of anthropometry.* Yellow Springs, OH: NASA.

Asfour, S., Ayoub, M. M., Mital, A., & Bethea, N. (1978). *Reach profiles for males and females under restrained and unrestrained conditions.* Paper presented at the Proceedings of he Human Factors Society 22nd Annual Meeting, Detroit, Michigan.

Astrand, P. O., Rodahl, K., Dahl, H. A., & Stromme, S. B. (2003). *Textbook of work physiology: Physiological bases of exercise* (4th ed). Champaign, IL.

Ayoub, M. M., Selan, J. L., Burford, C. L., Intaranont, K., Rao, H. P. R., Smith, J. L., et al. (1984). *Biomechanical and work physiology study in underground mining excluding low coal.* In U. S. D. O. T. I. Bureau of Mines (Ed.).

Baddeley, A. D., & Hitch, G. J. (1994). Developments in the concept of working memory. *Neuropsychology, 8,* 484–493.

Bailey, D. A., Carter, J. E. E., & Mirwald, R. L. (1982). Somatotypes of Canadian men and women. *Human Biology, 54* (4), 813–828.

Birren, J. E., Woods, A. M., & Williams, M. V. (Eds.). (1980). *Behavioral slowing with age: Causes, organization and consequences*. Washington, DC: American Psychological Association.

Boas, F. (1912). *Changes in bodily form of descendants of immigrants*. New York, NY: Columbia: University Press.

Borkan, G. A., Hults, D. E., & Glynn, R. J. (1983). Role of longitudinal change and secular trend in age differences in male body dimensions. *Human Biology, 55* (3), 629–641.

Bowles, E. A. (Ed.). (1993). *Semantic processes that serve picture naming*. San Diego, CA: Academic Press.

Charmess, N., & Bosman, E. A. (Eds.). (1992). *Human factors and age*. Hillsdale, NJ: Erlbaum.

Clark, M. C., Czaja, S. J., & Weber, R. A. (1990). Older adults and daily living task profiles. *Human Factors, 32* (5), 537–549.

Contreras, L. R., Pennathur, A., Ahmed, N., & Premkumar, K. S. (2004, May 15–19). *Upper extremity posture and grip strength in older Mexican American adults*. Paper presented at the Proceedings of the 2004 Annual Industrial Engineering Research Conference (IERC), Houston, Texas.

Craik, F. I. M. (1994). Memory changes in normal aging. *Current Directions in Psychological Science, 3,* 155–158.

Damon, A., Seltzer, C. C., Stoudt, H. W., & Bell, B. (1972). Age and physique of healthy white veterans at Boston. *Journal of Gerontology, 27* (2), 202–208.

Damon, A., & Stoudt, H. W. (1963). The functional anthropometry of old men. *Human Factors, 5,* 485–491.

Desrosiers, J., Herbert, R., Bravo, G., & Dutil, E. (1995). The Purdue pegboard test – normative data for people age 60 and over. *Disability and Rehabilitation, 75,* 751–755.

Desrosiers, J., Herbert, R., Bravo, G., & Rochette, A. (1999). Age-related changes in upper extremity performance of elderly people: A longitudinal study. *Experimental Gerontology, 34,* 393–405.

Engel, A., Murphy, R. S., Maurer, K., & Collins, E. (1978). *Plan and operation of the HANES I augmentation survey of adults 25–74 years, United States 1974–1975*. In P. H. Service (Ed.) (Vol. 1).

Fozard, J. L., Vercruyssen, M., Reynolds, S. L., & Hancock, P. A. (1990). *Longitudinal analysis of age related slowing: BLSA reaction time data*. Paper presented at the Proceedings of the Human Factors Society 34th Annual Meeting, Santa Monica, CA.

Friedlaender, J. S., Costa, P. T., Bosse, R., Ellis, E., Rhoads, J. G., & Stoudt, H. W. (1977). *Human Biology, 49* (4), 541–558.

Haward, B. M., & Griffin, M. J. (2002). Repeatability of grip strength and dexterity tests and the effects of age and gender. *International Archives of Occupational and Environmental Health, 75,* 111–119.

Hertzog, K. P., Garn, S. M., & Hempy, H. O. I. (1969). Partitioning the effects of secular trend and aging in adult stature. *American Journal of Physical Anthropology, 31,* 111–116.

HFES 300 Committee. (2004). *Guidelines for using anthropometric data in product design*. Santa Monica, CA: Human Factors and Ergonomics Society.

Houtkamp, J. J., & van Beijsterveldt, C. E. M. (Eds.). (1998). *Reaction time*. Delft: Delft University Press.

Howard, J. H. J., & Howard, D. V. (Eds.). (1997). *Learning and memory*. London: Academic Press, Inc.

Illmarinen, J. (2000). *Job design for aged with regard to decline in their maximal aerobic capacity: Part I–the scientific basis for the guide* (Vol. 1). Oxford: UK: Elsevier Science Ltd.

Kaplan, B. A. (1954). Environment and human plasticity. *American Anthropology, 56,* 780–800.

Kausler, D. H. (1994). *Learning and memory in normal aging*. San Diego, CA: Academic Press.

Koblianski, E., & Arensburg, B. (1977). Changes in morphology of human populations due to migration and selection. *Annals of Human Biology, 4,* 57–71.

Konz, S. (2000). *Work/rest: Part II–the scientific basis (knowledge base) for the guide* (Vol. 1). Oxford: UK: Elsevier Science Ltd.

Kroemer, K. H. E. (2006). *Extra-ordinary ergonomics: How to accommodate small and big persons, the disabled and elderly, expectant mothers, and children.* Boca Raton, FL: CRC Press.

Kroemer, K. H. E., Kroemer, H. J., & Kroemer-Elbert, K. E. (1990). *Engineering physiology: Physiologic bases of ergonomics* (2nd Ed.). New York, NY: Van Nostrand Reinhold.

Lahtela, K., Niemi, P., & Kuusela, V. (1985). Adult visual choice-reaction time, age, sex and preparedness: A test of Welford's problem in a large population. *Scandinavian Journal of Psychology, 26,* 357–362.

Light, L. L. (Ed.). (1992). *The organization of memory in old age.* Hillsdale, NJ: Erlbaum.

Martin, J. I., Sabeh, R., Driver, L. L., Lowe, T. D., Hintze, R. W., & Peters, P. A. C. (1975). *Anthropometry of law enforcement officers.* In N. B. O. S. Law Enforcement Standards Laboratory (Ed.): San Diego, CA: Naval Electronics Laboratory Center.

Mital, A., & Kumar, S. (Eds.). (2000). *Human muscle strength definitions, measurement and usage: Part II–the scientific basis (knowledge base) for the guide* (Vol. 1). Oxford: UK: Elsevier Science Ltd.

Mital, A., & Pennathur, A. (Eds.). (2000). *Perspectives on designing human interfaces for automated systems.* New York, NY: Marcel Dekker, Inc.

Parris, H. L., & McConville, J. T. (1983). *Anthropometric database for power plant design.* (No. NP-1918-SR). Palo Alto, CA: Electric Power Research Institute.

Pennathur, A., Contreras, L. R., Arcaute, K., & Dowling, W. (2003). Manual dexterity of older Mexican American adults: A cross-sectional pilot experimental investigation. *International Journal of Industrial Ergonomics, 32,* 419–431.

Pennathur, A., & Dowling, W. (2003). Effect of age on functional anthropometry of older Mexican American adults: A cross-sectional study. *International Journal of Industrial Ergonomics, 32,* 39–49.

Pheasant, S. (1996). *Bodyspace* (2nd Ed.). London, United Kingdom: Taylor & Francis.

Pheasant, S., & Haslegrave, C. M. (2006). *Bodyspace: Anthropometry, ergonomics and the design of work.* Boca Raton, FL: CRC Press.

Roberts, D. F. (1973). *Climate and human variability: An Addison-Wesley module in anthropology. Reading, No. 34.*

Robinette, K. M. (1998). *Multivariate methods in engineering anthropometry.* In Proceedings of the Human Factors and Ergonomics Society 42nd Annual Meeting, Santa Monica: CA.

Roche, A. F. (1990). Post-pubescent growth in stature. *Human Biology Council Poster Abstracts, 2* (2), 190.

Roebuck, J. A. (1995). *Anthropometric methods: Designing to fit the human body.* Santa Monica, CA: Human Factors and Ergonomics Society.

Roebuck, J. A., Kroemer, K. H. E., & Thomson, W. G. (1975). *Engineering anthropometry methods.* New York, NY: Wiley.

Salthouse, T. A. (1985). *A theory of cognitive aging.* Amsterdam: Elsevier Science.

Salthouse, T. A. (1994). The aging of working memory. *Neuropsychology, 8,* 535–543.

Saltin, B. (Ed.). (1990). *Cardiovascular and pulmonary adaptation to physical activity* (Part III: Human Adaptation to Physical Activity ed. Vol. 18). Champaign, IL: Human Kinetics.

Schaie, K. W. (1989). *Individual differences in rate of cognitive change in adulthood.* New York, NY: Springer.

Schaie, K. W. (1990). *Intellectual development in adulthood* (3rd ed.). San Diego, CA: Academic Press.

Schaie, K. W. (1994). The course of adult intellectual development. *American Psychologist, 49,* 304–313.

Schaie, K. W., & Willis, S. L. (1986). Can intellectual decline in the elderly be reversed? *Developmental Psychology, 22,* 223–232.

Shapiro, H. (1939). *Migration and environment.* London, UK: Oxford University Press.

Shock, N. W. (Ed.). (1972). *Energy metabolism, caloric intake, and physical activity of the aging.* Uppsala: Almqvist & Wiksell.

Small, A. (Ed.). (1987). *Design for older people.* New York, NY: John Wiley and Sons.

Smith, S., Norris, B., & Peebles, L. (January 2000). *Older adult data: The handbook of measurements and capabilities of the older adult.* England: Institute for Occupational Ergonomics, University of Nottingham.

Stelmach, G. E., & Nahom, A. (1992). Cognitive-motor abilities of the elderly driver. *Human Factors, 34* (1), 53–65.

Stoudt, H. W. (1981). The anthropometry of the elderly. *Human Factors, 23,* 29–37.

Stoudt, H. W., Damon, A., McFarland, R., & Roberts, J. (1965). *Weight, height, and selected body dimensions of adults, United States 1960–1962* (No. PHS Publication No. 1000, Series 11, No. 8). Washington, D.C.: U.S. GPO.

Stoudt, H. W., Damon, A., & McFarland, R. A. (1960). Heights and weights of white Americans, *ARS Anatomy of Manned-Space Operations Conference.* New York, NY: American Rocket Society.

Willis, S. L. (1990). *Contributions of cognitive training research to understanding late life potential.* Washington, D.C.: Gerontological Society of America.

Wright, U., Govindaraju, M., & Mital, A. (1997a). Reach profiles of men and women 65 to 89 years of age. *Experimental Aging Research, 23,* 369–395.

Wright, U., Govindaraju, M., & Mital, A. (Eds.). (1997b). *Reach design data for the elderly.* Santa Monica, CA: Human Factors and Ergonomics Society.

Chapter 10

INTELLIGENT SYSTEM TECHNOLOGY FOR ENHANCING THE QUALITY OF LIFE

CYNTHIA R. MARLING

INTRODUCTION

Intelligent systems technologies can appreciably enhance the lives of older persons. Such technologies enable elders to live more independently by compensating for diminished mobility, assisting those with memory impairment, and providing remote monitoring capabilities. They can also provide support for elders, family caregivers, and geriatric health care professionals in making the many important decisions that confront people as they age.

While relatively few products have already reached the market, many current research projects hold great promise. In the near future, it is possible that smart devices will automatically open doors, refill prescriptions, and control home comfort systems. Smart wheelchairs will enable those unable to operate standard wheelchairs to navigate smoothly. Reminder systems will help elders remember to take medications, to keep appointments, and to complete unfinished tasks. Caregivers will be able to remotely monitor living spaces to quickly detect problems, such as illness or falls. Decision support systems will help plan medical, nursing, and social interventions tailored to individual needs. In order to take advantage of today's intelligent technologies and to fulfill the promise of the future, it is important for gerontologists and technologists to work in tandem.

Smart Homes

Most elders prefer to *age in place,* or remain in their own homes, for as long as possible. There are strong social and economic incentives for them to do so. Moving to assisted living or nursing care facilities entails leaving a familiar environment, neighbors, shops, community resources, and places of worship behind. It reduces the degree of autonomy and control that elders have over their lives. For many, it raises the uncomfortable specter of approaching the end of life. Furthermore, the financial cost of quality assisted living or nursing home care is high. Many elders and their families do not have the means to comfortably afford this care.

Nevertheless, there are many pressing reasons why elders who live alone must leave their homes at some point. First and foremost is safety. When physiological and/or cognitive decline prevents elders from performing daily activities that keep them safe and healthy, they can not remain at home. An elder must be able to eat nutritious meals regularly, take medications on schedule, keep medical appointments, and summon help when needed. In addition, the demands of home upkeep may become too great for those with arthritis, impaired vision, hearing loss, mild cognitive impairment, or other common age-related deficits. For example, it may become difficult for elders to shop, to do light housekeeping, to manipulate the controls on home appliances or comfort systems, or to even use the telephone. Technological assistance can compensate for some of these problems, enabling elders to remain longer in their own homes in safety and comfort.

Toward this goal, Smart Home technology aims to embed assistive technology in the home environment. For example, the Aware Home Research Initiative at Georgia Institute of Technology has built a 5,040 square foot house as a *living laboratory* (Abowd, Bobick, Essa, Mynatt, & Rogers, 2002; Rogers & Mynatt, 2003). The Aware Home, shown in Figure 10.1, contains two separate apartments used to prototype different technologies for aging in place. Each apartment has two bedrooms, two bathrooms, a kitchen, a dining area, a living room, an office, and a laundry room. Sensors for tracking the activities of occupants are located throughout the living space. Video cameras and microphones allow sights and sounds to be captured and analyzed. In addition, a *smart floor* is embedded with special sensors that track the location within the house of each occupant. Radio frequency identification (RFID) is used

Figure 10.1. The Aware Home. Photo copyright Georgia Institute of Technology, used by permission.

to track the location of people and objects, especially objects likely to get lost, such as house keys. With RFID technology, small identification tags that can be detected using radio waves are placed on people and objects in the home. The house is extensively networked, so that all data collected from cameras, microphones and other sensors is immediately available for processing on high performance computers. The basement houses the computers that monitor the sensors, as well as the connecting cables and power supplies.

The Digital Family Portrait, shown in Figure 10.2, and the Gesture Pendant, shown in Figure 10.3, are two emerging technologies pioneered in the Aware Home. The Digital Family Portrait shares the information collected about an elder with the elder's children, or other remote caregivers, in the friendly form of a picture frame (Mynatt, Rowan, Jacobs, & Craighill, 2001). This allows for in-home monitoring by those who must make decisions about the elder's capacity to live alone. It can also help to provide peace of mind to family members who live apart but need and want to stay connected. In the Digital Family Portrait, a photograph of the elder is placed in a frame. Icons, or

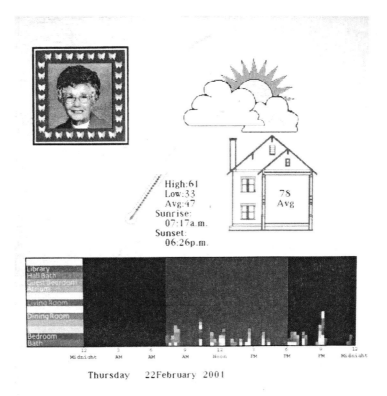

High:61
Low:33
Avg:47
Sunrise:
07:17a.m.
Sunset:
06:26p.m.

78
Avg

Library
Hall Bath
Guest Bedroom
Atrium
Living Room
Dining Room
Bedroom
Bath

12   3   6   9   12   3   6   9   12
Midnight   AM   AM   AM   Noon   PM   PM   PM   Midnight

Thursday   22February 2001

Figure 10.2. The Digital Family Portrait. Photo copyright Georgia Institute of Technology, used by permission.

indicators, surround the photo in the frame to represent the activities of the elder. Additional information about the elder can be displayed by touching the icons. Particular attention is paid to changes in typical activity level, so that remote observers will know if the elder is eating more or less than usual, is more active or sedentary than usual, or is more socially interactive or isolated than usual. Figure 10.2 shows an elder's framed portrait, the weather conditions surrounding the elder's home, the temperature inside the home, and the movement of the elder throughout the home.

The Gesture Pendant facilitates the control of home systems and devices, such as lighting, heating and televisions. Such systems may have controls with small buttons that are hard to manipulate and/or are in inconvenient locations for elders to reach. The Gesture Pendant promotes independent living by enabling the elder to control devices they might otherwise find difficult or impossible to use. This prototypical

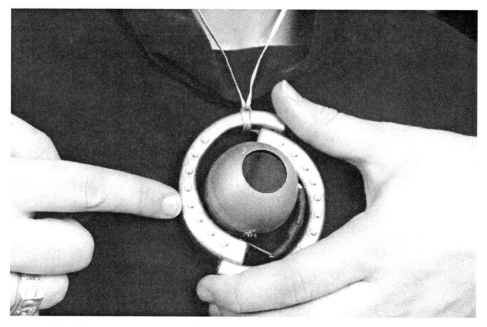

Figure 10.3. The Gesture Pendant. Photo copyright Georgia Institute of Technology, used by permission.

device is worn like a necklace, as shown in Figure 10.3. It contains a small, light-weight camera and uses infrared light to track the wearer's hand movements. The user can gesture to indicate, for example, that the thermostat should be set higher or that the television channel should be changed.

The Gator Tech Smart House, at the University of Florida, is another research laboratory home (Helal, Mann, El-Zabadani, King, Kaddoura, & Jansen, 2005). A virtual tour of this smart house is available online at http://www.icta.ufl.edu/gt.htm. The layout of the Gator Tech Smart House is shown in Figure 10.4. In this figure, technologies that currently exist and are operational in the home are denoted by E, for Existing. Technologies that are the focus of ongoing research and development projects are denoted by O, for Ongoing. Technologies slated for future research are denoted by F, for Future.

Technologies that are currently operational within the Gator Tech Smart House are described in Table 10.1.

Table 10.2 describes technologies that are under development or planned for future research.

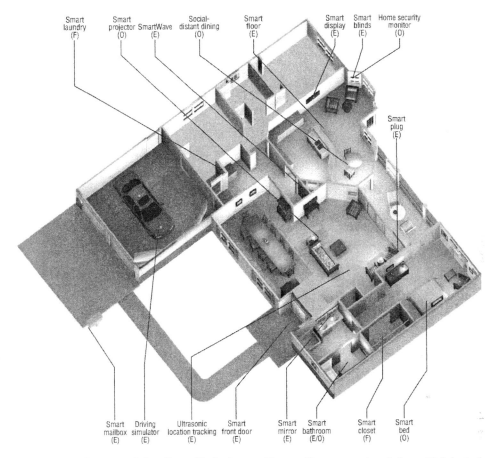

Figure 10.4. Layout of the Gator Tech Aware Home. Figure reprinted from Helal et al. (2005), with permission.

While living laboratories hold great promise for the future, costs prohibit most elders from living in smart homes today. For example, the cost of constructing the Aware Home was $600,000. However, some smart home technologies are already being transitioned for use in everyday homes. The Safe at Home project is a collaboration of the Alzheimer's Society of the United Kingdom (UK) with governmental agencies in Northampton (Woolham & Frisby, 2002). This project targets elderly dementia patients who live with family caregivers and are at risk of institutionalization. The Safe at Home project began by outfitting a demonstration house with relatively simple devices that could easily be installed in an ordinary home. These devices include a clock/calendar for patient orientation, a gas detector that shuts off gas

TABLE 10.1.
Technologies Implemented in the Gator Tech Smart House

Technology	Functionality
Smart floor	Tracks the movement of occupants within the house
Smart window Blinds	Can be remotely adjusted to control brightness and/or provide privacy
SmartWave microwave oven	Uses RFID technology to detect what kind of prepackaged frozen food the occupant wants to cook, displays a video showing how to open the package, automatically adjusts its settings to correctly prepare the food, and tells the occupant when the food is ready
Smart displays	Provide entertainment and information throughout the home, as the occupant moves from room to room
Smart mailbox	Informs the occupant when mail arrives
Driving simulator	Evaluates how safely a person is able to drive a car
Ultrasonic location tracking	Determines the locations of occupants within the house
Smart front door	Allows the occupant to see and hear approaching visitors and remotely admits approved visitor
Smart mirror	Displays reminder messages for the occupant in the master bathroom
Smart bathroom	Senses when toilet paper or soap has run out, detects when the toilet has been flushed, and regulates water temperature to prevent scalding
Smart plugs	Detect lamps and appliances and connect them to remote monitoring and control systems

should a stove be left on, a sensor that sounds an alarm when a patient gets out of bed at night, and a pressure sensitive doormat that sounds an alarm when a patient leaves the house. In an initial study, 14 dementia patients and their caregivers installed one or more of these devices in their own homes. When compared to a control group without access to these devices, the study group had a lower rate of institutionalization. Currently, this project has moved beyond the experimental stage, and the devices they tested are available for home use in the UK. Continuing collaboration among gerontologists and technologists, including rigorous field testing of smart home devices, will promote greater use of smart home technology.

Memory Aids

Memory loss, ranging from normal age-related forgetfulness to mild cognitive impairment, is a problem for many elders. Forgetting the

TABLE 10.2.
New Technologies Planned for the Gator Tech Smart House

Technology	*Proposed Functionality*
Smart laundry	Will help to sort laundry and tell occupants when clothes need to be washed
Smart projector	Will locate an occupant within the house and then display messages and reminders on the wall directly in front of them
Social-distant dining	Will use immersive audio and video techniques to enable an occupant to share a meal with a friend or relative who is physically elsewhere
Home security monitor	Will watch doors and windows and, upon request, inform the occupant if any are unlocked
Smart closet	Will suggest appropriate clothing to wear for the weather
Smart bed	Will monitor sleep patterns and track restlessness

names of friends and family members can be embarrassing, forgetting where the car keys are can be inconvenient, and forgetting to take medications on schedule can pose a serious health risk. Elders affected by dementia, such as Alzheimer's disease, typically have multiple impairments, including memory loss, personality change, wandering, hallucinations, and depression. Dementia often progresses over the course of five to ten years. Patients in the early stages are often able to live at home with assistance, while patients in the severe stage lose most communication abilities and are unable to perform even the basic activities of daily living such as toileting or bathing. Since computers, unlike people, have virtually limitless memories, they should be deployed to assist those with mild to severe memory loss.

One example of such a deployment is *Autominder*. Autominder is a prototypical *cognitive orthotic,* or memory aid, that aims to help elders with mild to moderate memory impairment by providing personalized reminders (Pollack, Brown, Colbry, McCarthy, Orosz, Peintner et al., 2003; Pollack, 2005). It reminds elders to complete routine daily tasks, such as taking medications on time, and to attend to periodic tasks, like ordering prescription refills or keeping doctor's appointments. Clock and calendaring systems currently available can remind elders to complete particular tasks at specific times, but they depend on following rigid schedules that cannot accommodate normal changes in daily patterns of activity. Autominder uses artificial intelligence techniques to model an elder's normal schedule, observes whether or not the elder is adhering to that schedule, and then selectively issues reminders as necessary and appropriate.

The Autominder researchers use an individual with urinary incontinence as an example. This individual needs to be reminded to void every three hours. If the next reminder is scheduled for 11:00 A.M., but the individual is observed to enter the bathroom at 10:40 A.M., then the 11:00 A.M. reminder is skipped. Furthermore, the schedule is adjusted, so that the next reminder will be issued at 1:40 P.M., not 2:00 P.M. Autominder also considers the scheduling of the older person's various daily activities. If the individual is normally watching a favorite television program at 1:40 P.M., Autominder automatically adjusts to issue the reminder shortly before the television program begins. Autominder is personalized to take each individual's daily requirements and leisure activities into account.

Autominder is not dependent on any particular type of hardware platform. It can run on a small handheld device or be incorporated into other computing platforms that are available to elders. Autominder has even been embedded in a mobile robot. Figure 10.5 shows this robot, called Pearl, being field tested in a Pennsylvania retirement community. Pearl was built for the Nursebot Project, a multi-disciplinary effort to build robotic aides for use in nursing homes and assisted living facilities. Prototypical robotic aides not only provide helpful reminders, but also direct and accompany elders to scheduled activities, such as meals and therapeutic appointments (Pollack, Engberg, Matthews, Thrun, Brown, Colbry et al., 2002).

Researchers at the Aware Home have taken a different approach to developing memory aids. They posit that it is especially difficult to remember recent actions, especially if distractions or interruptions occur. For example, if an elder is preparing to take medications when the phone rings, the elder may not recall whether or not he or she actually took the medications after finishing the conversation. *Déjà vu displays,* or photographic displays of recent actions, can help by showing exactly what a person was doing when an interruption occurred. The Cook's Collage is a prototypical *déjà vu display* implemented in the kitchen of the Aware Home (Tran & Mynatt, 2003; Tran, Calcaterra, & Mynatt, 2005). Cooking was selected as the target task, because it is cognitively demanding, requiring precise sequences of steps, and because it is an important activity of daily living. In the Cook's Collage, several video cameras are inconspicuously mounted under the kitchen cabinets to photograph cooking activities on the counter top. A flat panel video display is mounted on a kitchen cabinet. The output dis-

Figure 10.5. The Robot Pearl, in a Pennsylvania Retirement Community. Photo used by permission of the Nursebot Project.

play is always on, but it is passive, much like a kitchen clock, in that a person can consult it or not, as needed. The images displayed are sequential action shots of cooking steps. An elder can review the pictures, for example, to see whether or not they have already added eggs to the batter. Artificial intelligence techniques are used to select the shots displayed. While simply playing back the videos in their entirety might also have some value, this would take the elder more time to review and would provide less focused information.

Another related effort, the Assisted Cognition project at the University of Washington, focuses on the special needs of those with Alzheimer's Disease (AD) and related dementias (Kautz, Fox, Etzioni, Borrielo, & Arnstein, 2002; Philipose, Fishkin, Perkowitz, Patterson, Fox, Kautz et al., 2004). For example, in the middle stages of the disease, an AD patient may be capable of performing simple actions, like putting on socks or shoes, but may not be able to complete sequences of actions, like putting on socks before shoes. An Activities of Daily Living (ADL) Prompter is being developed to guide such individuals in the completion of sequential tasks, such as dressing, washing, toileting, and preparing simple snacks. The prototypical ADL Prompter analyzes sensor data to infer what the individual is probably trying to do. For example, if an elder goes into the bathroom in the morning, turns on the faucet, and stands there for several minutes, the system may infer that the elder intends to brush his or her teeth. Then it can prompt him or her to pick up a toothbrush.

While data could conceivably be collected by any type of sensor, including cameras, microphones and touch sensors, the Assisted Cognition group is currently experimenting with the use of RFID tags. These tags are small and inexpensive and can be attached to ordinary objects in an ordinary home. A wearable RFID reader senses when a person is near a tagged object, like a sink or a dresser drawer, giving valuable feedback about the person's intentions. Inferring the intentions and capabilities of an AD patient carrying out activities of daily living (ADLs) is useful to caregivers as well as to patients. Caregivers currently monitor the proficiency of AD patients at completing ADLs in order to assess the progression of the disease and to make decisions about the level of care required by the patient. This is a time-consuming and stressful manual task that could be eased by automated assistance. Assisted Cognition researchers project that practical tools based on their technology will be commercially available to AD patients and their caregivers within five years.

There is no cure for AD, but a large number of medical, nursing and social interventions are available to improve the quality of life for AD patients and their caregivers. As patients vary greatly in their symptoms, capabilities, and personalities, it is not always easy to know which interventions would be most efficacious for an individual patient. Intelligent decision support systems can help family caregivers and health care professionals to make the best choices for an individual with dementia who can no longer make independent decisions. Decisions that may need to be made include the following: the selection of drugs to treat behavioral aberrations, agitation, or depression; choosing appropriate daycare options; identifying and eliminating safety hazards in the home; determining that an individual is no longer competent to drive or to manage his or her own finances; and deciding when institutionalization becomes necessary.

In the Auguste Project, researchers at Ohio University and the University Hospitals of Cleveland Alzheimer Center prototyped a decision support system to help determine whether or not an AD patient would benefit from taking a neuroleptic drug, and if so, which of the Food and Drug Administration (FDA) approved alternatives would be best (Marling & Whitehouse, 2001; Whitehouse, Marling, & Harvey, 2003). Neuroleptic drugs may be used to control the behavioral problems that can beset AD patients, such as aggressiveness, sexual disinhibition, or wandering away from home. These behaviors can be uncomfortable and unsafe for the patient and can cause considerable caregiver stress. While most AD patients do not take neuroleptic drugs, it can be very helpful to identify those patients who would benefit from them. In the Auguste Project, an artificial intelligence approach called case-based reasoning was employed. Using this approach, treatments that proved effective for similar patients in the past were considered in planning care for current patients.

Practical adoption of intelligent decision support technology has been hindered by the difficulty of finding relevant patient data in paper-based patient charts. Accurate, up-to-date data is essential to good decision making, with or without computer assistance. The increasing use of electronic medical records will facilitate development of intelligent systems to assist in making the complex decisions that face elders and those who care for them.

Smart Wheelchairs

Impaired mobility due to frailty or disability can severely limit independent functioning for elders. While ordinary wheelchairs can help elders move from place to place, they can be difficult to operate without the assistance of a caregiver. Traditionally, the power wheelchair is offered as an alternative to those who are unable to operate a manual wheelchair without assistance. The commercial power wheelchair is controlled by means of a joystick, which is enabling for those who are not strong enough to manually turn the wheels on an ordinary wheelchair. However, this is also prone to problems for those with diminished visual acuity or lack of fine motor control in their hands. It can be especially difficult to maneuver power wheelchairs through narrow doorways or in crowded public places.

Work on smart wheelchairs, for the elderly and for younger disabled individuals, initially grew out of work by the autonomous robotics research community. The goal of autonomous robotics research is to have robots independently complete tasks that people would otherwise have to perform. An autonomous robot must be able to safely navigate from place to place using a variety of sensors to understand its environment, including video cameras, infrared sensors, laser sensors, and sonar. Many techniques developed to guide robot navigation have been applied to the development of smart wheelchairs. Additional techniques have been developed to allow for coordination between the rider and the wheelchair in which the rider, not the wheelchair, is in constant control of the destination. The role of intelligent technology in the wheelchair is to enable the rider to safely and easily reach the desired destination.

Wheelesley and NavChair were two early research platforms that formed the foundation for much of the research in smart wheelchairs today. Wheelesley, shown in Figure 10.6, was developed in the Massachusetts Institute for Technology's (MIT) Artificial Intelligence Laboratory (Yanco, 1998; 2001). A robotic wheelchair was custom built for this project by the KISS Institute for Practical Robotics (KIPR) and outfitted with a computer processor, infrared proximity sensors, ultrasonic range sensors, and shaft encoders. The processor is used to control the wheelchair, the sensors are used to detect obstacles in the way, and the shaft encoders are used to determine the wheelchair's position.

Wheelesley's main goals are: (a) to be able to navigate both indoors and outdoors, in new places as well as familiar ones; and (b) to provide a user friendly interface that allows a rider to issue high level commands to direct the wheelchair. It operates by accepting a command from the rider such as forward, left, right, back, or stop. It then follows that command until either it receives a new command to follow, or it

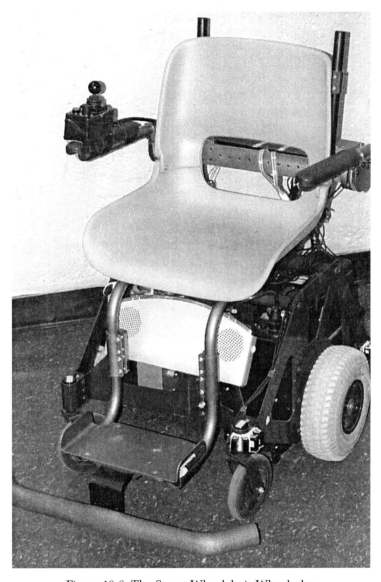

Figure 10.6. The Smart Wheelchair Wheelesley.

detects that there is an obstacle in the way. Common obstacles encountered in everyday environments include curbs, furniture, pets, and other people. When Wheelesley encounters an obstacle, it stops and waits for a new command from the rider. The rider can then either (a) remove the obstacle, for example, by asking a person to move out of the way; or (b) direct Wheelesley to circumvent the obstacle, using high level commands. Wheelesley was tested with a variety of interfaces for users with and without the use of hands. These included: (a) a standard graphical user interface on a Macintosh computer; (b) an interface that interprets the direction of a rider's glance as a command; and (c) a single switch scanning interface, which displays choices in sequence and allows the rider to depress a switch when a desired choice appears.

NavChair is another smart wheelchair project that continues to evolve with an emphasis on making commercially viable products (Levine, Bell, Jaros, Simpson, Koren, & Borenstein, 1999). The goals for this project are avoiding obstacles, following walls to aid navigation, and safely passing through narrow doorways. NavChair was built by modifying a commercially available power wheelchair. Sonar sensors were mounted on the wheelchair to detect obstacles, and a computer was added to run intelligent software routines. Initially, the wheelchair's standard joystick interface was used, with software routines intercepting the signals and modifying them as needed. Researchers from this project have experimented with a variety of different approaches, including using spoken commands as an interface. The benefits of allowing a rider to simply tell the wheelchair where to go are evident. This approach, however, is not yet commercially viable since commands may not be heard or correctly interpreted in noisy environments, leading to unsafe operating conditions.

Currently, the only commercially available smart wheelchairs are sold for disabled children by a UK-based company. These are expensive (starting at 7,700 British pounds), and depend on older technologies, including bump sensors, which only detect obstacles once they have already been touched, and special tracks laid out on the floor to indicate pathways from one place to the next. However, researchers from the NavChair project have a new component-based approach to commercialization that they expect to lead to reasonably priced products for elders in the very near term (Simpson, LoPresti, Hayashi, Nourbakhsh, & Miller, 2004). Their approach is to retrofit ordinary wheelchairs, both power and manual, with smart components to augment their capabilities. Their Smart Wheelchair Component System is meant to work with multiple brands of commercial wheelchairs with minimal modification. They are also being designed for use with any type of command input system, including joysticks and touch activated switches.

A new and exciting development from the NavChair group is their work on making manual wheelchairs smarter. To date, research in smart

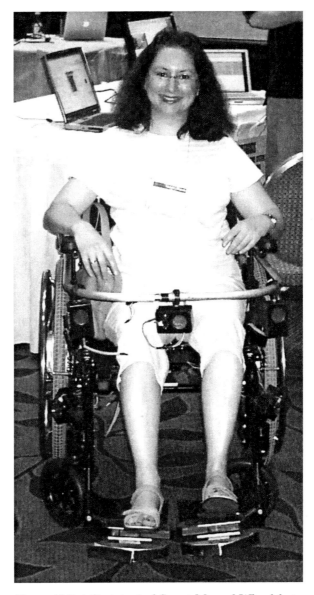

Figure 10.7. A Prototypical Smart Manual Wheelchair.

wheelchairs has been limited to power wheelchairs, although manual wheelchairs are less expensive and allow more portability, in that they can be folded up and placed in automobile trunks for travel. Figure 10.7 shows a prototype smart manual wheelchair that was displayed at the 2005 American Association for Artificial Intelligence (AAAI) National Conference held in Pittsburgh, Pennsylvania. This is a standard wheelchair except for its wheels and obstacle sensors. The wheels, which are already commercially available, contain motors and torque sensors. When a rider applies even a very light force to the wheels, the torque sensors detect just how much force has been applied, and then the motors add just enough boost to provide a smooth ride in the desired direction. Sonar and infrared sensors are mounted all around the wheelchair to detect obstacles. When an obstacle is detected, friction is applied to the wheels so that the wheelchair stops. This approach is especially promising for those who have the use of their hands, but lack the physical strength required to operate an ordinary wheelchair.

Leading Gerontechnologists

The paths selected by gerontechnologists are often instructive in learning about or assessing their growth in particular areas. To this end, the experiences and perspectives of three leading gerontechnologists are described.

Martha Pollack

Martha Pollack is a professor and Associate Chair of the Department of Electrical Engineering and Computer Science at the University of Michigan, Ann Arbor. She is the principal investigator for the Autominder project, and an expert in artificial intelligence, planning and execution, agent-based systems, and computational models of rationality. She is also a member of the multi-disciplinary, multi-university Nursebot project, which introduced the robot Pearl.

Dr. Pollack became interested in gerontechnology while a faculty member at the University of Pittsburgh. She was invited to represent Computer Science at a multi-disciplinary meeting that included faculty from the School of Nursing, faculty from Occupational Therapy, and roboticists from Carnegie Mellon. The purpose of this meeting was to brainstorm about how advancing technologies could be used to help the elderly, given the large demographic shift and the growing percentage of elderly people. One of the issues raised was memory difficulties and how elderly people may have difficulty making and executing daily plans. Dr. Pollack, as an expert in modeling and monitoring plans, assumed the lead in researching solutions to this problem.

Photo 10.1. Martha Pollock

The most difficult technical challenge she faces is activity recognition. In order for systems to be adaptive, and to issue appropriate reminders at the best times, it is important for them to recognize what people are doing. While it is possible to put sensors in an individual's home and to collect plentiful data, it is still a challenge to determine what that data means in terms of human activity. Automatically recognizing that a person has drunk a cup of coffee or made his or her bed is still a difficult technical problem.

The most difficult nontechnical challenge in her work is managing privacy concerns. An individual's activities are monitored for the purpose of providing that individual with appropriate reminders. Every precaution must be taken to ensure that the data collected is used only for its intended purpose, and that it is otherwise kept private and secure.

Dr. Pollack is currently pursuing three lines of research in her laboratory. The first line of research addresses the technical issue of activity recognition. Wireless sensor networks are installed in an environment to collect data. Different machine learning techniques are tested to determine how effective they are at recognizing specific human activities from the collected data. The second line of research involves developing efficient algorithms for handling rich models of plans. Developing more sophisticated models of people's plans will enable future reminder systems to consider conditional events, which only occur under certain conditions, and to take personal preferences into account. The third line of research is exploring machine learning techniques to make reminder systems more adaptive. The goal of this research is to build a system that can learn an individual's personal preferences and then determine the kinds of reminders that the individual would need.

Peter Whitehouse

Peter J. Whitehouse, M.D., Ph.D., is a clinical neurologist, neuropsychologist, and bioethicist. He is a professor at Case Western Reserve University and the Founding Director of University Hospitals of Cleveland Alzheimer Center. He served as the domain expert for the Auguste Project. His current research interests include biological, social, and technological interventions to enhance cognition in elders.

The University Hospitals of Cleveland Alzheimer Center is an early adopter of computer technology. The earliest technology adopted, over ten years ago, was the use of the Cleveland Free-Net to establish a support group for caregivers of patients with Alzheimer's Disease (Smith & Harris, 1993). The Cleveland Free-Net was one of the first city-wide public access computer networks. An early electronic bulletin board was set up on this network to allow caregivers to support each other. Caregivers coined the term "computer family" to describe it as they adopted the electronic bulletin board and incorporated it into their support networks. Work is currently underway at the Alzheimer Center on electronic reminiscence, which is the use of digital video discs (DVDs) to capture memories for people who have memory problems. Dementia patients can derive comfort and pleasure from reviewing significant personal and family events stored on DVDs.

Dr. Whitehouse predicts that, in the future, the computer will become an auxiliary memory and executive function enhancer for people. While computers may provide this capability to some extent today, when they are smart enough to deal with older people who are having

Photo 10.2. Peter Whitehouse

memory problems and can adapt to those people, computers will truly become symbiotic assistants. Devices will allow people to organize their lives when their illness is affecting their ability to do so.

Dr. Whitehouse feels that the main obstacle to wider adoption of intelligent gerontechnology is a pervasive sense that older people do not use computers. While younger people use computers more than older people do today, Dr. Whitehouse believes that the reluctance of elders to use computers has been overstated.

As an ethicist, Dr. Whitehouse sees three significant issues that may arise in developing intelligent technologies for elders with dementia. The first issue is maintaining patient confidentiality when sharing clinical information. The second issue concerns the digital divide, which gives the affluent greater access to computers. Since many older people may not be able to afford computers, there is a social justice issue with respect to accessibility to the latest technology. The third issue concerns the potential for the invasion of privacy. If an active video camera is omnipresent, could this be viewed as an intrusion into the private space of an individual, potentially leading to control rather than increasing autonomy and quality of life? Ensuring that ethical, as well as technical, considerations are addressed becomes an important responsibility.

Holly Yanco

Holly Yanco designed and implemented the smart wheelchair Wheelesley. She is an assistant professor in the Computer Science Department at the University of Massachusetts Lowell, where she heads the Robotics Laboratory. In addition to gerontechnology, she is interested in human-robot interaction and is active in educational robotics programs for middle school and high school students.

Dr. Yanco received her Master's degree and her Ph.D. while working in the MIT Artificial Intelligence Laboratory. This laboratory is best known for its humanoid robots that learn through interactions with people. She became interested in smart wheelchairs when she took time off between her Master's degree and her Ph.D. to teach at Wellesley College. She bought her first robotic wheelchair from the KISS Institute for Practical Robotics. Since she first began working on the chair with undergraduates at Wellesley College, the chair was subsequently dubbed Wheelesley. When Dr. Yanco returned to MIT to complete her graduate work, she took Wheelesley with her to use in her dissertation research.

Dr. Yanco recognizes at least two technical challenges that must be met before smart wheelchair technology can become available and can practically meet the needs of older consumers. First is the need to make the systems very stable and reliable. The occasional "computer crash" is unacceptable on a smart wheelchair. The chair must provide reliability. Second is the need for better computer vision. Current computer vision technology functions fairly well in constrained, regularly shaped, environments, such as hallways. However, the goal is for smart wheelchairs to operate successfully in unconstrained environments. For an elder to venture outdoors to travel on sidewalks, to shop in a mall, or to make home visits to friends, computer vision technology must surpass its present capabilities.

The latest work in Dr. Yanco's laboratory involves developing better computer vision algorithms. She is collaborating with researchers at

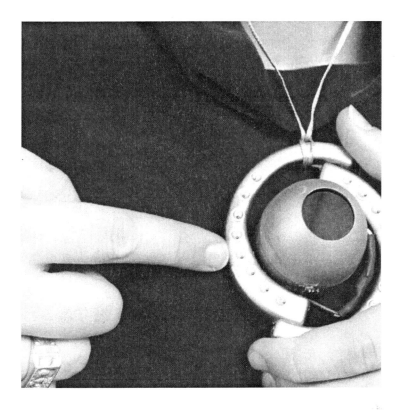

Photo 10.3. Holly Yanco

Swarthmore College on a new prototype that reads signs. The ability to read signs that occur regularly in the environment, such as street signs or signs on office doors, would enable better wheelchair navigation.

CONCLUSION

Intelligent systems technology is an important and powerful tool for enhancing quality of life for elders. It is an important responsibility to ensure that intelligent systems technology is used as effectively, appropriately, and beneficially as possible. Developing intelligent technologies that truly meet the needs of elders will require collaboration among gerontologists and technologists with frequent input and feedback from representative elders. Successfully deploying new technologies will require an understanding and accommodation of the ethical and social issues surrounding their use, as well as their technological capabilities. For example, many potentially dangerous activities can occur in the bathroom, and it is technologically possible to monitor activity in that area. It is natural for caregivers to want to know if an elder slips and falls in the shower, but it is also natural for a person to desire privacy in the bathroom. Control over what may be monitored, and for what purposes, must remain with the elder.

REFERENCES

Abowd, G. D., Bobick, A. F., Essa, I. A., Mynatt, E. D., & Rogers, W. A. (2002). The Aware Home: A living laboratory for technologies for successful aging. In K. Haigh (Ed.), *Automation as Caregiver: The Role of Intelligent Technology in Elder Care, Papers from the AAAI Workshop* (pp. 1–7). Menlo Park, CA: AAAI Press.

Helal, S., Mann, W., El-Zabadani, H., King, J., Kaddoura, Y., & Jansen, E. (2005). The Gator Tech Smart House: A programmable pervasive space. *IEEE Computer, 38* (3), 50–60.

Kautz, H., Fox, D., Etzioni, O., Borrielo, G., & Arnstein, L. (2002). An overview of the Assisted Cognition Project. In K. Haigh (Ed.), *Automation as Caregiver: The Role of Intelligent Technology in Elder Care, Papers from the AAAI Workshop* (pp. 60–65). Menlo Park, CA: AAAI Press.

Levine, S. P., Bell, D. A., Jaros, L. A., Simpson, R. C., Koren, Y., & Borenstein, J. (1999). The NavChair assistive wheelchair navigation system. *IEEE Transactions on Rehabilitation Engineering, 7* (4), 443–451.

Marling, C., & Whitehouse, P. (2001). Case-based reasoning in the care of Alzheimer's disease patients. In D. W. Aha & I. Watson (Eds.), *Proceedings of the Fourth International Conference on Case-Based Reasoning (ICCBR-01)* (pp. 702–715). Berlin: Springer-Verlag.

Mynatt, E. D, Rowan, J., Jacobs, A., & Craighill, S. (2001). Digital family portraits: Supporting peace of mind for extended family members. *Proceedings of the ACM Conference on Human Factors in Computing Systems* (pp. 333–340). Seattle, WA: ACM Press.

Philipose, M., Fishkin, K. P., Perkowitz, M., Patterson, D. J., Fox, D., Kautz, H., & Hahnel, D. (2004). Inferring activities from interactions with objects. *Pervasive Computing, 3* (4), 50–57.

Pollack, M. (2005). Intelligent technology for an aging population. *AI Magazine, 26* (2), 9–24.

Pollack, M. E., Brown, L., Colbry, D. McCarthy, C. E., Orosz, C., Peintner, B., et al. (2003). Autominder: An intelligent cognitive orthotic system for people with memory impairment. *Robotics and Autonomous Systems, 44,* 273–282.

Pollack, M. E., Engberg, S., Mathhews, J. T., Thrun, S., Brown, L., Colbry, D., et al. (2002). Pearl: A mobile robotic assistant for the elderly, in In K. Haigh (Ed.), *Automation as Caregiver: The Role of Intelligent Technology in Elder Care, Papers from the AAAI Workshop* (pp. 85–91). Menlo Park, CA: AAAI Press.

Rogers, W. A., & Mynatt, E. D. (2003). How can technology contribute to the quality of life of older adults? In M. E. Mitchell (Ed.), *The technology of humanity: Can technology contribute to the quality of life?* (pp. 22–30). Chicago, IL: Illinois Institute of Technology.

Simpson, R., LoPresti, E., Hayashi, S., Nourbakhsh, I., & Miller, D. (2004). The smart wheelchair component system. *Journal of Rehabilitation Research and Development, 41* (3B), 429–442.

Smith, K. A., & Harris, P. B. (1993). Using telecomputing to provide information and support to caregivers of persons with dementia. *The Gerontologist, 33,* 123–127.

Tran, Q., Calcaterra, G., & Mynatt, E. (2005). Cook's collage: Déjà vu display for a home kitchen. *Proceedings of Home Oriented Informatics and Telematics (HOIT 2005)* (pp. 15–32). York, UK: University of York.

Tran, Q., & Mynatt, E. (2003). What Was I Cooking? Towards Déjà Vu Displays of Everyday Memory. *Technical Report GIT-GVU-TR-03-33.* Atlanta, GA: Georgia Institute of Technology.

Whitehouse, P., Marling, C., & Harvey, R. (2003). Can a computer be a caregiver? *Geriaction, 21* (2), 12–17.

Woolham, J., & Frisby, B. (2002). How technology can help people feel safe at home. *Journal of Dementia Care, 10* (2), 27–29.

Yanco, H. (1998). Wheelesley, a robotic wheelchair system: Indoor navigation and user interface. In V. O. Mittal, H. A. Yanco, J. Aronis, & R. Simpson (Eds.), *Lecture notes in artificial intelligence: Assistive technology and artificial intelligence* (pp. 256–268). Berlin: Springer-Verlag.

Yanco, H. (2001). Development and testing of a robotic wheelchair system for outdoor navigation. *Proceedings of the 2001 Conference of the Rehabilitation Engineering and Assistive Technology Society of North America* (pp. 145–147). Arlington, VA: RESNA Press.

PART V

Chapter 11

ROBOTICS AND INDEPENDENCE
FOR THE ELDERLY

Nicholas Roy and Joelle Pineau

OVERVIEW

One of the critical issues facing the aging population is the significant shortage of nursing professionals. The Health Resources and Services Administration estimated that 30 U.S. states had already experienced shortages of registered nurses by the year 2000, a situation that had originally been predicted to start in 2007 (U.S. Department of Health and Human Services, 2002). In 2001, the Federation of Nurses and Health Care Professionals projected a need for 450,000 additional nurses by the year 2008 (Nurses & Health Professionals, 2001). In 2004, the U.S. Bureau of Labor Statistics predicted that more than one million new and replacement nurses would be needed by 2014 (Hecker, 2005). Furthermore, the fastest growing occupation from 2004 to 2014 was predicted to be "home health aides" (Hecker, 2005). With declining enrollment in nursing programs, it is unlikely that the nursing and health care work force will grow to the required level to provide sufficient patient care.

The technologies of robotics and artificial intelligence (AI) provide one possible solution to alleviating the demands placed on the health care work force. The goal is not to use the technology as a replacement for health care professionals, but to use the technology to provide specialized functions and increase the effectiveness of health care professionals. Most health care tasks can be placed in one of two broad categories:

- High-cognition tasks: These tasks require substantial cognitive ability, and interactivity with the patient. Examples include diagnosis, interaction,
- Low-cognition tasks: These tasks are frequently repetitive and mechanical and do not require the health caregiver to use a high level of cognitive ability. Examples of such tasks may be medication reminding, walking assistance, monitoring, et cetera.

The low-cognition tasks are good prospects for automation in caregiving in that these are the tasks that lead fastest to caregiver burnout. The hope is that by reducing the caregiver workload, robotics and artificial intelligence will permit the existing health care work force to redistribute its time, focusing on the human health care tasks, while the technology provides mechanical health care support. Such a focus is central to the utilization of robotics in providing care to the elderly.

Robotics

The precise definition of a robot is the subject of much discussion, as robots vary substantially in form and function. Broadly speaking, a robot is a computational device that can sense and act in the physical world. Early forms of robots were essentially remote-controlled mechanical devices that could take instructions from a human user and translate these instructions into basic motor actions. The majority of commercial robots are used in the manufacturing sector where a form of robot arm or "manipulator" assembles parts together at high speed and with high precision. In most cases, the basic sequence of actions has been designed by a human, but the robot is then used to ensure reliability and accuracy. There are pilot programs at hospitals in the United States to install robot arms in hospital pharmacies. The expectation is that a robot is capable of much more accurate dispensing of medication, allowing the human pharmacist to concentrate on detecting possible problems, such as drug interactions, and providing drug counseling.

As computers have increased in speed and power, robots have taken advantage of the faster computers to become more intelligent and, as a result, more autonomous. In particular, mobile robots are becoming capable of moving independently in an increasingly wider range of environments. Service robots have been used in businesses around the world to deliver mail. One notable example is the Helpmate robot (King & Weiman, 1990) used at hospitals to deliver charts and meals.

Robots have also been used as proxies for humans in hostile or remote environments. The Mars Exploration Rovers are an example of the successful use of robots to explore otherwise inaccessible environments, but rovers have also been used to clean-up Chernobyl and Three Mile Island. Rovers have also been tested in mapping underground mines in the wake of the Quecreek mine disaster.

Finally, there is a burgeoning market for entertainment robots. In particular, Japan has a strong tradition of humanoid mechanical devices in the theater, known as "Karakuri Ningyo." Unlike Western society, Asian societies in general are more accepting of robots and mechanical devices on the level of peers. Japanese companies such as Sony, Honda, and Toyota have invested heavily in humanoid robots, and Sony sells a variety of robots as toys.

Robot Hardware

In terms of shape or "morphology," robots vary widely. The majority of operational robots are either wheeled mobile bases or nonmobile robot arms, often referred to as manipulators. The wheeled bases are usually capable of simple carrying tasks and some limited human-robot interaction and have been used in office and industrial contexts. The manipulator robots are most commonly used in manufacturing. These two forms of robots are not exclusive, as there are mobile bases with useful arms and grippers.

The last 10 years have seen a growth in "humanoid" robots that walk instead of roll and have pairs of arms. Common examples are the Honda Asimo (Sakagami et al., 2002), the Sony Qrio (Geppert, 2004) and the Toyota Partner robot (Toyota, 2006). These humanoids generally have the appearance of walking space suits, although there have been a number of efforts to generate more realistic robots with very human features using modern synthetics to replicate skin, hair, and so on.

Task-specific kinds of robots are also starting to proliferate. Possibly the most successful robot in the world in terms of sales volume to date is the Roomba robotic vacuum cleaner, manufactured by iRobot (iRobot, 2006). This robot looks like a flat disc and contains very little computational hardware, but is capable of cleaning a room up to 1000 sq. feet. Robotic wheelchairs, walkers and other physical assistants have also been developed in the research setting, but these robots have not yet been commercially successful.

Robots also differ widely in terms of their sensing capability; the most common forms of robot sensors for autonomy and mobility are range sensors, such as sonars or low-power laser range finders that can detect the distance to objects held in front of the sensor, and, in some cases, determine the shape of the object. Robots do not yet have the ability to be able to interpret camera images fast enough or with enough reliability to use cameras as general-purpose sensors for interacting with the world.

Robot Software

Many robots function entirely "autonomously," in that the robot software has complete control over all aspects of the robot operation. At the other end of the spectrum are "tele-operated" robots, in which the software has little decision-making power but relies on a human operator for instructions. Most robots fall at some intermediate point along the continuum, such that a human operator gives general instructions to the robot but the software must determine for itself what the correct set of actions are to fulfill the instructions.

Most autonomous robot control software is divided into three main layers: a low-level *control* layer, an intermediate *motion planning* layer and a high-level *task planner*. Roughly speaking, the low-level control layer can be thought of as the nervous system, converting intended motions into motor commands, and reacting to unexpected events. The intermediate layer has some basic understanding of the environment, and can assemble sensor signals into a consistent picture (or map) of the world. The motion planner converts the robot's high-level goals (e.g., "Go to the kitchen" or "Pick up the book") into a trajectory through the world, which the control layer converts into a set of motor commands. The high-level planner consists of software processes that operate at approximate the same level of understanding as human cognition, and, generally, it is at this level where human-robot interaction takes place. The high-level planner may only have a coarse understanding of the world in terms of travel routes, and approximate locations of objects, and so on. However, good high-level planners have an understanding of time, how the world can be ambiguous, that the system may not have enough information, and that people can be contradictory.

One of the major recent advancements in robot technology has been the application of statistical modeling, or "machine learning" at all levels of robot software. Robots are increasingly learning how to control their own motors; legged robots are successfully using learning from past experience to improve their gaits to a level greater than human programmers could. Robots are now capable of learning their way around indoor environments and building maps by themselves, leading to very reliable mobility. Similarly, machine learning techniques are being used to teach robots basic knowledge of how the world operates, in order to enable high-level, task planning. Good techniques for interacting with people is one of the last frontiers still to benefit from machine learning, but it is reasonable to expect that robotic technology will become most effective when machine learning plays a role in how robots understand people.

Robotics and Elder Care

In the early 1990s, progress in sensor and computer technology prompted a new wave of activity in the development of personal robotics. The first efforts to apply robotics in the care of the elderly occurred in this context. There is a wide range of services a robot can offer to an elderly client, from monitoring vital signs, to helping a person navigate in a new environment, to reminding someone when to take his or her medication. Most robot platforms developed to date do not attempt to be everything to everyone, but rather provide a specific class of services to a specific type of client. Three broad classes of robotic assistants include health-care assistants, physical assistants, and cognitive assistants.

Health Care Assistants

One of the priorities, when dealing with a vulnerable population, is to ensure their good health and welfare. As such, health care assistance has been a strong focus for the development of robotic technology for the elderly. Health care assistance refers to those services which can be provided by a robot with the explicit purpose of maintaining or improving the physical health of the user.

A key problem currently faced in the health care sector is the inability to collect data for people living in private homes. Such data include statistics on medication (when did the person take what?), daily living activities, and factors related to the prediction of specific medical risks (blood sugar, leg diameter). Assuming that the necessary mechanisms are in place to guarantee the privacy of this information, such data could be of great value to professional caregivers in the diagnosis and selection of treatment.

Monitoring and Safeguarding

The concepts of monitoring and safeguarding are the core of medical practice. Devices for monitoring biological functions are in every hospital and nursing home, as well as in many home environments. Health monitoring in living environments can be done either through wearable sensors and devices which record activity and physiological systems, or through sensors which are embedded in the home environment. In both cases, the sensors may be passive, in that they only take measurements, but never initiate action. Other systems are active: for example, an alarm is activated when out-of-range measurements are observed. Robotics technology can be used to produce monitoring and safeguarding systems with much broader capacities and less invasive interfaces than standard wearable or embedded sensors.

One of the goals of monitoring is to be able to automatically detect unusual behaviors. Changes to daily patterns are often a good predictor of a change in the health of the person. Caregivers frequently use such information to detect potential problems. To build a robot that would do the same, it is necessary to have a robot that can (a) learn the person's normal patterns; (b) detect deviance from these patterns; and (c) carry-out an appropriate follow-up action. This set of components is fairly general, and there have been many specific applications of these ideas, such as biological sign monitoring (Inada, Horio, Sekita, Isikawa, & Yoshida, 1992; Celler et al., 1995), the detection of sleep patterns (Tamura, Togawa, & Murata, 1988; Loos, Ullrich, & Kobayashi, 2003), as well as to the detection of falls (Doughty, 2000; Noury et al., 2000). Some researchers have also investigated using subjective information, such as complaints and answers to carefully timed questions, to automatically identify health issues as they arise (Inada et al., 1992; Intille, Larson, & Kukla, 2002).

In most of these cases, the system is focused on identifying the baseline patterns, and identifying deviances from those. The question of how to raise alerts is not yet tackled. This is in part a question of whom to contact, but, more importantly, *when* to activate an alarm. This may seem an easy question, but there are trade-offs involved. It is not sufficient to say that a person will be alerted when patterns deviate from normal. If an alert is raised every time there is a small deviation (e.g., person wakes up 5 minutes later than usual), there is a risk of annoying both the elderly person and his or her caregiver. If an alert is raised only in cases of extreme deviation (e.g., person has not woken up in 3 days), then the likelihood of a useful intervention occurring is reduced. Thus there should be a careful trade-off between the threshold at which alarms are raised. In addition, it would be even more useful if, upon detecting a deviance from normal behavior, the system could not only raise an alarm but attempt to prevent further deviance (e.g., if the person is 20 minutes late in taking medication, the system should try to achieve medication compliance before emitting an alert). Of course, this is a much more complicated task. Some of these issues are discussed below in the section on cognitive assistance.

Smart Living Environments

Throughout North America, home visits by health care professionals are extremely rare, due to the high costs involved. The idea of robotic tele-presence is to use Internet technology to relay live video and audio stream from the doctor's office to the patient's living room, thereby enabling the doctor to establish a tele-presence in the patient's home. Most of the smart living facilities involve tracking and monitoring patients. For example, Oatfield Estates, an assisted living facility in Oregon monitors medical data and living patterns and provides internet-based feedback for elders who can monitor their own health. Similar efforts by Richardson et al. (1993a, 1993b) involved installing sensors to detect activities of daily living.

Projects such as the Aware Home (Abowd, Bobick, Essa, Mynatt, & Rogers, 2002; Kidd et al., 1999), the SmartHouse (Barger, Brown, & Alwan, 2005), the Independent LifeStyle Assistant (Haigh, Geib, Miller, Phelps, & Wagner, 2002; Haigh, Phelps, & Geib, 2002) and others (Celler et al., 1995; Yamaguchi, Ogawa, Tamura, & Togawa, 1998; Glascock & Kutzik, 2000) use a set of basic sensors to monitor the in-house movements of an elderly person living alone. The preference is for simple motion detection sensors (e.g., infrared, magnetic switch), rather than more invasive sensors such as video recordings. Sensors are placed strategically to detect entry and exit from rooms (e.g., kitchen, bedroom, bathroom, office, living room, front door) as well as on key objects (e.g., refrigerator door, toilet, pill bottle). The sensor data is then used to build a statistical model of behavioral patterns. These patterns have a natural correspondence to plausible everyday activities (e.g., sleep, meal preparation, toilet use, medication adherence). The statistical model corresponding to a given activity defines its expected location, start time, time of duration, and frequency of activity. The health condition of the person on any given day can then be estimated by comparing the duration of stays in specific rooms, such as the bathroom or bedroom, with previously recorded data.

More sophisticated than the basic sensing and tracking systems are intelligent homes that can reason at a higher level about the users. For example, the system can learn the regular patterns itself from data analysis and then carry out actions such as alerting family members or caregivers itself. The Neural Network House (Mozer, 1998) used neural networks to learn user preferences of environment settings and could choose settings that minimized energy consumption. Similarly, the Intelligent Home project (Lesser et al., 1999) developed a multi-agent system that was also designed to minimize resource utilization. The ability to move (and manipulate) provides an enhanced degree of flexibility currently lacking in sensing, tracking, video-conferencing and other, competing alternatives. Jung et al. (2005) developed a smart home system in which individual components of the system were mobile and connected, including a smart bed and smart wheelchair. In all the smart home systems, comfort and usefulness of the devices and their interfaces is an issue. Edge et al. (2000) developed a system called "Custodian" designed to improve the ability of elder people to use smart technology, such as with larger buttons, et cetera (Edge et al., 2000; Ferreira, Amaral, Santos, Agiannidis, & Edge, 2000).

Caregiver Assistance

While much attention has been devoted to the question of using robotic technology for the support and care of the elderly, it is interesting to look at the problem from another angle. Namely, can robotic technology be used to alleviate the load of the caregiver? This is an important question, given what we know of the stress and fatigue that befall caregivers looking after an elderly person (Barr, Johnson, & Warshaw, 1992; Gallagher, Rose, Rivera, Lovett, & Thompson, 1989; Gallienne, Moore, & Brennan, 1993; Hughes, Giobbie-Hurder, Weaver, Kubal, & Henderson, 1999). An important category of tasks with which a robot can be helpful are fetch-and-carry tasks (Ettelt, Furtwangler, Hanebeck, & Schmidt, 1998). This means that the robot is dispatched to gather certain objects and to return with them. Walky (Bolmsjo, Neveryd, & Eftring, 1995) was one of the first robots to provide fetch-and-carry tasks for nurses and health care workers. This type of assistance requires a complex set of abilities on the part of the robot. First, it must be able to understand the command (i.e., what object is being requested), and second, it must have the ability to find that object, e.g., navigate to its location, pick it up and return. Each of these steps can be challenging under a realistic set of assumptions. It can also be made easier by limiting the robot to a small set of objects that are always in known places and easy to pickup. In such a case, a robot can be expected to perform reasonably well. Under more realistic assumptions, such as noisy communication between the caregiver and the robot, objects that are moved around, and obstacles that can arise in the path of the robot, work remains to be done to ensure robust performance on the part of the robot.

Physical Assistants

One of the major functions that robotics can play in assisting the elderly is compensating for loss of physical motion. There have been a number of studies of using robotic technology as physical prosthetics and physical orthotics in a variety of ways; Miller (1998) describes the physical assistance that robots can provide in three approximate categories: mobility, manipulation and sensing. The most common form of assistant is helping the elderly with mobility, but the interesting thing is that this assistance can range from simple walking assistance to actual collision avoidance, way finding and full navigation.

Sadly, the research and technological development has two shortcomings. Firstly, there has been very little research into the integration of good human-computer interaction and the physical assistance. For instance, ensuring the effectiveness of guided navigation requires addressing issues of display, representation, and situation awareness. To date, there does not appear to have been much effort to provide good human-computer interaction in physical assistive robots, with the exception of some of the wheelchair efforts (Yanco, 2000). As a result, much of the robotic technology described below has not matured to the product level yet. The Manus robot wheelchair (Rosier et al., 1991) is one of the few commercially available robotic platforms, but the use of intelligent control in this system is relatively limited.

Intelligent Walkers

One of the major technologies helping the elderly preserve independence is the relatively simple walker. However, as the elderly start to suffer cognitive and perceptual decline, the usefulness of the walker also declines. A number of research efforts have augmented walkers with navigation aids, both for sensing obstacles, but also for attempting to recognize user intent and provide cognitive guidance.

One of the first intelligent walkers was the PAM-AID, shown in Figure 11.1. The walker was designed as a navigation aid for the elderly, in particular the visually impaired, but Lacey and MacNamara (2000) recognized the importance of inferring user intent, especially with an assistive device that has a fairly loose physical connection to the user. The developers state: "the provision of feedback about objects in the environment must be based on the needs of the user (reassurance, information) and the needs of the robot (user safety)" (Lacey & Dawson-Howe, 1998, p. 251). A number of assistive devices have continued to address the issue of inferring user intent from forces exerted on the device, but for many of the early devices, the assumption was that either the user or the robotic device assumed full authority over the direction of motion, and many devices developed today share this shortcoming (Park, Jang, & Han, 2003; Shim, Lee, Shim, Lee, & Hong, 2005).

A number of assistive walking devices were developed at MIT, starting with the smart cane (Dubowsky et al., 2000), a motorized base with a cane-like handle that could provide collision avoidance and navigation assistance for the blind. The SmartCane effort was one of the first devices that attempted to provide active guidance to the user and addressed the problems of user intent combined with directional control. Similarly, Wasson et al. (2001) developed an intelligent walker for inferring user intent from the forces on the walker and used sensing technology to provide obstacle avoidance.

More recently, two research groups have developed complete mobile robots that can also act as assistive walking devices. Morris et al. (2003) equipped a mobile base with force sensing in order to provide

Figure 11.1. The PAM-AID walker. Figure reprinted with permission. Source: Provided courtesy of S. Dubowsky (MIT).

walking guidance, and then created the CMU walker by retrofitting a conventional walker with a full suite of sensing and computation in order to learn user activity patterns (see Figure 11.2). More recently, Glover, Thrun, and Matthews (2004) demonstrated that this robotic walker could provide more activity-centered guidance by understanding user intent such as intended destination based on past history.

Figure 11.2. The CMU walker. Figures reprinted with permission. Source: Provided courtesy of J. Glover (MIT), S. Thrun (Stanford University) and J. Matthews (University of Pittsburgh).

The Care-O-Bot (Graf, Hans, & Schraft, 2004) is the other mobile robot developed to be a multi-purpose aid to the elderly, as a carrying robot, manipulator and walker. As in the early incarnations of the CMU walker, the robot is not a retrofitted walking frame but a large mobile robot, using force feedback to make the robot have the responsive feel of a light walker. Users reported the Care-O-Bot to be too large to be practical, and the force that each user must exert was reported to be larger than for a normal walker. Nevertheless, as robotic technology improves and components decrease in size and weight, the Care-O-Bot approach may prove successful.

Intelligent Wheelchairs

For a large portion of the elderly population, assisted walking devices are no longer sufficient, and mobility must be provided through a wheelchair. Typically the wheelchair is powered in order to give the

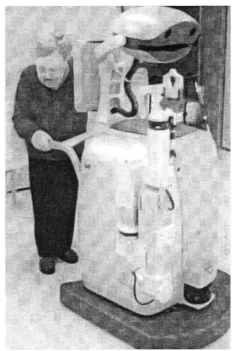

Figure 11.3. Care-o-Bot II. Figure reprinted with permission. Source: Provided courtesy of B. Graf (Fraunhofer IPA).

user as much independence as possible. Just as intelligent walkers can give cognitive assistance with navigation, robotic wheelchairs can provide the same assistance. Wheelchair control can also be a challenge for many, as operating the wheelchair without collisions in most indoor environments requires good perception, attention, and good muscular control. As a result, much of the research into robotic wheelchairs has also addressed the problem of navigation and collision avoidance.

However, most robotic wheelchairs operate in indoor environments only. Kettle et al. (1992) report that "a survey of powered and manual wheelchair users found that 57 percent used their wheelchair only outside and 33 percent used their wheelchair both inside and outside" (Haigh and Yanco, 2002, p. 43). Haigh and Yanco (2002) point out that "even considering that some of the target population may be institutionalized which may increase the number of people using their systems indoors only, a large number of users still need a system that will work outdoors" (p. 43).

One of the most basic capabilities of a robotic wheelchair is the ability to sense obstacles and to provide a measure of collision avoidance. Scott and Munro (1985) used sonar range sensors to detect obstacles, but the automatic control would only slow down the wheelchair instead of coming to a full stop. This behavior was designed to allow a user to pull the chair under a desk. However, it is not likely that such an approach will be successful in the long term, as the wheelchair operator has to be fully aware that for obstacles that are *not* desks, the wheelchair will still not stop.

Sonar-based collision avoidance was similarly a key capability of the NavChair system, which also provided rudimentary navigation in terms of wall- and corridor-following (Simpson et al., 1998). The TinMan series of wheelchairs integrated sonar range sensing with infrared sensing and bump sensing for collision avoidance (Miller & Slack, 1995). The CALL Center Smart Wheelchair Collision (Nisbet, Craig, Odor, & Aitken, 1996) used a control model known as "behavior-based" control to mimic biological or natural responses to collisions and bumps; in particular, the response to collisions and bumps was trained for each individual user. However, it is hard to see how using bumpers to detect collisions will be a popular technology; the priority should be avoiding collisions before the bump has occurred.

In contrast, Alanen et al. (1996) developed a package that could allow a standard powered wheelchair to be retrofitted with sonar range sensors to provide collision avoidance capabilities. This would appear to be a very viable approach when coupled with appropriate feedback to the user.

In addition to collision avoidance, robotic wheelchairs can provide full navigation capability, wherein the user selects a destination, and the robot then assumes full control of the wheelchair until the user deliberately seizes control, or the chair arrives at the destination. A number of wheelchair projects actively developed autonomous navigation for robotic wheelchairs, including the TAO project (Gomi & Griffith, 1998) which used computer vision and infrared sensing to track landmarks and distinctive places in the environment. Similarly, the VAHM project (Bourhis & Agostini, 1998a, 1998b) provides full path planning in addition to collision avoidance. Both the TAO project and the VAHM project gave the user supervisory override capability. In contrast, the navigation system developed by Yoder et al. (1996) learned from experience to predict the route that the user would take to get to some destination, but this system did not have collision avoidance—when an obstacle appeared in the path of the robot, control would be returned to the user. The Arizona State University wheelchair (Madarasz, Heiny, Cromp, & Mazur, 1991) provided capability for planning routes, with the addition of collision avoidance using sonar. This system used an additional video camera to ensure the chair stayed in the center of corridors, tracked room numbers and detected elevator lights. The PSUBOT (Perkowski & Stanton, 1991; Stanton et al., 1991) provided a similar set of indoor navigation capabilities with route planning from room to room by tracking landmarks using a camera. In contrast to these indoor robotic wheelchairs, the Wheelesley wheelchair (Yanco, 2000) was the first wheelchair to provide general navigation for both indoor and outdoor, giving the user basic but all-purpose navigation and obstacle avoidance capabilities using gaze control.

One of the critical issues in the successful implementation of a robotic wheelchair is the interface mechanism used to convey the user intent to the control system. One of the most common interface mechanisms is gaze control, where the system tracks the user's gaze direction to infer the user's desired direction of motion; Adachi et al. (1998) integrated such a control system with sonar collision avoidance to give command-and-control to users with limited range of motion (Kuno, Nakanishi, Murashima, Shimada, & Shirai, 1999a). Jaffe (1981) used sonar transducers to track the head position, rather than gaze direction (Jaffe, 1983; Jaffe, Harris, & Leung, 1990). While this system provides an interesting demonstration of technology, it is unlikely that it would be a practical system as sonar is audible to the human ear, and a constant sonar pulse to track the head would most likely be a significant source of annoyance to the user. Other wheelchair systems use speech interaction such as the Vocomotion system (Amori, 1992), or a combination of voice and face tracking, as in the UMIDAM system (Mazo et al., 1995; Bergasa et al., 1999). Integrating voice commanding with a simple point-and-click interface (using a joystick or other pointer) would seem to be the most reliable interface, such as the Scenario wheelchair system (Katevas et al., 1997; Beattie & Bishop, 1998), which used a combination of voice and joystick commanding. This system unfortunately did not provide full motion planning capability, but would warn of impending collisions and stop the chair before a collision occurred. In an attempt to reduce the overall cognitive load on the wheelchair user, Crisman and Cleary (1998) investigated a specialized form of tele-operation that allowed the user to give commands in the robot reference frame, in a form of commanding known as "deictic commanding." Because all symbols are relative to each other, then potential ambiguities in instructions such as "go over there" can be more easily resolved. While the deictic interface style may lead to very efficient interaction, the driving interface modality must also be addressed satisfactorily. Finally, a topic of ongoing research is different ways for wheelchairs to move around. Wada and Asada (1999) developed a wheelchair capable of moving in any direction without rotating, a concept known as "holonomic" motion. The advantage to holonomic motion is that the wheelchair can move sideways more easily, making it easier to move in tight spaces. Borgolte et al. (1995) also developed a holonomic wheelchair, and showed that a smoother ride resulted when performing collision avoidance (Borgolte, Hoyer, Buhler, Heck, & Hoelper, 1998; Buhler, Heck, & Jumann, 1997; Hoyer, Borgolte, & Hoelper, 1997). Additionally, the MIT Omnidrive chair can change its "footprint" so that the chair wheels take up less space in tight quarters. Wider wheelchair footprints are more stable, but narrower footprints are easier to control. The changeable footprint allows the wheelchair to trade off between the two (Mascaro & Asada, 1998; Tahboub & Asada, 1999).

Intelligent Robot Arms

Mobility is not the only form of physical assistance that robots can provide. Allowing people to move around their homes as long as possible is clearly one of the best ways to allow them to maintain a sense of independence. However, as the ability to walk declines, often so does the ability to reach and to carry objects. As a result, there have been a number of studies that combine mobility assistance with a robot arm or manipulator.

The Wessex robot (Hillman, Hagan, Hagan, Jepson, & Orpwood, 1999) is one of the first successful integration of a robotic wheelchair and a flexible robot arm. The best example of a successful arm on a wheelchair is the Manus system, shown in Figure 11.5. The Manus system is largely tele-operated—the user must use a joystick interface to control both the wheelchair and the robotic arm. The technical challenge that the Manus system addresses is how to ensure that the arm is both capable but also lightweight. The Manus arm moves contains the motors in the wheelchair base and uses a belt-drive system to move the

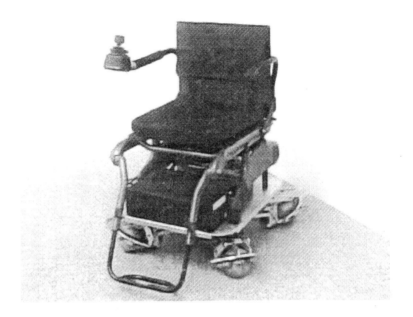

Figure 11.4. The MIT Omnidrive Wheelchair. Figure reprinted with permission. (© IEEE 1999). Source: Provided courtesy of M. Wada, H. H. Asada (MIT). Appeared in "Design and control of a variable footprint mechanism for holonomic omnidirectional vehicles and its application to wheelchairs." *IEEE Transactions on Robotics and Automation, 15:* 6, pp 978–999. (© IEEE 1999).

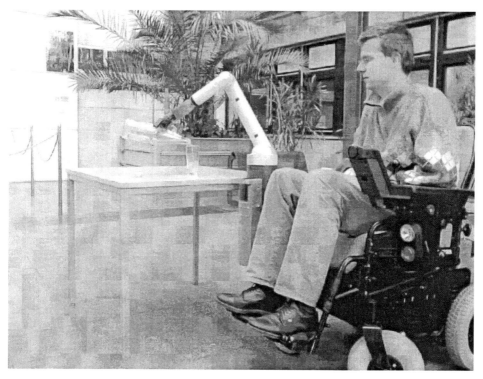

Figure 11.5. The Manus Arm. Figure reprinted with permission. Source: Provided courtesy of A. Graeser (Institut fur Automatisierungstechnik).

power to the individual joints. The Manus system is commercially available from Exact Dynamics in the Netherlands.

In contrast to these robots, the Kares system (Song, Lee, Kim, Yoon, & Bien, 1998) is an integrated wheelchair and robot arm that has a much clearer interface. The Kares I and II systems (Bien et al., 2004) both accept natural, spoken word commands to move around and pick up objects. The more recent Kares II system does not require the different objects in the environment to have special markers, and can also be controlled using gaze directions and facial expressions if the user has speech difficulties.

The Care-o-Bot walking system (Graf et al., 2004) has the ability to perform fetch-and-carrying tasks, and has also been demonstrated to assist with business card exchange. The Telecare Robotic System (Jia, Hada, & Takase, 2003) includes a mobile robot arm intended for a remote user to provide assistance. The system consists of the mobile base, the arm, and a video camera–the interface issues of such a system

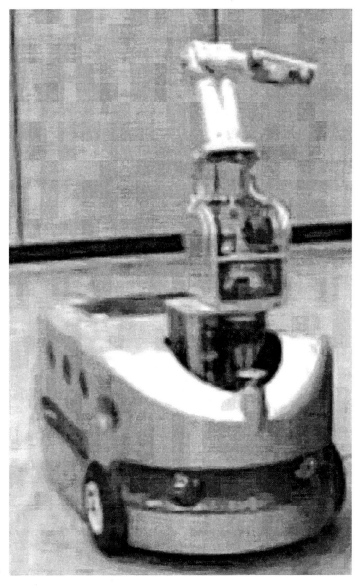

Figure 11.6. The Kares Wheelchair. Figure reprinted with permission. Source: Provided courtesy of Z. Z. Bien (Korea Advanced Institute of Science and Technology).

are an open problem, and this system is not likely to be as useful in preserving the independence of the elderly.

Finally, a number of robot arms have been developed that are not designed for integration with a mobile base. Suzuki et al. (2000) developed an arm that travels around the room on a ceiling-mounted track.

They demonstrated that this arm could in fact provide walking assistance (e.g., as a ceiling-mounted walker), but could also provide fetch-and-carry assistance, and could help answering the phone. Topping (1999) developed the Handy movable arm for providing hygiene and eating assistance. A more unusual device is the arm developed by Gimenez et al. (2003) that is mobile by itself–the arm can crawl around the environment. This arm currently must be operated directly by the user and has no intelligence of its own. While different arm configurations are interesting, it is also difficult to imagine ready acceptance by the general public of a crawling arm as a health care assistant.

Exoskeletons

One final form of physical assistance that robots can provide is as an "exoskeleton," where the robot provides powered assistance to the user's skeleton and musculature. Exoskeletons have been developed in North America largely for the military, to allow soldiers to carry greater loads and to walk further distances. In Japan, however, exoskeletons became commercially available in November of 2005 as assistance for the elderly.

Pratt et al. (2004) describes the three key capabilities that an exoskeleton device must possess to be useful:

- The device must determine user's intent.
- The device must apply forces where and when appropriate.
- The device must present low impedance, that is, "get out of the way."

The RoboKnee (Pratt et al., 2004) shown in Figure 11.7 is an example of one exoskeleton device. The device is a robotic knee with series-elastic actuators. The device estimates the user intent from forces applied on the ground, and then helps rotate the human knee forward during the swing phase of the gait. In contrast, Kiguchi, Iwami et al. (2003) have developed exoskeleton shoulder support. The controller learns the correct response from EMG signals in the shoulder, and provides assistance in rotating the shoulder joint during reaching and carrying tasks (Kiguchi, Tanaka, Watanabe, & Fukuda, 2003; Kiguchi, 2004).

Finally, two interesting motion assist devices are wheelchairs that provide standing assistance. Nagai et al. (2002) developed a mobile device that can assist people in transitioning from either a prone or seat-

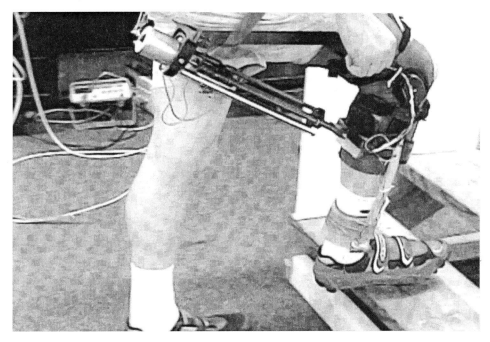

Figure 11.7. The RoboKnee. Figure reprinted with permission. Source: Provided courtesy of J. Pratt (Institute for Machine and Human Cognition).

ed position to standing. The Vivax wheelchair (Vivax, 2006) is a powered wheelchair that can transition the user to a fully standing position. The Vivax system is commercially available, although addresses a simpler problem than assisting during general transfer motion.

Cognitive Assistants

The decline of cognitive functions in the elderly usually results in an increased need for caregiver involvement. Simple activities of daily living, such as taking one's medication, preparing a meal, or attending to a pet, can be severely compromised without proper guidance. Robotic technology can be helpful to provide the kind of round-the-clock gentle monitoring and assistance that is required in such situations.

Cognitive assistance needs not be limited to memory functions. Socially assistive robots are playing an increasingly active role in providing social stimulation to the elderly. Such robots are typically designed to take on certain characteristics of a human, or pet, to provide a familiar interface for the human. They can facilitate expression of emotional and social behaviors on the part of an elderly person, thereby helping to reduce stress and depression.

Cognitive and social assistance are discussed separately in this section in order to draw a clear picture of the challenges and possibilities associated with each. In reality, however, it is often most effective to design robots that combine both types of assistance, and a few such examples are discussed below.

Cognitive Prosthesis–Planning, Scheduling, Medication Reminding

A large fraction of the elderly population suffers from varying degrees of dementia. The inability to remember can have severe consequences. For example, subjects may forget to take their medicine; they might forget to use the bathroom, et cetera. When conditions become too severe, patients need regular supervision in carrying out their daily activities, which often means moving into a nursing home. People also might use a robot for lesser purposes, such as finding out what is on TV. Reminding is an important (and time-consuming) activity in a health care professional's life.

Cognitive assistants are designed to help with planning and scheduling activities. This can include both daily activities (such as taking medication, eating, drinking, using the bathroom, washing one's hands), as well as occasional activities (such as doctor's appointments or family visits). The cognitive assistant can be useful to remind the person of *when* to conduct these activities, but it can also provide guidance as to *how* to complete them correctly.

The idea of using computer technology to enhance the performance of cognitively disabled people dates back over 40 years (Englebart, 1963). More recently, cognitive orthotics have enabled reminders to be provided using the telephone (Friedman, 1998), personal digital assistants and pagers (Hersh & Treadgold, 1994). Very inexpensive electronic pillboxes have also recently appeared on the market (Cadex, 2006; MedGlider, 2006; MedReminder, 2006), which simply provide appropriately-timed medication reminders. These are important devices since medical reminder systems have been formally proven to improve medical compliance (Fulmer et al., 1999). However, they are in effect glorified alarm clocks, and cannot be viewed as full cognitive assistants since the interaction is only one-way (from the device to the patient).

An integral part of robotics is the ability to receive, and to reason about, input from the environment (including the user). More sophisticated systems, such as the Autominder system installed on-board the robot Pearl (Pollack et al., 2003; Pineau, Montemerlo, Pollack, Roy, & Thrun, 2003) use artificial intelligence technology to issue reminders that are tailored to each individual, based on data it has received and interpreted concerning what the person has done and is supposed to do. In this system, the goal of the cognitive assistant is to make principled decisions about what reminders to issue and when, balancing the following potentially competing objectives: (a) ensure that the user is aware of activities she/he is expected to perform, (b) increase the likelihood that she or he will perform the required activities (e.g., taking medicine), (c) avoid annoying the user, and (d) avoid making the user overly reliant on the system. To attain these goals, the system must be flexible and adaptive, responding to the actions taken by its user. The system uses a Plan Manager to store the user's plan of daily activities. It also uses a Client Modeler to maintain information about the user's observable activities to see whether or not the user is following instructions. The system can then reason about any disparities between what the user is supposed to do (as reported by the Plan Manager) and what the user is actually doing (as reported by the Client Modeler), and make the final decision about when to issue reminders.

The Assisted Cognition Project at the University of Washington (Kautz, Arnstein, Borriello, Etzioni & Fox, 2002) is another ongoing research effort in the development of cognitive assistants, which also maintains an extensive Client Model and uses it to make decisions about whether or not to intervene. Its Client Model includes both information about the person's position (tracked by GPS) as well as about his or her activities (tracked by RFID).

Other projects have taken a more focused view and are aimed at providing cognitive support for specific key tasks. The COACH system is specifically designed to monitor progress and provide assistance during handwashing for older adults with dementia (Boger et al., 2005). A vision system is used to estimate the person's hand position and the water flow from the tap. Based on this imprecise information, the system can decide to issue any of a number of verbal prompts that gently guide the user through the appropriate sequence of steps.

Social Assistance

A large proportion of elderly people live alone, and in many cases lack social interaction. Social engagement can significantly delay the deterioration and health-related problems. Robotic technology can be a useful tool to alleviate the social isolation that affects many older adults. Social isolation can be the result of many factors. For example, when mobility problems restrict the activities of an individual, including leaving the house, there can be a profound negative impact on that individual's ability to maintain a social network and have frequent interactions with others.

Technology has been used to enhance contact with family and friends. For example, the elder-friendly email programs Generations on Line provides a simplified interface for emailing that uses familiar images and large type instructions to guide the elderly user. Robotics can enrich such technology by offering a more versatile interaction platform. The robot's physical presence commands attention to a much greater degree than a standard screen. In addition, a robot's ability to move means that the videoconferencing is not limited to a single location, and that the robot can provide multiple viewpoints on a scene. Recent work on such technology is reported by Leigh (2000).

In some instances, a simplified robot can be just as effective in promoting socialization. It is well documented that pet companions can reduce depression and isolation in the elderly. Therefore, it is an interesting question as to whether or not robotic pets can be used for a similar purpose. The advantage of a robotic pet is that it requires much less daily care (no need to clean, feed, take for a walk) and is accepted in all residential environments. These robotic pets sometimes take the form of a well-known animal, such as the highly successful AIBO line of robot dog produced by Sony. However, in other instances, they are designed as generic "fuzzy" animals such as the highly popular Furby toy. Whether or not these robotic pets can have a meaningful impact on the social life of the elderly remains to be seen. Most current results are purely anecdotal, and there has not yet been a long-term study on this question.

The area of socially assistive robotics is very recent and, more than other applications discussed above, already has strong economic potential. Between 1999 and 2004, Sony sold 130,000 AIBO robot dogs to customers worldwide (*News Release: AIBO Celebrates Five Years of Innovation and Intelligence,* 2004). Such market demand is driving the development of the technology, bringing enhanced functionality and social features in response to customer demand. While this growth is not driven primarily by older adults, the new developments that are demanded by the younger consumers are likely to benefit elderly users. From improved interfaces, to more robust hardware, to better adaptivity to the user, there are many directions in which entertainment robotics are moving which will have a long-term impact on the development of socially assistive robots for all segments of the population.

While it is well-recognized that robots cannot replace humans, it is useful to understand the degree to which robots can augment humans, either by directly interacting with individuals, or by providing a communication interface between different people that is more usable than current alternatives. Several factors make interaction a challenging one for a robot to accomplish successfully. First, many elderly have difficulty understanding the robot's synthesized speech, as well as articulating an appropriate response in a computer-understandable way. In addition, walking abilities vary dramatically between individuals. People with walking aids are usually an order of magnitude slower than people without, and people often stop to chat or catch their breath along the way. It is therefore imperative that the robot adapt to individuals–an aspect of interaction that has been poorly explored in AI and robotics.

In systematic experiments conducted by Pineau et al. (2003) at a nursing home, a combination of techniques was found to be highly effective in dealing with elderly test subjects. This study focused on the robot Pearl shown in Figure 11.8, which was primarily designed to interact with the world through speech, visual displays, facial expressions, and physical motion. It differed from earlier workplace robots in that it went beyond simply interacting with an (often static) environment, to interacting with human users and bystanders. In particular, during a sequence of one-on-one interactions between Pearl and residents of the nursing home, the robot demonstrated the ability to contact a resident, remind him or her of an appointment, accompany her or him to that appointment, as well as provide information of interest to that person, such as weather reports or television schedules.

This project also demonstrated the importance of high-level intelligence in interactive robots. The ability to represent the uncertainty inherent in a person's behavior and to formulate plans accordingly, allowed the robot to robustly handle difficult situations, including noisy communication and crowded environments. One of the key lessons

Figure 11.8. The Nursebot Pearl. Figure reprinted with permission. Source: Provided courtesy of S. Thrun (Stanford University).

learned while developing the robot was the need for techniques that can cope with individual differences. This lesson is especially significant in designing robots for elderly users who exhibit a great range of skills as a result of age-related decline.

AREAS OF CONCERN

Ethical Issues

By their very nature, robots acquire enormous amounts of information about their surroundings, both the physical world and the humans who populate it. The issue of confidentiality naturally arises whenever data is being collected about a person. The monitoring systems in particular, whether they are monitoring biological functions or behavioral activities, are based on the collection of large amounts of data over time. One way to alleviate the privacy concerns is to reduce the quantity and specificity of the data being collected, for example, by using motion sensors rather than video recordings to acquire information about a person's patterns of activity. The resulting data is much sparser, and, generally, requires more advanced techniques to analyze (thus making it less tempting as a target for fraud).

Usability

One of the greatest challenges for the smooth integration of robotic technology in the area of personal assistance is in providing a usable interface between the technology and person. Since older adults often have greater difficulty in learning new skills, interfaces that are poorly designed can cause rejection of an otherwise useful product. The question of product usability for the elderly has been studied in the context of non-robotic technologies (e.g., accessibility of the internet, remote controls, phones, etc.) Many of the lessons learned through these simpler products can better guide the design of the robot interface. There is also significant interest in developing new interface paradigms, including multimodal communication, the modeling of emotions and anthropomorphic agents, to enrich interactions between robots and humans. Most of this work is currently being conducted with nonelderly populations, but in the long run may generalize to this group as well.

Long-term Impact

While a number of robotic assistants for the elderly have been tested and validated with the target population, few have been deployed for extended periods of time. There are some factors that can be tested in short interactions, such as ease of operation, initial satisfaction, and comfort level. However, other outcomes can only be measured during and after a long-term exposure: for example, the social impact, the compliance with robot's instructions, and long-term usage patterns. Such long-term studies have not been conducted as yet, but will be required to test the true impact of robotic technology on the elderly population.

CONCLUSION

Robotics contains great promise in helping the elderly to maintain a sense of independence. As robots become more intelligent, more capable and more autonomous, they will become increasingly useful both to the general public and to the elderly. Although most elder-care robots have been developed in the laboratory setting as research projects, user studies and small-scale deployments are occurring with increasing frequency, and commercially viable products have gradually begun to appear on the market.

However, some nontechnical obstacles must also be addressed in order to ensure the wide-scale adoption of robotic technology for health care and elder care. Dario et al. (1994) observed that the medical community is reluctant to accept robots in medical settings, as they are seen as dangerous, competitive, and technical. Moreover, the medical community tends to think of robots as mechanical arms, and not as mobile assistants. Clearly, part of the process of developing robots for health care will involve a large educational component.

A second substantial obstacle is the cost of the technology. Harmo et al. (2005) demonstrated that there is interest in technological solutions to the worsening shortage of caregivers, but the cost is currently perceived as prohibitive, especially with regard to installation costs. In order to make a convincing economic argument for the use of technology, cost-benefit analyses are required. Different levels of technology present differences in different cost effectiveness. Using technology to mediate communication and "remote presence" between outside caregivers and the elderly seems to be the easiest in the short-term, while providing manipulation assistance would seem to be the most difficult and suited for special needs. One possible approach suggested by Kawamura and Iskarous (1994) is that government programs are needed to transfer technology into commercial successes. Regardless of the economic, social, and technical challenges, robots represent one of the best tools for allowing the elderly to maintain their independence and to live safely and comfortably in their own homes.

REFERENCES

Abowd, G. D., Bobick, A. F., Essa, I. A., Mynatt, E. D., & Rogers, W. A. (2002). The aware home: A living laboratory for technologies for successful aging. In *Proceedings of the AAAI-02 Workshop "Automation as Caregiver"* 1–7.

Adachi, Y., Kuno, Y., Shimada, N., & Shirai, Y. (1998). Intelligent wheelchair using visual information on human faces. In *Proceedings of the IEEE International Conference on Robotics and Automation (ICRA)*, 354–359.

Alanen, J., Karasti, O., Mattila, P., Santti, V., & Virtanen, A. (1996). A drive assistant for a wheelchair. In *Proceedings of the IEEE Conference on Systems, Man and Cybernetics*, 376–381.

Amori, R. D. (1992). Vocomotion–An intelligent voicecontrol system for powered wheelchairs. In *Proceedings of the Rehabilitation Engineering Society of North America Annual Conference*, 421–423.

Barger, T., Brown, D., & Alwan, M. (2005). Health status monitoring through analysis of behavioral patterns. *IEEE Transactions on Systems, Man and Cybernetics, Part A. 35* (1), 22–27.

Barr, J. K., Johnson, K. W., & Warshaw, L. J. (1992). Supporting the elderly: Workplace programs for caregivers. *The Milbank Quarterly, 70* (3), 509–533.

Beattie, P., & Bishop, J. (1998). Self-localisation in the scenario autonomous wheelchair. *Journal of Intelligent and Robotic Systems, 22,* 255–267.

Bergasa, L., Mazo, M., Gardel, A., Garcia, J., Ortuno, A., & Mendez, A. (1999). Guidance of a wheelchair for handicapped people by face tracking. In *Proceedings of the 7th IEEE Conference On Emerging Technologies and Factory Automation*, Vol. 1, 105–111.

Bien, Z., Chung, M.-J., Chang, P.-H., Kwon, D.-S., Kim, D.-J., Han, J.-S., et al. (2004). Integration of a rehabilitation robotic system (Kares II) with human-friendly man-machine interaction units. *Autonomous Robots, 16* (16), 165–191.

Boger, J., Poupart, P., Hoey, J., Boutilier, C., Fernie, G., & Mihailidis, A. (2005). A decision-theoretic approach to task assistance for persons with dementia. In *International Joint Conference On Artificial Intelligence (IJCAI)*, 1293–1299.

Bolmsjo, G., Neveryd, H., & Eftring, H. (1995). Robotics in rehabilitation. *IEEE Transactions on Rehabilitation Engineering, 3* (1), 77–83.

Borgolte, U., Hoyer, H., Buhler, C., Heck, H., & Hoelper, R. (1998). Architectural concepts of a semiautonomous wheelchair. *Journal of Intelligent and Robotic Systems, 22,* 233–253.

Borgolte, U., Hoelper, R., Hoyer, H., Heck, H., Humann, W., Nedza, J., et al. (1995). Intelligent control of semiautonomous omnidirectional wheelchair. In *Proceedings of the 3rd International Symposium On Intelligent Robotic Systems*, 113–120.

Bourhis, G., & Agostini, Y. (1998a). Man-machine cooperation for the control of an intelligent powered wheelchair. *Journal of Intelligent and Robotic Systems, 22,* 269–287.

Bourhis, G., & Agostini, Y. (1998b). The VAHM robotized wheelchair: System architecture and human-machine interaction. *Journal of Intelligent and Robotic Systems, 22* (1), 39–50.

Buhler, C., Heck, H., & Jumann, W. (1997). User-driven human-machine interface configuration for a wheelchair with complex functionality. *Advancement of Assistive Technology*, 375–380.

Cadex. (2006). http://www.responselink.com/medication.htm.

Celler, B. G., Earnshaw, W., Ilsar, E. D., Betbeder-Matibet, L., Harris, M. F., Clark, R., et al. (1995). Remote monitoring of health status of the elderly at home: A multidisciplinary project on aging at the University of New South Wales. *International Journal of Bio-Medical Computing, 40,* 147–155.

Crisman, J. D., & Cleary, M. E. (1998). Progress on the deictically controlled wheelchair. In V. Mittal, H. A. Yanco, J. Aronis, & R. C. Simpson (Eds.), *Lecture notes in Artificial Intelligence: Assistive Technology and Artificial Intelligence*, Berlin: Springer, 137–149.

Dario, P., Guglielmelli, E., & Allotta, B. (1994). Robotics in medicine. In *Proceedings of the IEEE/RSJ International Conference on Intelligent Robots and Systems*, Vol. 2, 739–752.

Doughty, K. (2000). Fall prevention and management strategies based on intelligent detection, monitoring and assessment. *New Technologies in Medicine for the Elderly*, 1–20.

Dubowsky, S., Genot, F., Godding, S., Kozono, H., Skwersky, A., Yu, H., et al. (2000). PAMM– A robotic aid to the elderly for mobility assistance and monitoring: A "helping-hand" for the elderly. In *Proceedings of the IEEE International Conference on Robotics and Automation (ICRA)*, Vol. 1, 570–576.

Edge, M., Taylor, B., & Dewsbury, G. (2000). The potential for "smart home" systems in meeting the care needs of older persons and people with disabilities. *Senior's Housing Update, 10* (1), 6–7.

Englebart, D. (1963). Vistas in information handling. In *A conceptual framework for the augmentation of man's intellect*. Washington: Spartan Books 1-29.

Ettelt, E., Furtwangler, R., Hanebeck, U. D., & Schmidt, G. (1998). Design issues of a semi-autonomous robotic assistant for the health care environment. *Journal of Intelligent and Robotic Systems, 22* (3–4), 191–209.

Ferreira, J. M. M., Amaral, T., Santos, D., Agiannidis, A., & Edge, M. (2000). The Custodian tool: Simple design of home automation systems for people with special needs. In *Proceedings of EIB Event 2000, Technische Uni. Munchen*, 1–10.

Friedman, R. (1998). Automated telephone conversation to assess health behavior and deliver behavioral interventions. *Journal of Medical Systems, 22,* 95–101.

Fulmer, T. T., Feldman, P. H., Kim, T. S., Carty, B., Beers, M., & Putnam, M. (1999). An intervention study to enhance medical compliance in community-dwelling elderly individuals. *Journal of Gerontological Nursing, 25* (8), 6–14.

Gallagher, D., Rose, J., Rivera, P., Lovett, S., & Thompson, L. W. (1989). Prevalence of depression in family caregivers. *The Gerontologist, 29* (4), 449–456.

Gallienne, R. L., Moore, S. M., & Brennan, P. F. (1993). Alzheimer's caregivers, psychosocial support via computer networks. *Journal of Gerontological Nursing, 19* (12), 15–22.

Geppert, L. (2004, May). Qrio, the robot that could. *IEEE Spectrum, 41* (5), 34–37.

Gimenez, A., Balaguer, C., Sabatini, A., & Genovese, V. (2003). The mats robotic system to assist disabled people in their home environments. In *Proceedings of the IEEE/rsj International Conference on Intelligent Robots and Systems*, Vol. 3, 2612–2617.

Glascock, A. P., & Kutzik, D. M. (2000). Behavioral telemedicine: A new approach to the continuous nonintrusive monitoring of activities of daily living. *Telemedicine Journal, 6* (1), 33–44.

Glover, J., Thrun, S., & Matthews, J. (2004). Learning user models of mobility-related activities through instrumented walking aids. In *Proceedings of the IEEE International Conference on Robotics and Automation (ICRA)*, Vol. 4, 3306–3312.

Gomi, T., & Griffith, A. (1998). Developing intelligent wheelchairs for the handicapped. In V. Mittal, Yanco, H. A., Aronis, J. & Simpson, R. C. (Eds.), *Lecture notes in artificial intelligence: Assistive technology and artificial intelligence,* Berlin: Springer-Verlag, 150–178.

Graf, B., Hans, M., & Schraft, R. D. (2004). Care-o-bot II development of a next generation robotic home assistant. *Autonomous Robots, 16* (16), 193–205.

Haigh, K. Z., Geib, C. W., Miller, C. A., Phelps, J., & Wagner, T. (2002). Agents for recognizing and responding to the behaviour of an elder. In *Proceedings of the AAAI-02 Workshop "Automation as Caregiver,"* 31–38.

Haigh, K. Z., Phelps, J., & Geib, C. W. (2002). An open agent architecture for assisting elder independence. In *First International Joint Conference On Autonomous Agents And Multiagent Systems (AAMAS),* 578–586.

Haigh, K. Z., & Yanco, H. A. (2002). Automation as caregiver: A survey of issues and technologies. *Proceedings of the AAAI-02 Workshop "Automation as Caregiver,"* 39–53.

Harmo, P., Taipalus, T., Knuuttila, J., Vallet, J., & Halme, A. (2005). Needs and solutions–Home automation and service robots for the elderly and disabled. In *Proceedings of the IEEE/RSJ International Conference on Intelligent Robots and Systems,* 2721–2726.

Health and Human Services, U.S. Department of, Health Resources & Services Administration, N. C. F. H. W. A., Bureau of Health Professions. (2002, July). *Projected supply, demand, and shortages of registered nurses: 2000–2020.* ftp://ftp.hrsa.gov/bhpr/nationalcenter/rnproject.pdf.

Hecker, D. E. (2005, November). Occupational employment projections to 2014. *Monthly Labor Review Online, 128* (11).

Hersh, N., & Treadgold, L. (1994). Neuropage: The rehabilitation of memory dysfunction by prosthetic memory and cueing. *NeuroRehabilitation, 4,* 187–197.

Hillman, M., Hagan, K., Hagan, S., Jepson, J., & Orpwood, R. (1999). A wheelchair mounted assistive robot. In *Proceedings of the International Conference on Rehabilitation Robotics (ICORR),* 86–91.

Hoyer, H., Borgolte, U., & Hoelper, R. (1997). An omnidirectional wheelchair with enhanced comfort features. In *Proceedings of the International Conference On Rehabilitation Robotics (ICORR),* 31–34.

Hughes, S. L., Giobbie-Hurder, A., Weaver, F. M., Kubal, J. D., & Henderson, W. (1999). Relationship between caregiver burden and health-related quality of life. *The Gerontologist, 39* (5), 534–545.

Inada, H., Horio, H., Sekita, Y., Isikawa, K., & Yoshida, K. (1992). A study on a home care support information system. In *Proceedings of the Seventh World Congress on Medical Informatics,* 349–353.

Intille, S. S., Larson, K., & Kukla, C. (2002). Just-in-time context-sensitive questioning for preventative health care. In *Proceedings of the AAAI-02 Workshop "Automation as Caregiver,"* 54–59.

iRobot. (2006). Roomba. http://www.irobot.com/.

Jaffe, D. L. (1981). Smart wheelchair. In *Proceedings of the 4th Annual Conference on Rehabilitation Engineering,* 91–93.

Jaffe, D. L. (1983). Ultrasonic head control unit. In *Proceedings of the 6th Annual Conference on Rehabilitation Engineering,* 242–243.

Jaffe, D. L., Harris, H. L., & Leung, S. K. (1990). Ultrasonic head controlled wheelchair/interface: A case study in development and technology transfer. In *Proceedings of the RESNA 13th Annual Conference,* 23–24.

Jia, S., Hada, Y., & Takase, K. (2003). Telecare robotic system for support of elderly and disabled people. In *Proceedings of the IEEE/ASME International Conference On Advanced Intelligent Mechatronics (AIM),* Vol. 2, 1123–1128.

Jung, J.-W., Do, J.-H., Kim, Y.-M., Suh, K.-S., Kim, D.-J., & Bien, Z. (2005). Advanced robotic residence for the elderly/the handicapped: Realization and user evaluation. In *Proceedings of the International Conference on Rehabilitation Robotics (ICORR),* 492–495.

Katevas, N., Sgouros, N., Tzafestas, S., Papakonstantinou, G., Beattie, P., & Bishop, J. (1997). The autonomous mobile robot scenario: A sensor-aided intelligent navigation system for powered wheelchairs. *IEEE Robotics and Automation Magazine,* 60–70.

Kautz, H., Arnstein, L., Borriello, G., Etzioni, O., & Fox, D. (2002). An overview of the assisted cognition project. In *Proceedings of the AAAI-02 Workshop "Automation as Caregiver,"* 60–65.

Kawamura, K., & Iskarous, M. (1994). Trends in service robots for the disabled and the elderly. In *Proceedings of the IEEE/RSJ International Conference on Intelligent Robots and Systems,* Vol. 3, 1647–1654.

Kettle, M., Rowley, C., & Chamberlain, M. A. (1992). A national survey of wheelchair users. *Clinical Rehabilitation, 6,* 67–73.

Kidd, C. D., Orr, R., Abowd, G. D., Atkeson, C. G., Essa, I. A., MacIntyre, B., et al. (1999). The aware home: A living laboratory for ubiquitous computing research. In *Proceedings of the Second International Workshop on Cooperative Buildings,* 191–198.

Kiguchi, K. (2004). Actuated artificial joints for human motion assist—An inner skeleton robots. In *First IEEE Technical Exhibition-based Conference on Robotics and Automation (TExCRA)*, 29–30.

Kiguchi, K., Iwami, K., Yasuda, M., Watanabe, K., & Fukuda, T. (2003). An exoskeletal robot for human shoulder joint motion assist. *IEEE/ASME Transactions on Mechatronics, 8* (8), 125–135.

Kiguchi, K., Tanaka, T., Watanabe, K., & Fukuda, T. (2003). Exoskeleton for human upper-limb motion support. In *Proceedings of the IEEE International Conference on Robotics and Automation (ICRA)*, Vol. 2, 2206–2211.

King, S. J., & Weiman, C. F. R. (1990, Nov.). Helpmate super (tm) autonomous mobile robot navigation system. In *Proceedings of the SPIE Conference on Mobile Robots*, 190–198.

Kuno, Y., Nakanishi, S., Murashima, T., Shimada, N., & Shirai, Y. (1999). Intelligent wheelchair based on the integration of human and environment observations. In *Proceedings of the International Conference on Information Intelligence and Systems*, 342–349.

Lacey, G., & Dawson-Howe, K. (1998). The application of robotics to a mobility aid for the elderly blind. *Robotics and Autonomous Systems, 23*, 245–252.

Lacey, G., & MacNamara, S. (2000). User involvement in the design and evaluation of a smart mobility aid. *Journal of Rehabilitation Research and Development, 37* (6), 709–723.

Leigh, J., Rawlings, M., Girado, J., Dawe, G., Fang, R., Verlo, A., Khan, M., Cruz, A., Plepys, D., Sandin, D., & DeFanti, T. (2000). Accessbot: an enabling technology for video conferencing. In *The 10th annual Internet Society Conference (INET)*. Yokohama, Japan CD-ROM.

Lesser, V., Atighetchi, M., Benyo, B., Horling, B., Raja, A., Vincent, R., et al. (1999). A multi-agent system for intelligent environment control. In *Proceedings of the Third International Conference on Autonomous Agents*, 291–298.

Loos, H. M. V. der, Ullrich, N., & Kobayashi, H. (2003). Development of sensate and robotic bed technologies for vital signs monitoring and sleep quality improvement. *Autonomous Robots, 15*, 67–79.

Madarasz, R. L., Heiny, L. C., Cromp, R. F., & Mazur, N. M. (1991). The design of an autonomous vehicle for the disabled. *Autonomous Mobile Robots: Control, Planning, and Architecture*, 351–359.

Mascaro, S., & Asada, H. (1998). Docking control of holonomic omnidirectional vehicles with applications to a hybrid wheelchair/bed system. In *Proceedings of the IEEE/RSJ International Conference on Intelligent Robots and Systems*, Vol. 1, 399–405.

Mazo, M., Rodriguez, F. J., L'azaro, J. L., Na, J. U., Garcia, J. C., Santiso, E., et al. (1995). Wheelchair for physically disabled people with voice, ultrasonic and infrared sensor control. *Autonomous Robots, 2*, 203–224.

MedGlider. (2006). http://www.dynamic-living.com/medgliderlpill box.htm.

MedReminder. (2006). http://www.medreminder.com/.

Miller, D. P. (1998). Assistive robotics: An overview. In V. Mittal, H. A. Yanco, J. Aronis, & R. C. Simpson (Eds.), *Lecture notes in artificial intelligence: Assistive technology and artificial intelligence*, Berlin: Springer-Verlag, 126–136.

Miller, D. P., & Slack, M. G. (1995). Design and testing of a low-cost robotic wheelchair prototype. *Autonomous Robots, 2*, 77–88.

Morris, A., Donamukkala, R., Kapuria, A., Steinfeld, A., Matthews, J., Jacob, J., et al. (2003). A robotic walker that provides guidance. In *Proceedings of the IEEE International Conference on Robotics and Automation (ICRA)*, Vol. 1, 25–30.

Mozer, M. C. (1998). The neural network house: An environment that adapts to its inhabitants. In AAAI Spring Symposium on Intelligent Environments, 110–114.

Nagai, K., Hanafusa, H., Takahashi, Y., Bunki, H., Nakanishi, I., Yoshinaga, T., et al. (2002). Development of a power assistive device for self-supported transfer motion. In *Proceedings of the IEEE/RSJ International Conference on Intelligent Robots and Systems,* Vol. 2, 1433–1438.

News release: Aibo celebrates five years of innovation and intelligence. (2004, May). Distributed by PR Newswire on behalf of Sony Europe GmbH.

Nisbet, P., Craig, J., Odor, P., & Aitken, S. (1996). "Smart" wheelchairs for mobility training. *Technology and Disability, 5,* 49–62.

Noury, N., Herve, T., Rialle, V., Virone, G., Mercier, E., Morey, G., et al. (2000). Monitoring behavior in home using a smart fall sensor. In *Proceedings of the IEEE-EMBS Special Topic Conference on Microtechnologies in Medicine and Biology,* 607–610.

Nurses & Health Professionals, Federation of (2001, April). *The nursing shortage: Perspectives from current directcare nurses and former direct care nurses.* http://www.aft.org/fnhp/download files/Hart Report.pdf.

Park, T.-J., Jang, J.-H., & Han, C.-S. (2003). Walking assistant service mobile robot using lever mechanism and wireless internet communication. In *Proceedings of the IEEE/ASME International Conference On Advanced Intelligent Mechatronics (AIM),* Vol. 1, 657–662.

Perkowski, M. A., & Stanton, K. (1991). Robotics for the handicapped. In *Northcon Conference Record,* 278–284.

Pineau, J., Montemerlo, M., Pollack, M., Roy, N., & Thrun, S. (2003). Towards robotic assistants in nursing homes: Challenges and results. *Special issue on Socially Interactive Robots, Robotics and Autonomous Systems, 42* (3–4), 271–281.

Pollack, M., Brown, L., Colbry, D., McCarthy, C., Orosz, C., Peintner, B., et al. (2003). An intelligentcognitive orthotic system for people with memory impairment. *Robotics and Autonomous Systems, 44,* 273–282.

Pratt, J. E., Krupp, B. T., Morse, C. J., & Collins, S. H. (2004). The roboknee: An exoskeleton for enhancing strength and endurance during walking. In *Proceedings of the IEEE International Conference on Robotics and Automation (ICRA),* 2430–2435.

Richardson, S. J., Poulson, D. F., & Nicolle, C. (1993a). Supporting independent living through adaptable smart home (ASH) technologies. In *Human welfare and technology: Papers from the human service information technology applications (HUSITA) 3 Conference on Information Technology and the Quality of Life and Services,* 87–95.

Richardson, S. J., Poulson, D. F., & Nicolle, C. (1993b). User requirements capture for adaptable smarter home technologies. In *Rehabilitation Technology: Proceedings of the 1st TIDE Congress,* 244–248.

Rosier, J., Woerden, J. van, Kolk, L. van der, Driessen, B., Kwee, H., Duimel, J., et al. (1991). Rehabilitation robotics: The Manus concept. In *Fifth International Conference on Advanced Robotics: Robots in Unstructured Environments,* Vol. 1, 893–898.

Sakagami, Y., Watanabe, R., Aoyama, C., Matsunaga, S., Higaki, N., & Fujimura, K. (2002). The intelligent ASIMO: System overview and integration. In *Proceedings of the IEEE/RSJ International Conference on Intelligent Robots and Systems,* Vol. 3, 2478–2483.

Scott, J. B., & Munro, J. L. (1985). Collision-avoidance system for a motorized wheelchair. In *Proceedings of the RESNA 8th Annual Conference,* 51–52.

Shim, H.-M., Lee, E.-H., Shim, J.-H., Lee, S.-M., & Hong, S.-H. (2005). Implementation of an intelligent walking assistant robot for the elderly in outdoor environment. In *Proceedings of the International Conference on Rehabilitation Robotics (ICORR),* 452–455.

Simpson, R. C., Levine, S. P., Bell, D. A., Jaros, L. A., Koren, Y., & Borenstein, J. (1998). Navchair: An assistive wheelchair navigation system with automatic adaptation. In V. Mittal, H. A. Yanco, Aronis, J., & Simpson, R. C. (Eds.), *Lecture notes in artificial intelligence: Assistive technology and artificial intelligence,* Berlin: Springer, 235–255.

Song, W.-K., Lee, H.-Y., Kim, J.-S., Yoon, Y.-S., & Bien, Z. (1998). Kares: intelligent rehabilitation robotic system for the disabled and the elderly. In *Proceedings of the 20th Annual International Conference of the IEEE,* Vol. 5, 2682–2685.

Stanton, K. B., Sherman, P. R., Rohwedder, M. L., Fleskes, C. P., Gray, D. R., Minh, D. T., et al. (1991). PSUBOT–A voice-controlled wheelchair for the handicapped. In *Proceedings of the 33rd Midwest Symposium on Circuits and Systems,* Vol. 2, 669–672.

Suzuki, N., Masamune, K., Sakuma, I., Suzuki, M., Yahagi, N., Tuji, T., et al. (2000). System assisting walking and carrying daily necessities with an overhead robot arm for in-home elderlies. In *Proceedings of the 22nd Annual International Conference of the IEEE Engineering in Medicine and Biology,* Vol. 3, 2271–2274.

Tahboub, K. A., & Asada, H. H. (1999). A semiautonomous control architecture applied to robotic wheelchairs. In *Proceedings of the IEEE/RSJ International Conference on Intelligent Robots and Systems,* 906–911.

Tamura, T., Togawa, T., & Murata, M. (1988). A bed temperature monitoring system for assessing body movement during sleep. *Clinical Physics and Physiological Measurement, 9,* 139–145.

Topping, M. (1999). The development of Handy 1, a robotic system to assist the severely disabled. In *Proceedings of the International Conference On Rehabilitation Robotics (ICORR),* 244–249.

Toyota. (2006). *Partner robot.* http://www.toyota.co.jp/en/special/robot/.

Vivax. (2006). *Vivax mobility system.* http://www.vivaxmedical.com/mobilitysystem.htm.

Wada, M., & Asada, H. (1999). Design and control of a variable footprint mechanism for holonomic omnidirectional vehicles and its application to wheelchairs. *IEEE Transactions on Robotics and Automation, 15* (15), 978–989.

Wasson, G., Gunderson, J., Graves, S., & Felder, R. (2001). An assistive robotic agent for pedestrian mobility. In *International Conference On Autonomous Agents,* 169–173.

Yamaguchi, A., Ogawa, M., Tamura, T., & Togawa, T. (1998). Monitoring behaviour in the home using positioning sensors. In *Proceedings of the 20th Annual IEEE Conference on Engineering in Medicine and Biology,* 1977–79.

Yanco, H. A. (2000). *Shared user-computer control of a robotic wheelchair system.* Doctoral dissertation, Massachusetts Institute of Technology, Cambridge, MA.

Yoder, J.-D., Baumgartner, E. T., & Skaar, S. B. (1996). Initial results in the development of a guidance system for a powered wheelchair. *IEEE Transactions on Rehabilitation Engineering, 4* (3), 143–151.

Chapter 12

KEEPING AN OLDER POPULATION MOBILE

Rozanne M. Puleo

INTRODUCTION

The question, What is mobility? would elicit a variety of responses. Professionals, such as physicians or civil engineers, would have different interpretations, while a grandmother might provide yet another definition. Each of the responses would be correct although each would probably be regarded as incomplete.

In the professional world, mobility is regarded in terms of segmented subsystems. A physician may discuss mobility in terms of gait and physical mobility. A civil engineer may be more inclined to talk about mobility as it relates to transportation and getting from point "A" to point "B." For the grandmother, mobility includes each of these concepts on a continuum. It is equally important that she have the ability to get up from her chair to get milk from her refrigerator as it is for her to get to the store to buy milk. If one looks at mobility from the individual's point of view, it is clear that mobility is a key component to quality of life. Mobility is the glue that holds lives together. If one cannot move, one cannot participate in the activities that "life" presents. With limited mobility, the quality of life decreases as does independence.

Iezzoni et al. (2001) define mobility difficulties on four levels.

- *None:* No reported difficulty walking or climbing stairs and no use of a mobility aid.
- *Minor:* Some difficulty with walking or climbing stairs or reports the use of a cane or crutches.

- *Moderate:* A lot of difficulty walking or climbing stairs or reports using a walker.
- *Major:* Unable to walk or climb stairs. Uses a manual or powered wheelchair or a scooter.

While correct, these definitions are incomplete with regard to the term "mobility." If a person does not have difficulty walking, and does not use a mobility aid, yet has a vision impairment that makes driving impossible, is it fair to say that this person has no mobility difficulties?

Because mobility is such a broad concept, it is helpful to break the word down into two definable concepts:

- Micromobility defines movements related to gait and physical mobility. Micromobility can be defined as the form of mobility needed to move around in small areas by walking, through personal mobility aids, or even as slight as sitting up from a supine position.
- Macromobility describes the manner in which persons travel. Macromobility is the form of mobility used to get from one place to another using some form of transportation.

It is important to maintain distinct terms for each concept because both are essential for quality of life. As persons age, their environments tend to stay the same. Homes remain the same, cars remain relatively similar, and the driving task changes minimally. Communities typically remain quite similar. However, as they age, people change. As discussed at length earlier in this book, one's functional capacity changes and, therefore, the ability to navigate through these common places becomes more difficult. Understanding both micro- and macromobility provides a holistic view of an important component in the quality of life that helps define quality living.

MICROMOBILITY

Movement in its every form is the essence of freedom. The freedom to move allows one the independence of not having to rely on others to provide mobility. Years ago, an acquaintance became a quadriplegic from an accident. When asked what he missed the most, he stated "I miss being able to turn myself over in bed at night without assistance." In an instant, he lost most of his physical independence. Accidents, birth defects, and other illnesses can result in the loss of functioning to the extreme. In many cases, full-time caregivers must provide assistance to those who can no longer care for themselves. This level of immobility is at the most extreme end of the spectrum. The following discussions will not cover the needs of those who can no longer care for themselves, rather, it will focus upon the needs of those whose mobility is degenerating, but who remain mobile and independent in some capacity.

Walking is the basic form of human transportation and locomotion. Before the wheel was invented, humans walked the earth to conduct their daily lives. Communities were not as vast, and distances traveled were not as large. The development of alternative forms of transportation beyond walking allowed for the incredible expansion of communities. Walking remains crucial, but is less vital than before. People still need to be mobile to cover shorter distances, but, in theory, daily lives could be conducted via the internet, through delivery and online services.

However, independence and the quality of life would drastically decrease. The need to keep the population moving is critical. When abilities begin to decline, one must find ways to adapt.

Limiting Factors on Micromobility

Walking is a complex biomechanical task, incorporating many neuromuscular, kinesthetic, and proprioceptive tasks in addition to demanding cardiovascular capacity. While walking may seem to be an intuitive motion, many different areas of the body are responsible for its actions. Because of the tendency of bodies to experience natural functional decline through aging, walking can become more difficult. The brain experiences an overall decrease in function in its motor control centers, such as the basal nuclei, cerebellum, and the cerebral cortex. This can result in impaired locomotor function such as a slowed rate of fine motor tasks, decreased postural reflexes, and an altered walking pattern (Chop & Robnett, 1999). Decreased functioning in the musculoskeletal system has a major impact on overall functional capacity. Reduction in bone density, joint mobility and strength can cause postural changes and can increase the risk of fractures, which in itself can reduce the ability to walk. Changes in the skeletal muscle tissue can result in decreased strength, efficiency and muscular endurance. The number and size of each muscle fiber decreases with age, with the greatest loss found in muscles used less frequently (Chop & Robnett, 1999). These changes can result in impaired locomotion.

In addition to the natural decline of functional capacity, older persons are at greater risk for a variety of chronic diseases that can affect the ability to walk. These conditions may be cognitive, neurological or musculoskeletal in nature (Cook & Hussey, 2002). The various forms of cardiovascular disease can affect one's endurance, making any form of extended walking difficult. Chronic pain conditions such as osteoarthritis, gout, lupus among others can make walking a challenge. These diseases can cause pain and stiffness in the joints involved in walking.

Osteoporosis occurs commonly as people age. Osteoporosis is the gradual loss of bone mass, which puts one at great risk for fractures. Osteoporosis has very few obvious symptoms, without a diagnostic exam, individuals usually will not discover that they have the condition until they experience a painful fracture. A person with osteoporosis can experience a fracture simply by bumping into a table or wall with enough force. However, most fractures that occur with osteoporosis result from falls. A fracture in old age can severely limit locomotion. At younger ages, walking around with crutches is very difficult. As persons age, they have less strength which makes the use of crutches extremely difficult. Hip fractures are a common occurrence when one has osteoporosis. Recent statistics suggest that once a person has experienced a hip fracture, his or her life expectancy is reduced by 1.8 years (Braithwaite, Col, & Wong, 2003). This statistic could suggest that the loss of mobility interferes with health to such an extent that life expectancy is reduced.

Ranges of Micromobility

The degree of micromobility impairments exist on a continuum. At one end of the spectrum exist no limitations at all, while at the other end exist severe mobility impairments (Cook & Hussey, 2002). Warren (1990) and Cook and Hussey (2002) define the different levels of micromobility impairment which can help determine which mobility aids are most appropriate in maximizing a person's functioning.

- *Full ambulator:* A full ambulator is a person with no limitations at all. These individuals are fully capable of walking and maneuvering without assistance within their environments.

- *Marginal ambulator:* A marginal ambulator has the ability to walk short distances, such as those within the home. They may use a cane or a walker while trying to cover short distances, but they do have some capacity to remain upright. However, while outside the home, this person may need wheelchair assistance.
- *Manual wheelchair user:* Manual wheelchair users are functional enough to propel themselves in a manual wheelchair. They have adequate use of their upper extremities and possibly their lower extremities, but they have some limitation that makes walking difficult.
- *Marginal manual wheelchair user:* These users may have some ability to propel themselves in a manual wheelchair, but are limited enough that a powered wheelchair allows for greater independence.
- *Totally/severely mobility-impaired user:* These users cannot propel themselves in a manual wheelchair. In order to be independent, they must use a powered wheelchair for mobility in all situations.

Improving Micromobility

HISTORY OF MOBILITY AIDS: Personal mobility aids date back to early civilization. Although life expectancy was shorter, diseases that limited mobility, such as polio, were more common and had a significant impact on people's micromobility. At the Carlsberg Sculpture Museum in Copenhagen, an Egyptian stele depicts a female physician with her disabled male patient. To get himself around, he used a long pole (Childress, 2002). In many areas around the world where poverty is rampant and polio is still a threat, these primitive, yet effective aids are still in use.

Historically, mobility aids were designed for those with disabilities. In general, people did not live long enough to experience extensive age-related physical decline. Micromobility impairments were more a result of disease, injury, and warfare (Childress, 2002). The increase in war-related injuries prompted technological solutions. Ambroise Paré (1510–1590) was a French military surgeon who established guidelines for amputation surgery and their associated prosthetics which were developed by the knights' armor makers (Childress, 2002). As wars continued throughout history, advances in prosthetics continued as well. Improved limb prosthetics and methods of operation blossomed, yet it was during the American Civil War that the industry exploded. New facilities needed to be established to respond to the demand for prosthetic services. After World War I, the collaboration of limb makers and surgeons gained greater acceptance, with many principles applied in the early days remaining in place today (Childress, 2002).

Today, the need for prosthetics still exists; however, the need for personal mobility aids such as canes, walkers, and wheelchair far outnumbers prosthetic use. Data from 1994 show that 199,000 Americans have some sort of artificial limb, while 7.4 million use some sort of personal mobility aid (National Center for Health Statistics, 1994). Artists first depicted the use of wheelchairs in the early 1500s showing disabled individuals being transported in carts, and the first literary reference to wheelchairs was in 1588 in Europe (Cook & Hussey, 2002). The first formal record of a wheelchair is a patent from 1853 for an "Invalid Locomotive Chair" (Minniss, 1853). Thomas Minniss of Pennsylvania developed a wheelchair so that those with disabilities could become more mobile. It was not until 1932 that wheelchair development was formalized into a bona fide industry. Mr. H.A Everest, a mining engineer who had a spinal cord injury, collaborated with mechanical engineer, Mr. H.C. Jennings. They created the first folding chair, and this led to the formation of E & J Wheelchair Company, which is still one of the largest wheelchair manufacturers in the United States (Cook & Hussey, 2002).

As time evolved and life expectancy began to increase, the need for personal mobility aids also increased. The first patent for the electric wheelchair was issued in 1940. The electric wheelchair first started by using an automobile motor, and applying it to the standard wheelchair with power coming from the automotive battery (Warren, 1990). Engineers went from adding motors and battery packs onto existing manual wheelchairs to creating chairs designed to be inclusive of electronic capabilities (Cook & Hussey, 2002).

Recent developments in wheelchair technology have included the development of wheelchairs that are more maneuverable, lighter, and easier to use. This has helped wheelchair users to be more independent. Wheelchair use has sprung an entire movement devoted to those whose mobility is improved through wheelchair use. There exist wheelchair advocacy groups, wheelchair sports organizations, and even a Ms. Wheelchair America competition.

Technological advancements have allowed the creation of better mobility aids with greater capabilities that ever before. Future generations of mobility aids will go beyond mobility, but will extend to independence as a whole, providing features that make the technologies "smart."

MOBILITY AIDS: The use of personal mobility aids progresses in a hierarchical fashion (Iezzoni, McCarthy, Davis, & Siebens, 2001). As one's need for assistance increases, the complexity of mobility aids tends to increase as well. Typically, someone with diminishing function will began with a simple cane for balance. From there, as abilities begin to decrease, one might go from a cane to crutches to a walker to a wheelchair as function continues to decline.

Recent statistics state for adults 65+, 1.1 million use a cane, 863,000 adults use a wheelchair, and 295,000 adults use a walker (National Center for Health Statistics, 1994). This represents almost two-thirds of the American population over 65 who have an activity of daily living (ADL) disability (Cornman, Freedman, & Agree, 2005). Since one out of every five Americans will be over age 65 by 2030, the use of mobility aids is certain to increase (Molnar, Eby, & Miller, n.d.).

Canes range from the simple one-legged version to those that have four contact points. Canes are typically the first form of mobility aid that a person will use until his or her functioning decreases to the point at which greater support is necessary. Most are used strictly for balance, although some canes provide some weight-bearing support.

The standard cane is an inexpensive, lightweight device. The ones made of wood must be custom fit, and those that are made of aluminum are more expensive yet they can be adjustable in length (Hook, Demonbreun, & Weiss, 2003). These canes are designed for those who need little weight-bearing support. Offset canes are designed to take a greater amount of weight bearing. They are designed with a "C" curve from the handle which allows the person's weight to be displaced over the shaft.

Multiple-legged canes have four points of contact on the floor which also provides a greater ability to bear weight. They are designed like the offset cane to displace weight over the cane shaft. These canes can stand upright even if the person is not holding it because of the larger support base. The main disadvantage of these canes is that the person must have all four contact points on the ground. This can prove to be difficult if the person has a fairly quick gait; however, if the base of support can be made smaller, this problem can often be overcome (Hook et al., 2003).

Crutches can be used for those who need full weight-bearing assistance. Axillary crutches are those typically used for people who need ambulation assistance on a temporary basis. These crutches are designed to rest under the armpit, with much of the weight placed in the person's hands. These require a good amount of strength and, therefore, are not often used long-term. It is rare that an older person who has mobility difficulties will be asked to use crutches; they are more often used for younger adults recovering from an injury.

Forearm crutches are used for those who require bilateral upper-extremity support (Hook et al., 2003). Because these crutches provide support at the forearm, the person's hands can be free without putting the crutches down. These are much easier to use than axillary crutches and require much less strength.

Walkers range from those that have four wheels as contact points to those that do not have any wheels. The standard walker does not have any wheels; rather, their legs have rubber tips to keep the walker as stable as possible. Users must have the strength to lift the walker to propel it forward, which also requires that the user maintain a slowed, controlled gait.

Front-wheeled walkers are best for those who cannot lift a standard walker and whose gait may be too fast for a standard walker (Hook et al., 2003). These walkers allow for a more normal gait pattern, but, because of the wheels, they are less stable than the standard walker.

Four-wheeled walkers are for those people who do not require much weight bearing, but who need a larger base of support (Hook et al., 2003). Only high functioning individuals can use four-wheeled walkers because if they rely on the walker for too much support, the walker can roll away and cause a fall.

Wheelchairs are divided into four different types: manual wheelchairs, powered wheelchairs, scooters and "smart" wheelchairs. Very few "smart" wheelchairs are commercially available, most are still in the research and development phase. Deciding which wheelchair is best suited for a person's needs depends primarily upon a person's current level of functioning. The main consideration is whether or not the person has the strength and stamina to push a manual wheelchair, or whether he or she needs the convenience of a power wheelchair (Iezzoni, 2003). The benefits of a manual chair include weight, cost, and ease of use. Because there are no electronics attached, manual chairs are lighter weight, which also makes them easier to transport. They are much less expensive because of the lack of electronics, and, because of this, there is no risk that the chair will lose its battery charge.

However, power wheelchairs have their own benefits. There is less risk that the user will fatigue over long journeys or up steep hills. Power wheelchairs require one hand at most for steering. Some chairs do not require any hand control; rather they can be controlled by a mouthpiece or even by voice.

Scooters are similar to power wheelchairs in that they are controlled by battery; however, the steering mechanism differs in that the person "drives" a scooter and has all controls in the front. This is called a tiller-type control, and acceleration and braking occur with levers on the handlebars, similar to what one might find on a bicycle, or sometimes a button system. When users release the levers or the buttons, the scooter comes to a stop (Cook & Hussey, 2002). Marginal ambulators most commonly use scooters, and they typically use them on "as needed" basis. Shopping malls and amusement parks usually offer scooter rentals for their customers as a service to those who may not be capable of covering distances.

There exists an additional electronic mobility aid that is unlike any other wheelchair or scooter. In July 2005, Independence Technology released the iBOT® 4000, making cutting-edge, patented technology available to the general public. The iBOT® has five unique functions: balance, stair, four-wheeled, remote, and standard. The balance function allows the user to be elevated to eye-level with those who are standing. The front wheels rotate up and over the back wheels, while the user remains seated. This can improve independence by allowing the user to reach for shelves and items previously unreachable while in a seated level in a traditional chair. The stair function provides users the ability to climb up and down stairs without assistance. The four-wheeled function enables independent travel over a variety of terrain, such as sand, gravel, grass, thick carpeting, and also allows users to climb curbs up to five inches in height. This function provides significant opportunity for independence. With this function, users can more easily access places that are typically not so accessible to wheelchair users, such as the beach and other recreational areas. The remote function allows the unit to be driven unoccupied into a vehicle or other storage space. The standard function allows the user to operate the device in a manner similar to any other powered wheelchair. Users can fit their chairs underneath a table or desk without having to transfer to a smaller chair (Independence Technology, 2005).

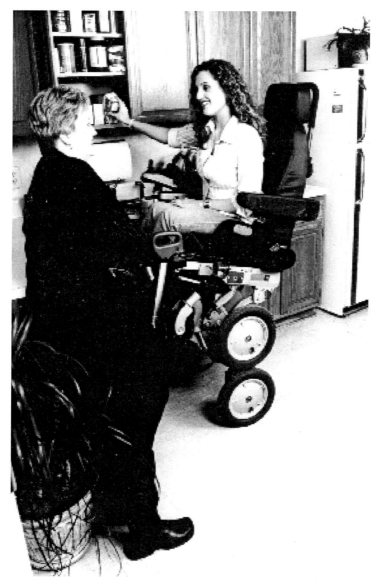

Picture of iBOT® 4000. Photo courtesy of Independence Technology.

The iBOT® 4000 Mobility System is a gyro-balanced personal mobility system with patented iBALANCE® Technology. The electronic balance system is an integrated combination of sensor and software components that work together to maintain balance (Independence

Picture of iBOT® 4000. Photo courtesy of Independence Technology.

Technology, 2005). The user operates the iBOT® with a joystick, similar to those on other commercially-available powered wheelchairs. The iBOT® Mobility System is powered by rechargeable batteries, and, with typical usage, it can run all day on a single charge.

Future Research

The "Smart" concept in all forms of mobility aids is the direction in which research is heading. Although there exist a few commercially available models of sensor-enabled devices (Simpson, 2005), there is much research being done to enhance their technological capabilities. Research on technology that can be applied to canes, walkers, and wheelchairs continue to evolve at institutions around the world.

At the Massachusetts Institute of Technology, researchers are developing an innovative robotic device that not only provides mobility assistance, but will also allow for health monitoring. This system, called PAMM (Personal Aid for Mobility and Monitoring) not only provides physical support, but can also monitor the users' vital signs.

The PAMM is designed for use in assisted living facilities. The intended users are marginal ambulators who are comfortable using a wheeled walker or a cane. The PAMM system has been integrated into both a cane and walker format. The cane configuration, called a "SmartCane" is intended for those with minor mobility challenges while the walker prototype, called the "SmartWalker," will serve the needs of those with greater mobility challenges.

Designed with the assisted living population in mind, the PAMM is ultimately intended to assist the older population to live independently longer. The SmartCane is a motorized cane system that operates using a battery, computer, camera, and sensors. The PAMM system is designed to provide navigational assistance to users, to help them avoid obstacles that might be in their way and to assist them in getting around the facility. This latter function would be particularly useful to users new to an assisted living environment. PAMM also has the capability to provide health information to the user. Information would be fed through a central computing facility which would provide information back to the user on the map of the facility, medical appointment scheduling, and even medical instructions such as medication reminders (Dubowsky, 2000).

While there exist a few Smart Wheelchairs on the market, there is much more research being done to give these technologies greater capabilities. Research on smart wheelchairs has been conducted since the 1980s and is taking place at academic and commercial institutes around the world (Simpson, 2005). Smart wheelchair concepts have been born out of the technology that has gone into robotic design.

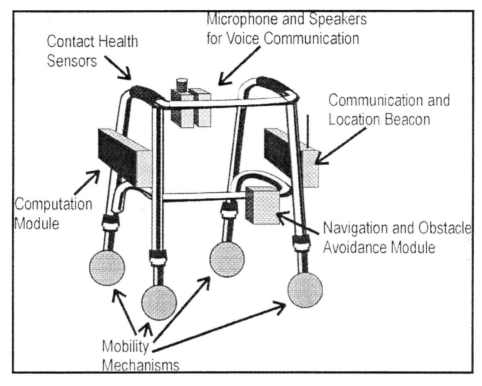

Figure 12.1. PAMM (Personal Aid for Mobility and Monitoring). Source: Dubowsky, S. (2000). Personal Aid for Mobility and Monitoring: A Helping Hand for the Elderly, *Progress Report No.2-5:* MIT Home Automation and Healthcare Consortium.

Robotic devices are designed to have certain characteristics that mimic human action in some way; this is why the technology that drives robotic devices can sometimes be referred to as "artificial intelligence." While power wheelchairs and scooters allow the user to exert less energy, smart wheelchairs are designed to help those who may need greater assistance, due to visual impairments, cognitive deficits, or other physical impairments (Simpson, LoPresti, Hayashi, Nourbakhsh, & Miller, 2004). Some estimate that up to 40 percent of the disabled community find standard powered wheelchairs to be too difficult to use (Simpson et al., 2004).

The basic concept of a smart wheelchair is the incorporation of sensors and a computer onto a standard form wheelchair. This sensor and computer system can then assist the user with navigation in various means, whether it is through collision avoidance, or through mapping assistance.

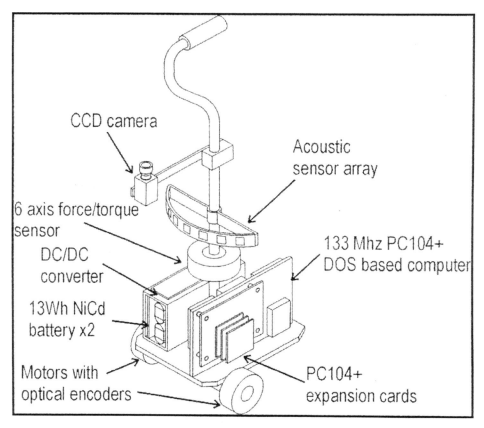

Figure 12.2. PAMM (Personal Aid for Mobility and Monitoring). Source: Dubowsky, S. (2000). Personal Aid for Mobility and Monitoring: A Helping Hand for the Elderly, *Progress Report No.2-5:* MIT Home Automation and Healthcare Consortium.

Technologies to improve maneuverability need to consider the entire person. However, some research is exploring how to make certain joint areas more mobile, which can oftentimes be a source of limited mobility. There two particular research initiatives at MIT that are directed at improving joint-specific mobility. The Active Ankle Foot Orthoses (AAFO) team at MIT is interested in developing a robotic orthotic device to improve ankle mobility (Blaya, Newman, & Herr, 2001). The Active Joint Brace team is developing a robotic elbow brace that can help improve upper body mobility.

The AAFO project is based upon previous work to develop assistive devices for the ankle that help prevent drop foot and can help with dorsiflexion. There are a few commercially available Ankle Foot Orthoses

(AFO) that combine a rigid brace with a spring mechanism to assist in ankle movement. Several manufacturers including Tamarack Joints and Becker Orthoses produce these devices. These devices help people lift their toes in the initial phase of walking, but are limited in that they do not adequately control plantar flexion (Blaya et al., 2001). The AAFO tries to remedy this limitation by using robotics.

The AAFO is equipped with sensors to determine the physiological needs of the user with regard to the gait cycle. The AAFO is powered by a Series Elastic Actuator which has been developed by the Leg Laboratory at MIT (Blaya et al., 2001).

The Active Joint Brace team is looking at improving upper extremity mobility. Their current working prototype is an elbow brace. It allows for flexion and extension of the elbow joint. This can help people with limited upper body mobility to feed themselves or take a drink of water. The goal of this brace is to enhance muscle strength. Surface electromyogram sensors (SEMG) sense existing muscle contraction. Then, the sensors determine how much force the muscles are trying to exert. A functional electrical stimulation (FES) system then takes the information from the sensors and moves the joint. Rather than supplementing the existing strength of the user, the bracing system applies an amount of force proportional to what the muscles exert which helps avoid any atrophy of the muscle (Puleo, 2005).

The innovation in this bracing system is that the brace is used to enhance existing movement as opposed to replacing a missing limb as in a prosthetic. In addition, the brace is wearable and can be taken on and off by the user, and nothing needs to be implanted under the skin (Puleo, 2005).

Much more is being done to ensure adequate micromobility as the population ages. Through computers, sensors and other electronic-based technologies, mobility devices are become more like systems that can go beyond just physical support. However, to fully integrate some of these innovative technologies, a larger systematic infrastructure must be in place. For systems that require a central computer processing facility, who will manage this? For systems that provide two-way communication with the caretaker, how will this be implemented? What industries will have to collaborate in order to make these visions a reality? These questions are what make engineering innovations a challenge to go from the lab bench to homes. Systems that consider many stakeholders must be designed in order to effectively implement new

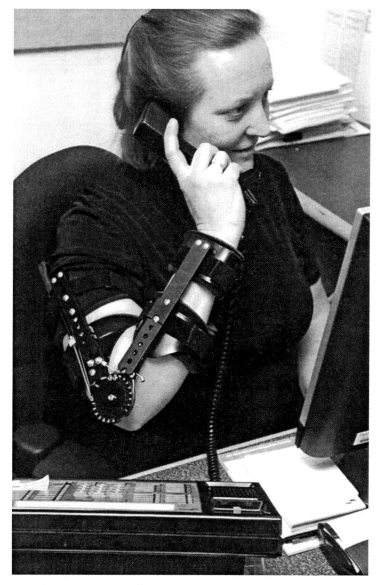

Photo AJB (Active Joint Brace). Source: Justin Allardyce Knight, photographer.

technologies. Manufacturers must comply with established regulations for privacy of information, or new policies must be put into effect. The industries that will support these innovations, such as the communications or computer software industries, will have to look beyond what their current business model is to enter the "white space" of businesses that support healthy aging and mobility. Without collaboration and practical thought leaders, these technological innovations will only serve to be impressive ideas.

MACROMOBILITY

As defined earlier, macromobility is the way in which persons travel. Whether it be by car, bus, train, airplane, these modes of mobility allow one to get from point A to point B, no matter how great the distance. For the purposes of this chapter, the focus is upon the forms of macro-mobility that allow for local trips, those that take place in the car or by public transportation, and the systems in which they must exist in order to be accessible and adaptable for those with functional limitations.

State of Older Adult Driving

Driving is an essential utility for independence, no matter what an individual's age. Just prior to entering adulthood, many obtain a driver's license which gives them the freedom to travel anywhere, at anytime, with anyone of choice. People become accustomed to this freedom very early in life. With age, this freedom becomes engrained in daily lives, and it becomes more of a right than a privilege. In one MIT- Hartford Insurance Company focus group, when asked of the importance of his driver's license, an older male participant answered, "You can always get another wife, but you can only get one driver's license" (Puleo & Reimer, 2005). This statement alone suggests the significance that driving represents for older adults. Yet, with age, the driving task remains relatively similar (aside from certain technological advances which will be addressed later), while people change. The loss of functional abilities may make the driving task more difficult.

Safe driving requires the integration of complex motor, visual, and cognitive tasks; however, overtime, these tasks become instinctive (Beers & Berkow, 2000). When a driver experiences severe functional loss, driving may become unsafe, and, therefore, the driver's license may need to be surrendered. It is then that the risk for depression and isolation can occur. Quality of life at this point can rapidly decline, and all these factors can lead to ill health. Without the ability to drive, the

TABLE 12.1.
Predicted number of daily trips taken by car

Adults Aged 65–84	Total Daily Trips Taken By Car	
	1995	2030
Male and Female combined	2.38	2.72
Female only	2.19	2.73
Male only	2.69	2.66

Source: Bush, S. (2003). Forecasting 65+ travel: An integration of cohort analysis and travel demand modeling. Massachusetts Institute of Technology, Cambridge.

freedom to visit a friend, to go to the shopping mall, or go out for an ice cream cone disappears. While public transportation in an option, most Americans live in areas where it is not available. Because of the suburbanization of America, 70 percent of adults live in areas where there is no public transportation (Rosenbloom, 2003). For those ages 65–84, 90 percent of all local travel takes place in a private automobile, whereas only 3 percent takes place in public transportation (U.S. Department of Transportation, 2003). Travel demands of older adults aged 65–84 are expected to rise by 2030. As shown in Table 12.1, in 1995, adults aged 65–84 made an average of 2.38 trips per day in a car or other motor vehicle. In 2030, this number is projected to rise to 2.72 (Bush, 2003). Therefore, it is critical that the driving experience be improved for older drivers.

While automobile accidents occur at all ages, there is a misconception that older adults are less safe drivers. In fact, older drivers are some of the safest drivers on the road. As one ages, the number of total accidents decreases (Coughlin, Mohyde, D'Ambrosio, & Gilbert, 2004). However, when tragic accidents that involve older drivers occur, the media often sensationalizes them, which perpetuates the stereotype of older drivers as poor drivers. The reality is that most older drivers choose to self regulate their driving because they know that their functional capacity is diminishing. They choose to drive less at night, drive less in bad weather, and/or avoid left hand turns which tend to be the most difficult driving maneuver to execute (Coughlin et al., 2004).

There is a certain level of responsibility that public policy exerts to oversee some of the issues that accompany older drivers, and when they may be too impaired to continue to drive. However, there exists very little consensus as the best way to create a unified policy. Each state has its own way of dealing with the older driver issue. Some states have licensing provisions for older drivers, some do not. Some states require physicians to report when a driver may be too risky to drive, others do not (Molnar et al., n.d.). Maryland is developing a pilot program to recognize early warning signs for prevention and intervention to prolong safe mobility (TRB, 2005). The program includes screening tests of vision, physical ability, and cognition. The program is not intended to take away licenses, but to make determinations about the need for possible driver remediation (TRB, 2005).

While public policy is seeking ways to make older adult mobility more accessible, safe, and acceptable, it is going to take more than a few regulations to impact the system. Leveraging technology for the car and the roadways to compensate for decline in function are essential to "driver longevity." Much has been done over the years to make driving safer, not only for older drivers, but for drivers of all ages.

The Evolution of the Automobile

The automobile dates back to 1769 and was built by Nicolas Joseph Cugnot, with a steam engine to be used in military operations in France. After seeing the usefulness of this tool, many inventors followed Cugnot's lead and tried to build a better car. In the 1830s, Scotland's Robert Anderson created the first car to use rechargeable batteries to power a small electric motor. Many innovations followed, including the invention of the gasoline powered vehicle, which ultimately became the dominant type of engine installed in cars. The Curved Dash Oldsmobile was the first car to be mass produced in America (Bellis, n.d.). Shortly thereafter, Henry Ford formed the Ford Motor Company in 1903. He set out to improve production, and in 1908, the Model T was born, and was produced in 93 minutes. Ford improved assembly line production, and, in 1913, he made Ford the world's largest auto manufacturer (Bellis, n.d.).

Cars have had quite an evolution since the early days of the American auto industry. In the early days of auto manufacturing, life expectancy was shorter, and no one ever took into consideration the "older driver." As the population's demography continues to shift, and as driving becomes more engrained in daily lives, older drivers' needs must be considered. Yet car companies have traditionally focused on the younger adult market. The belief that "capturing" a younger driver will lead to brand loyalty throughout the lifespan is myopic. The baby boomers have not demonstrated the brand loyalty that previous generations had shown, and younger generations will most likely continue this trend. Because of the aging of the population, proportionally fewer younger adults are buying cars. In 1994, one in ten cars was bought by 20-somethings; today, the number is one in sixteen (Coughlin, 2005).

However, the challenge lies in designing a car suitable and acceptable for older adults without making the "old man's car." Today's baby boomers, those born between 1946–1964, are heading toward a more active and robust lifestyle than previous generations. People are not only living longer, but are living healthier lives for a longer period of time beyond their working years. While illness, disability, and functional decline still exist, the attitudes and beliefs of what is means to be old have shifted in the baby boomer population. Therefore, while the needs of an older driver may remain, the demands may not mirror their reality. Previous generations of older adults accepted that old age meant the lack of activity (Coughlin, 2005). Today's older adults are more active, better educated, and wealthier than previous generations. These attributes contribute to an attitude that raises their expectations for products and services that do not label them as "old." It is essential to acknowledge that the graying of the baby boomer population could help shape product design and innovation.

Technologies to Meet the Needs of the Older Driver

Getting in and out of the car is a critical part of the driving task. If drivers cannot safely or easily get in or out of the car, they will look elsewhere for a more suitable car. Older adults have a higher incidence of joint stiffness and inflexibility than their younger counterparts, so the ingress and egress of a vehicle must be high priority for auto manufacturers. For example, Toyota has taken the initiative to improve accessibility of their vehicles for both older drivers and those people with disabilities. In their Welcab vehicle models, a series which began in 1995, they have widened the door openings, and made these vehicles wheelchair accessible through an electronic "lift-up" passenger seat, that comes out of the car, allows the person to transfer into the seat, and it then lifts the seat and the passenger into the car. General Motors has a similar motorized seat that can be installed in certain GM model vehicles.

Ford has paved one of the most useful paths to creating a car design appropriate for older drivers. Along with researchers in the UK, Ford created a Third Age Suit, which is a jumpsuit designed to simulate the feeling of being "old." In an industry where many engineers are in their thirties, getting to experience how it feels like to have limited mobility can significantly improve the design process. The suit is designed in a jumpsuit fashion, and reduces a person's strength, flexibility, and dexterity. The suit also includes yellow goggles to diminish a person's vision, to aid in the design of displays, font size, and color selection.

The Third Age Suit was used by engineers to help design the Ford Focus. The use of the suit helped the engineers to see where improvements could be made to aid older drivers. More headroom was added, engineers identified the "H" point where the hips swivel to get in and out of the car, and they redesigned some of the knobs and buttons to make their usage less difficult for arthritic hands (Coughlin, 2005).

Researchers at the MIT AgeLab have also designed an empathy suit, built in a modular fashion, to simulate what an aging body feels like. Researchers use this tool to educate engineers in training and those who are working in the field regarding the limitations an older adult experiences.

Because of the diminished vision that may accompany aging, Nissan has developed its own font design to make displays easier to read (Coughlin, 2005). Night vision actually begins to decline at around age 40, so tools to assist drivers to see better help more than just those in the higher age range. Cadillac has teamed up with Raytheon to offer night vision technology into its vehicles. Based on technology designed for use by the military, sensors that use infrared technology detect objects that lie in front of the vehicle. These images are projected onto a head-up display that is seen on the windshield so the driver does not need to take his/her eyes off the road. This technology can help drivers identify possible hazards in the roadway before they can identify them with their own eyes.

Certain technologies are designed with universal safety in mind, not just older drivers. Though currently available on higher end luxury vehicles, in time, most technologies will make their way into more modestly priced vehicles, in a trickle-down effect that happens with any new technology. Collision avoidance systems are designed to help drivers avoid a crash by giving them a warning signal. Sensors installed throughout the exterior of the car can warn drivers if they may be approaching something too closely, or backing up into something that is beyond the field-of-view. These systems can incorporate advanced brake warning systems, which will automatically depress the brake if a driver is not fast enough in doing it him or herself. This can clearly benefit older drivers who may have a slowed reaction time. It can also benefit any driver who may not be paying attention properly to brake quickly enough.

Adaptive cruise control is another technology aimed at reducing the number of crashes on the road. Sensors detect the speed at which the vehicle is approaching the car up ahead, and it will adjust the speed of the car to avoid a collision. This technology is currently available on certain Jaguar, Lexus, Infiniti, and Mercedes-Benz models (Karr, 2004).

Navigational aids and advance traveler information systems help people reach their destinations, through mapping and GPS (Maltz, Sun, Wu, & Mourant, 2002). These can enhance safety by keeping people from needing to look down to check a map or written directions; the aid can guide persons to their destination through audible instructions. This technology has already started to trickle down from being offered in only high-end vehicles; mid-range offerings like Honda are beginning to offer these systems.

Currently in development are cars that receive feedback from the driver's physical state, with the intention of preventing drowsy or stressed drivers. BMW is researching a camera that tracks eyelid movements to alert drowsy drivers through an alarm system. Daimler-Chrysler, Ford, and GM are researching how to track high-stress driving behavior, and then block any nonessential information going to the driver in order to reduce additional stress (Dizikes, 2003). Both of these innovations could become commercialized by 2008.

The development of all of these technologies is to enhance the driver experience and to promote safety. However, for the older driver, many of these technologies pose a new challenge. Older drivers have years of experience in driving cars that remained fundamentally unchanged and relatively low-tech for decades. With all these advances in technology, will the systems designed to help keep people safer actually become a greater distraction?

When comparing younger and older drivers in a study on the use of in-vehicle alerting systems, researchers found that younger subjects tended to trust the technology too much, and older adults find the technology more distracting (Maltz et al., 2002). Younger drivers may have an overreliance on technology because they have grown up in an era with so much automation. Older adults, on the other hand, may be less familiar with technological devices because they have had to learn them at later stages in life. This does not suggest that they are incapable of learning the technology, but because of decades of driving experience, there may be less value in learning the new technology which they may not perceive to be beneficial.

Technology Beyond the Car

Innovations in the car can also be complemented when combined with systems outside of the car. Smart cars alone will not be the panacea to keep drivers safe. The integration of the car with the system through which it travels must also be considered when trying to increase safe driving. Intersection collision avoidance systems are being investigated as a possible technological improvement to roadways. The United States Department of Transportation and a wide variety of stakeholders including government bodies, academic institutions, and auto manufacturers are addressing this potential.

Communication between the car and the traffic signals would allow for earlier detection and avoidance of potential crashes. With one in four fatal crashes occurring at intersections, there must exist some improvements to these systems (Zennaro & Misener, n.d.). These "intelligent intersections" have the potential to help drivers judge the size of gaps between cars when trying to turn, in addition to warning drivers of a possible collision. With auto manufacturers rushing to "smarten" up the car, it is important that the infrastructure around it keeps up with the car's "intelligence" to keep the roadways safe.

CONCLUSION

Across the entire continuum, adequate mobility results in the opportunity to participate in the road of life. Recreation, work, relationships, health care and all other aspects of quality living typically require persons to go outside the home. Micromobility is the form of mobility that allows people to move around in smaller areas, usually by walking or by some form of personal mobility aid. Devices that can aid in micromobility are becoming smarter, and are becoming capable of assisting with more than just movement. Macromobility is the way in which people travel. Driving is the key manner in which most Americans travel, and technology is moving ahead rapidly to try to keep drivers on the road for a lifetime. While these technologies do not come without their challenges, they certainly allow for great possibilities. Ultimately, the ability to be mobile will not rely solely on the car, or the person, or the community. Seamless and safe mobility from the chair to the kitchen and out into the community will require the integration of the segmented subsystems from which most mobility innovations derive.

REFERENCES

Beers, M. H., & Berkow, R. (2000). *The Merck Manual of Geriatrics.* Whitehouse Station, NJ: Merck Research Laboratories.

Bellis, M. (n.d.). *The History of the Automobile.* Retrieved March 15, 2006, from the World Wide Web: www.about.com.

Blaya, J., Newman, D., & Herr, H. (2001). *Active Ankle Foot Orthoses (AAFO).* Cambridge: Massachusetts Institute of Technology.

Braithwaite, R. S., Col, N. F., & Wong, J. B. (2003). Estimating hip fracture morbidity, mortality and costs. *Journal of the American Geriatrics Society, 51* (3), 364–370.

Bush, S. (2003). *Forecasting 65+ travel: An integration of cohort analysis and travel demand modeling.* Massachusetts Institute of Technology, Cambridge.

Childress, D. S. (2002). Development of rehabilitation engineering over the years: As I see it. *Journal of Rehabilitation Research and Development, 39* (6, Suppl.), 1–10.

Chop, W. C., & Robnett, R. H. (1999). *Gerontology for the healthcare professional.* Philadelphia: F.A. Davis Company.

Cook, A. M., & Hussey, S. M. (2002). *Assistive technologies: Principles and practices* (2nd Ed.). St. Louis: Mosby.

Cornman, J. C., Freedman, V. A., & Agree, E. M. (2005). Measurement of assistive device use: Implications for estimates pf device use and disability in late life. *The Gerontologist, 45* (3), 347–358.

Coughlin, J. (2005). Not your father's auto industry? Aging, the automobile and the drive for product innovation. *Generations, 28* (4), 38–44.

Coughlin, J., Mohyde, M., D'Ambrosio, L. A., & Gilbert, J. (2004). *Who Drives Older Driver Decisions?* Cambridge: Massachusetts Institute of Technology.

Dizikes, P. (2003, October). Building a safer driver. *Technology Review.*

Dubowsky, S. (2000). Personal Aid for Mobility and Monitoring: A Helping Hand for the Elderly, *Progress Report No.2-5:* MIT Home Automation and Healthcare Consortium.

Hook, F. W. V., Demonbreun, D., & Weiss, B. D. (2003). Ambulatory devices for chronic gait disorders in the elderly. *American Family Physician, 67* (8), 1717–1724.

Iezzoni, L. (2003). *When walking fails.* Berkeley: University of California Press.

Iezzoni, L., McCarthy, E., Davis, R. B., & Siebens, H. (2001). Mobility difficulties are not only a problem of old age. *Journal of General Internal Medicine, 16,* 235–243.

Independence Technology. (2005). *INDEPENDENCE® iBOT® 4000 Mobility System Fact Sheet.* Warren, NJ: Johnson & Johnson.

Karr, A. (2004, March 2). "Smart" cars are learning to avoid collisions. *The Wall Street Journal.*

Maltz, M., Sun, H., Wu, Q., & Mourant, R. (2002). *Use of an in-vehicle alerting system for older and younger drivers: Does experience count?* Cambridge: MIT AgeLab.

Minniss, T. S. (1853). *Patent for Invalid Locomotive Chair.* Retrieved February 22, 2006, from the World Wide Web: http://www.disabilitymuseum.org/lib/docs/2097.htm.

Molnar, L. J., Eby, D. W., & Miller, L. L. (n.d.). *Promising Approaches for Enhancing Elderly Mobility.* Ann Arbor: University of Michigan Transportation Research Institute.

National Center for Health Statistics. (1994). *National Health Interview Survey on Disability.* CDC. Retrieved February 22, 2006, from the World Wide Web: http://www.cdc.gov/nchs/about/major/nhis_dis/ad292tb1.htm.

Puleo, R. (2005). Adapting assistive devices for seniors. *Provider, 60.*

Puleo, R., & Reimer, B. (2005). *Keeping an older population mobile.* Lecture presented at the Aging By Design, Bentley College, Waltham, MA.

Rosenbloom, S. (2003). *The mobility needs of older Americans: Implications for transportation reauthorization.* Washington, DC: The Brookings Institute.

Simpson, R., LoPresti, E., Hayashi, S., Nourbakhsh, I., & Miller, D. (2004). The smart wheelchair component system. *Journal of Rehabilitation Research and Development, 41* (3B), 429–442.

Simpson, R. C. (2005). Smart wheelchairs: A literature review. *Journal of Rehabilitation Research and Development, 42* (4), 423–436.

TRB. (2005). *Safe mobility for older Americans.* Washington, DC: Transportation Research Board of the National Academies.

U.S. Department of Transportation. (2003). *Safe mobility for a maturing society.* Washington DC.

Warren, C. G. (1990). Powered Mobility and Its Implications. *Journal of Rehabilitation Research and Development* (Health Module Supplement), 74–85.

Zennaro, M., & Misener, J. A. (n.d.). *A "state map" architecture for safe intelligent intersections.* Berkeley: California PATH, University of California.

PART VI

Chapter 13

TECHNOLOGY, AGING, AND COMMUNICATION

JAMES L. FOZARD AND WILLIAM D. KEARNS

INTRODUCTION

Communication technology relates to almost every human activity. Advances in communication technologies are improving personal security, telemedicine, and creating novel options for maintaining health, treating and managing illness, and communicating with health care professionals. Gerontechnology theory identifies four ways that technology affects human activity (Bronswijk, Bouma, & Fozard, 2003). Communication technology is involved in all four.

Prevention and engagement refers to technology that delays or averts age-associated physiological and behavioral changes restricting human functioning. With respect to engagement, communication technology reduces isolation of the homebound, increases opportunities for entertainment, education, remote shopping, business transactions of all kinds, and working at home (Fozard 2005a).

Second, communication technology is involved in "compensation and assistance–technology that compensates for age-associated losses in strength and perceptual-motor functioning" (Bronswijk, Bouma, & Fozard, 2003, p. 171). Third, communication technology has specific applications for the frail elderly. "Care support and organization–use of technology for self-care by elderly persons with physical limitations or by caregivers–often elderly themselves–of elderly persons with disabilities. Technological support of caregiving activities includes devices that

271

lift and move physically disabled persons, machines that administer and monitor medication use, and equipment that provides information about physiological functioning" (Bronswijk, Bouma, & Fozard, 2003, p. 171).

Fourth, communication technology concerns new options for social communication via internet-facilitated human and virtual companions. It also concerns opportunities for communication with machines–computers, environmental control devices, and robots. "Enhancement and satisfaction–the innovative uses of technology; e.g., virtual reality, interactive communication devices and self-adapting equipment that expands the range and depth of human activities with respect to comfort, vitality and productivity. It is most relevant to applications of work and self-fulfillment–artistic activities, education. Because enhancement emphasizes the roles of technology for expanding human activities, it transcends and encompasses the other three classifications of technology impact" (Fozard, 2005b; Mollenkopf & Fozard, 2004).

Demographic and Psychological Factors Affect Use of Communication Technology

According to the Pew Internet and American Life Project report (Fox, 2004), 22 percent of American men and women 65 and older report using the internet as compared to 58 percent, 75 percent, and 77 percent in age groups 60–64, 30–49, and 18–29, respectively. In contrast to an earlier Pew Foundation study, Internet use by persons 65+ has increased from 17 percent to 22 percent in four years. The jump from 22% to 58% in internet use between adjacent cohorts 65 and older vs. 60–64 provided strong evidence that the percentage of older users will increase rapidly as younger cohorts enter the oldest age range represented in the survey. Similar findings have been reported for the United States and Canada (Opalinski, 2001; Brodie et al., 2000) and other industrialized countries (Selwyn, Gorard, & Furlong, 2005). The degree to which internet use among old persons could or should be increased is unknown. The current 75–77 percent user prevalence among adults aged 18-49 may provide an estimate of the upper limit.

Incentives for increased internet use come from businesses, government, and external user organizations. Many banks, insurance companies, and other businesses impose user fees for conventional transactions requiring human involvement. Government incentives include provision of health care information, e.g., Medicare, Medicaid, and the National Institutes of Health (Rideout, Neuman, Kitchman, & Brodie, 2005), and government business, e.g., income tax preparation and submission. Seniornet and some companies provide internet-based services for senior communities (Dunning, 2003).

Two lines of psychological research are being pursued: the first links measures of personality and psychopathology to overuse of online activities; the second explores self-esteem, well-being, and personality traits as predictors of amount and pattern of internet use. Chen and Persson (2002) noted that earlier studies of older adult Internet use were associated with positive outcomes in relationships and enjoyment. Well-being was defined in terms of Ryff's (1989) scales for autonomy, environmental mastery, personal growth, positive relations with others, purpose in life, and self-acceptance. Compared to older adults, young adults scored higher on personal growth and purpose in life, but lower on autonomy and environmental mastery. Within both the younger and older computer user groups, no significant correlations among the measures of well-being and amount of time spent on the internet emerged. Older users were higher in personal growth, purpose in life and a trait measure of openness to new experience than were older nonusers.

One survey of internet use by 1000 British adults (Selwyn, Gorard & Furlong, 2005) included interviews with a subsample of users and nonusers about amount and patterns of use. As in other studies, use of e-mail is the most frequent application in all groups. Consistent with other surveys, use of the internet was greater among younger cohorts, persons who were married, had no long-term illness or disability, had education beyond age 16, and had home computer access. Demographic differences between users and nonusers were insignificant. The percentage of internet nonusers increased with age: 40 percent, 47 percent, and 85 percent for age groups 21–40, 41–60, and 61+, respectively. Selwyn and colleagues conclude that ". . . there is a pressing need for politicians, policymakers and technologists to develop reasonable expectations of the internet and its use. The internet is unlikely to lead to a new, equitable and efficient version of modern society but is more likely . . . to reflect the same society as ever–just via different means" (pp. 23–24).

Selwyn, Gorard, Furlong and Madden (2003) conducted a more detailed analysis of the participants in the oldest age group of the larger study described above and found that ". . . using the Internet for banking and finances, shopping and dealings with government agencies was not evinced. . . . Sustained use of computers in public sites such as libraries . . . was not in evidence" (p. 576). They stressed that the Internet is not perceived by older persons as highly attractive, relevant, or useful and is clearly a minority activity. Simply training elderly persons to become users fails to address the need to reshape the Internet to be more attractive and useful to the older adult. This comment is consistent with the emphasis in gerontechnology theory to involve the user in technology development (Fozard, 2005a).

The research by Selwyn and colleagues indicated that improving internet access will not by itself increase internet use by older persons. A survey by the Kaiser Family Institute (Rideout, Neuman, Kitchman, & Brodie, 2005) found accessing health and medical information was an important goal for the minority of elderly adults who used the internet, but many complained about the poor quality of the materials found. Nevertheless, the Kaiser report echoed frequent recommendations (see Morrell, Mayhorn, & Echt, 2004) to increase internet use by the elderly by ". . . providing classes in how to use the internet, toll-free technical help lines, volunteers to assist with technical problems, and financial assistance for lower-income seniors" (p. 11).

Matanda, Jenvey, and Phillips (2004) administered questionnaires probing loneliness, computer anxiety, and education to a convenience sample of 158 Australian adult internet users. The predicted variable was category of internet use–communication, entertainment, information, and commerce. Earlier findings linking loneliness with more internet use for communication were only weakly corroborated; greater internet use for entertainment was found for younger vs. older men and for more men than women. These results support the contention that the computer and internet facilitate the pursuit of ongoing user activities.

Karavidas, Lim, and Katsikas (2002) related computer anxiety and computer knowledge to self-efficacy and life satisfaction among elderly computer club members in Florida. Path analysis indicated computer use lowered computer anxiety and increased self-efficacy and overall life satisfaction. Although similar in computer use, women reported more computer anxiety and less knowledge than men. The primary computer uses were: e-mail (56%) browsing internet (29%), and tracking investments (25%). The typical website sought contained product information (42%), health (29%), news (29%), hobbies (25%), and investments (24%). For self-selected members of computer clubs, the computer can contribute to life satisfaction.

The low use of computers and internet has multiple determinants. Morrell (2002) interprets the pattern of results as indicating that: Older adults are not less interested in learning about the internet than younger; they are capable of learning how to use the internet; and they are no more anxious about computer use than younger adults. Older users take a utilitarian approach to computer use. Low internet use by older persons is attributed to limited access to computers, unavailable broadband internet service, lack of training, poor accessibility to elder-friendly web sites, overly complex navigational tools, and motivational issues related to relevance and trustworthiness of internet information. Trustworthiness of internet information is a serious issue for all internet users (Benbow, 2004; Morrell, 2002).

Compensating for Functional Limitations Using Communication Devices

Many difficulties in using computers are shared by users regardless of age and even experience using computers (Landauer, 1995; Norman, 1998; Thomas, 2003). Many age-related perceptual motor limitations can be offset by improved computer displays and controls and others can be compensated for by training (Fozard, 2001). Because using the internet involves navigation through complex paths of related and unrelated information, research has focused on age-related limitations in working memory and other complex cognitive functions. Improving the ergonomics of display and control devices is very specific to the device in question. Most of the recent studies address desktop and laptop computers—display quality and use of input devices, e.g., mouse, keyboard, voice, light pen, and Bluetooth enabled pen.

Computer Displays

VISUAL DISPLAYS AND AIDS: Most computer displays are visual although there are recent developments in auditory displays by the machine as well as adaptive programs which can recognize and act on speech inputs by designated users. Universal but nonuniform age related changes in vision that increase the difficulty of older adults using a visual LCD or CRT display result from: poorer static and dynamic acuity; higher light requirements; poorer tolerance of glare, particularly veiling glare; and loss of accommodation. Charness and Dijkstra (1999) found the customary levels of illumination in home and public buildings are inadequate for many computer tasks. The amount and sources of ambient illumination are strong determinants of screen visibility, particularly in LCD and plasma emissive displays. Ambient lighting falling directly on the screen causes veiling glare that may greatly reduce screen visibility. As anyone who has attempted to use an outdoor ATM machine knows, ambient illumination and contrast strongly influence legibility of screen displays. Reviews of the magnitude and explanations for these changes (Charness, 2001; Fozard, 2001, 2003; Fozard & Gordon-Salant, 2001; Morrell, Dailey, & Rousseau, 2003; Scialfa, Ho, & Leberge, 2004; Schieber, 2003) also discuss ergonomics that could improve their usefulness.

Age associated accommodation losses are compensated for by magnifying spectacles that optimize acuity at specific viewing distances. Typical bifocal lenses improve acuity for materials at 45–60 cm and acuity at optical infinity, about 6m. The viewing distance for the typical keyboard is about 45–60 cm, roughly the same as reading a conventional book. The viewing distance for the screen may be two to three times that of the keyboard, thus spectacles optimizing acuity at 160–200 cm may be required as a substitute or in addition to the usual bifocal lens. Currently lenses are machined to precise optical values, but adjustable lenses which can be dynamically modified by the wearer have been patented (Kearns, 2000).

Age associated eye diseases—cataracts, macular degeneration, glaucoma, and diabetic retinopathy—all may affect static and dynamic acuity. Lens clouding due to cataract formation requires surgical substitution of a synthetic lens. Current implants do not readily change focal length, and users may retain glasses for near or far vision. Specialized low vision aids allowing retention of residual functions exist and are available to the legally blind (Snellen fraction of 0.1); some instruments would be also be valuable to persons with intermediate acuity levels. Text to speech converters are available for computerized documents, Adobe, Inc. provides this feature free of charge with their Acrobat Reader (Adobe, 2006) and hand-held devices which can read printed text from paper using a scanner and computer are available. Cellular telephones (Nokia, 2006; Vodaphone, 2006; Cingular, 2006) are now being distributed which read aloud the telephone's small display, the key pressed, received e-mail, instant messages, notes, and also transcripts of printed documents sent via the network using onboard software such as the Cingular "Talks" program. These phones may also employ voice recognition technology to initiate calls for the user.

AUDITORY DISPLAYS AND AIDS: As a result of the integration of digital audio processing into hearing aids, these instruments can be programmed to compensate for losses in specific frequency ranges (Fozard & Gordon-Salant, 2001) New versions with artificial intelligence automatically compensate for multiple sources of extraneous noise (Oticon, 2006) restoring hearing to near normal levels. Because of the trend towards miniaturization and the growth in wireless networking (Bluetooth, 2006) hearing aids now act as wireless receivers of audio data (Qian, Loizou, & Dorman, 2003; Starkey Laboratories, 2005) and may soon act as transmitters as well. Cellular and other telephones can transmit to hearing aids using traditional T-coil technology, and Qian, Loizou, and Dorman (2003) have tested a Bluetooth telephone interface for persons who have cochlear implants which allow cellular audio to be transmitted directly to the implant. Cellular phones support traditional TTY interfaces (Nokia, 2006) and speech to text translation devices are available but they require substantial training to achieve even modest performance levels and must be retrained for each speaker. Accurate speech recognition across individuals with minimal or no training will permit further miniaturization of devices whose current size is largely determined by the need for a usable keypad interface. Reducing the number of user responses to a limited set ("yes/no" and numbers from 0 to 10) has helped businesses automate many telephone-based services previously supported by call center support personnel.

HAPTIC DISPLAYS: Proprioception that determines accurate placement of limbs for support and walking diminishes with age increasing the likelihood of falls. Research using accelerometers and audio feedback communication allows elders to recognize when their body is adopting an unstable attitude and helps them correct (see Fozard, 2005a for a review). Artificial limbs are being tested with haptic interfaces allowing distal perception of pressure and touch aiding correct placement. Haptics have been used in virtual environments to enhance the sense of reality and the remote control of robotic and other devices.

Computer Controls

The major input devices for computers are the keyboard and mouse. For specialized computers, pointers or specially labeled keypads are used, and voice activated input devices are becoming widely available. Wireless mouse and keyboard inputs, keyboards with varying layouts, trackball and joystick controls, and Bluetooth enabled data pen devices provide alternatives. Ergonomic studies of the usefulness of these devices relative to age (Czaja & Lee, 2003; Morrell, Dailey & Rousseau, 2003) extend the well-known finding of age-related slowing of manual responses to computer displays. The extent, however, is modified by prior typing experience, use of computers, as well as by training.

Charness, Holley, Feddon, and Jastrzembski (2004) compared a light pen to a mouse in two tasks—menu selection requiring pure pointing and mixed pointing and data entry. Older adults were slower than younger on both tasks but the light pen yielded faster response times for both age groups. Practice improved the performance of older adults over that of younger adults.

Electronic Information Seeking and Web Navigation

Research studies indicated in comparison to younger adults, older adults use less efficient navigation strategies, have more difficulty in completing tasks and in remembering where and what they searched in the process (Czaja & Lee 2003; Morrell, Park, Mayhorn, & Kelley, 2000; Sharit et al., 2004). Lin (2003) compared young and elderly computer literate Chinese adults on internet navigation using three hypertext organizational schemes—hierarchical, network and a hybrid. Older users in all three conditions opened fewer nodes, reopened previously visited nodes more frequently, and were less efficient in navigation. The optimal hypertext organization for older users depends on the task, but hierarchical and hybrid organizational structures are superior.

Lazar, Dudley-Sponaugle, and Greenidge (2004) and Morrell, Dailey, and Rousseau (2003) reviewed published guidelines for Web design visibility, ease of understanding, and ease of navigation. They found that existing guidelines were too general and not inclusive of older users' needs and abilities. They summarized National Institute on Aging sponsored research to improve Website usability for elders obtaining health-related information—The NIHSeniorHealth.gov Project. Morrell et al. (2004) provided guidelines and implementation rules for factors affecting legibility of Web materials: clarity of writing; use of active voice; organization and repetition; the use of illustrations, photos, animation and video, and text alternatives to video and other illustrated materials. Morrell and colleagues (2003) evaluated ease of use and satisfaction with the NIH website by a panel of older adults. Satisfaction with the site was quite high, but navigating difficulties persisted.

INTERNET ACCESS FOR ELDERLY PERSONS WITH SPECIAL NEEDS: Egan, Warrall and Oxenham (2005) evaluated a training program to increase Internet use in seven patients with Traumatic Brain Injury. The seven participants were tutored by trained volunteers in a teaching program used with patients with aphasia. Participants improved in all areas of the training program with two becoming virtually independent internet users. Despite its small size and use of self-selected participants, the study is valuable because of its detailed descriptions of each patient's limitations and motivations. Sohlberg, Fickas, Ehlhardt and Todis (2005) reported that training combined with a simplified e-mail program enabled four adults (ages 37–65 years) with severe cognitive impairments to use e-mail. The beneficial effects persisted over a nine-month follow-up period.

Freeman, Clare, Savitch, Royan, Litherland and Lindsay (2005) compared ease of use and satisfaction with an unmodified website to one that was altered to address reported cognitive impairments associated with dementia. The major findings were that limiting the amount of information on a page to negate the need for scrolling and limiting the number of choices needed to navigate the website made navigation easier for dementia patients.

Functional Limitations in Telephone Use

In a German study, Ziefle (2002) compared ease of use of three mobile phones–Nokia, Siemens and Motorola. The complexity of the menus, expertise of the user, and ease of learning to use the device were all important determiners of the usability of the systems. Age was not systematically studied. A survey of French mobile phone users by Licoppe and Heurtin (2001) demonstrated that the increased accessibility between users made possible by ease of reaching one person by another was an important contributor to the rapid increase of use of such devices, a trend most obvious in teenagers, but also among older adults. The extreme miniaturization of the display and the alphanumeric telephone keypad poses significant problems for older users. Omori and colleagues (2002) found that only three out of six mobile phones tested had displays with characters that met the visual requirements for legibility of older Japanese users. Sending text messages is complicated because the user has to press a button the right number of times to designate a specific letter, e.g., one to four presses of the nine key to designate "w," "x," "y" or "z," respectively. Some mobile phones are now equipped with 'T9' Predictive Text Input software that attempts to reduce the number of keystrokes needed to create a text message. The software uses a dictionary to choose likely letters that follow the one originally typed in by the user (Biersdorfer, 2006).

INTERACTIVE VOICE RESPONSE (IVR) SYSTEMS: Dulude's (2002) review indicates the development of ergonomically sound guidelines for IVR has been slow and often inconsistent. Gardner-Bonneau (1992, 1999) and others agree the memory burden of menus should be limited to no more than three levels and no more than four choices per level. The ability to skip over spoken alternatives is also recommended. Error messages should never blame the caller and should provide explicit information for completing the call or reaching a human operator.

In Dulude's research, 22 young (18–27 years) and 22 older (65–86) women completed information seeking tasks on six existing systems–Regional Municipality, Canadian Airlines, Income Security, Statistics Canada, AccuRate Foreign Exchange and United Airlines (the only system that allowed for voice input instead of keystrokes). Measures of perceived usability of each system as well as success completing the task were obtained. The median number of successes by the older group was 2.8 vs. 5 for the younger; the comparable percentages of participants succeeding on at least five of the six tasks were 32 percent and 82 percent. The number of successes for each system varied widely, more so for the older adults. The two groups were equally successful using the Income Security system, the system on which performance was best. Older adults were much less successful with the United Airlines voice activated system. Younger adults gave higher usability ratings to all systems except the Income Security system for which the rated usability was the same in both groups. Older adults experienced much greater difficulty with the caller ignoring prompts, to the means of recovering from an error, and caller confusion about the task. Older adults experience greater difficulty using a variety of existing telephone menu systems to accomplish a transaction or reach a human respondent (Czaja & Sharit, 2002). Of various interventions explored, providing older adults with a graphical aid of the menu was more effective than providing a visual display. Slowing the speech rate did not improve the performance of the older users.

USE OF PHONES BY PERSONS WITH DEMENTIA: Ala, Berck, and Popvich (2005) studied the ability of outpatients with Alzheimer's disease or mild cognitive impairment (measured by MMSE scores) to use a telephone to call for help in an emergency either when a standard emergency number—911 or 0—was called or a specified 7-digit number written on a piece of paper was provided. Performance was better in all ability groups when the number was provided. Successes increased from 0 to 100 percent as MMSE scores rose from 0–9 to 26–30 when the number was provided; the corresponding percentages increased from 0 to 76 percent as MMSE scores rose from 10–15 to 26–30. Failure to remember the standard emergency number was the major limiting factor in the successful use of the telephone by these patients. Similar conclusions were reached in a Swedish study (Nygard & Starkhammer, 2003).

Technology for Elderly with Severe Illness and Functional Limitations

Research on traditional communications technologies such as hearing aids, visual aids, text to speech processors, speech to text processors, and electronic memory aids and telephone has a long history. More recently research has focused on nontraditional and developing technical products and environments, e.g., telemedicine, robots and smart houses.

PERSONAL SERVICE ROBOTS: According to Thrun (2004), ". . . the number of deployed personal service robots will grow from 176,500 in 2001 to 2,021,000 in 2005—a stunning 1,145 percent increase. Personal service robots assist or entertain people in domestic settings or in recreational activities. Examples include robotic vacuum cleaners, lawn mowers, receptionists, robot assistants to elderly and people with disabilities, wheelchairs, and toys" (p. 12). Worldwide industrial robot sales (the most numerous type) amounted to $1.4 billion in 2000 (Tanie, 2004) showing consistent gains as corporations adapt to an aging work force. Honda, Inc. has developed a humanoid robotic companion, Asimo, which performs basic chores and simple caregiving under voice, hand gesture, or network control. The bipedal device can walk at speeds up to 4 mph (see http://world.honda.com/ASIMO/) and is highly agile. Its level of deployment in the community is not known, however.

Montemerlo, Pineau, Roy, Thrun, and Varma (2002) have tested a robotic assistant named "Pearl" in an assisted living facility. The robot is tasked with reminding patients of upcoming doctor visits, escorting them to the physician's office, and providing a stable platform to support slow moving patients as they ambulate. The robot uses speech recognition software to respond to patient requests and can provide updated weather reports upon demand. Montemerlo's patients reported being generally pleased with the functionality of the robot. The investigators stressed the importance of having the robot precisely estimate the pace of an accompanied walker in order to minimize the risk of injury to the elder.

Yoshimi et al. (2004) have devised a mobile robotic information home appliance which comes when spoken to by the user, can operate other home appliances via infrared controller and present e-mail or other communications through the home's network infrastructure. Jung et al. (2005) have constructed a complete smart house for the elderly and handicapped that employs wireless video and physiological monitoring of the resident, an intelligent bed, robotic wheelchairs, and mechatronic lifting devices to assist in transfer. Preliminary evaluation of the home by a partially disabled 50-year-old test subject was generally positive.

TELEMEDICINE: With a video presence in the home, telemedicine applications may improve health care for the elderly because health professionals can observe the person's physical condition. Because of recent advances in cellular telephone design, health-related imagery may be increasingly sent by wireless mobile devices. IBM Researchers Husemann, Narayanaswami and Nidd (2004) have described a "Mobile Health Toolkit" integrating cellular telephones having Bluetooth or 802.11 capabilities with wireless medical devices such as blood pressure cuffs, pill reminders, digital blood glucose monitors, activity monitors, respirometers, and even needle injection monitors. In practice, a wireless connection would be established between the cellular telephone and any or all of the medical devices within approximately 10 meters.

Each time a device was used the time, date, and parameters measured would be relayed by phone to the patient's medical records at a remote server. Failure to adhere to a regimen would be detected by a correlation engine running on the cellular phone. Poor compliance with medical regimens in home care environments was cited as a primary motive for the development of this technology by the investigators.

Networked microprocessor devices like the "Health Buddy" which link service providers directly to elders at home (telemedicine) have demonstrated improved compliance with medication regimens, and computerized stand alone medication reminders capable of retaining several medication schedules are also available. A recent study by the Rand Corporation (Bigelow et al., 2000) evaluated the Health Buddy on a sample of 139 persons with congestive heart failure living in the community. The participants responded electronically to frequent health management queries delivered via the device over monitoring periods of up to four months. The investigators found that participants' rate of compliance to the health-related queries matched those of telephone delivered queries: 90 percent of participants indicated they were satisfied with the technology; 70 percent felt no improvements were needed; 70 percent also said they would continue using the technology if given the opportunity.

In home settings, telemedicine has been demonstrated to improve mental health outcomes. Heeter and colleagues (Heeter, Gregg, Climo, Biocca, & Dekker, 2002) have described three case studies of elders whose attendance at senior centers was curtailed due to illness. Each senior had bidirectional video and audio installed in his or her home to allow the continuous interaction in realtime with friends at the centers. Heeter et al.'s subjects reported a diminished isolation and feelings of depression. Smyth and Kwon (2004) reviewed several studies using communication technology to facilitate information sharing and support group activities among and between professional and non-professional caregivers of elderly persons (see also Meier, 2000).

DEMENTIA PATIENTS AND THEIR CAREGIVERS: Location aware cuing can be used to prompt behaviors. Several demonstration projects, including the University of Florida's "Smart House" employ tiny radio frequency identification devices (RFID) located in the physical environment or occupants' clothing to prompt wearer behavior contingent on their location (Helal, Mann, El-Zabadani, King, Kaddoura, &

Jansen, 2005). In practice such devices might warn an elder with dementia that he or she was in the kitchen, and that the hot stove would potentially burn them. When the RFID scanner device has been incorporated into a glove it provides cues to the wearer with dementia as to the uses of touched objects (Philipose, Fishkin, Perkowitz, Patterson, Fox, Kautz, & Hähnel, 2004), increasing the likelihood that a user might successfully carry out an ADL. Similarly, intelligent devices incorporating computer vision can verbally prompt the resumption of complex behavioral sequences like handwashing which can be interrupted if the elder with dementia becomes distracted (Mihailidis, Carmichael, & Boger, 2004).

Outside of the home, location aware services may rely on Global Positioning System (GPS) enabled devices. Patterson, Etzioni and Kautz's (2002) Activity Compass verbally prompts the elder with dementia or mild cognitive impairment to perform an ADL at that set of geographical coordinates. This system is sophisticated enough to recognize when a person becomes lost on the way to a commonly traveled destination and can prompt him or her "Were you going to the store? If so you'll want to turn right just up ahead." In a novel application of GPS enhanced cybernetic technology, Digital Angel, Inc. has developed an entire system to manage wandering in persons with moderate dementia. Digital Angel's solution uses a cellular telephone's onboard advanced computational abilities and built-in GPS to establish a perimeter (termed a "geofence") around the home (Munson & Gupta, 2002). Wanderers wearing the cellular telephone who cross the geofence, automatically reveal their position to their caregivers through a server-based notification system of e-mail, pager, and automated telephone calls using synthesized voices. Caregivers can locate the missing wanderer to within 100 feet, and coverage is dependent upon cellular telephone service and GPS satellite availability. One intriguing variant of their approach is that a wanderer who crosses a geofence could be redirected to his home by verbal directional cues delivered by a networked system similar to the Patterson, Etzioni and Kautz's (2002) "Activity Compass." Such a system would acquire data on a wanderer's location and vector and might issue specific prompts contingent on their response to verbal instructions. For example: "Please turn around and face the house. Walk back to the house. Enter the house."

Simpler technologies can also offer relief to caregivers. Robotic dolls may play a role by stimulating communications in persons with dementia, but they can also provide programmed cues and guidance to persons with memory disorders and act as a type of electronic guide dog. Sony's newest version of AIBO (Sony, 2006) includes touch sensors, cameras, wireless networking and artificial intelligence that learn its environment causing the robot's "personality" to change over time. It also presents six unique "emotions" happiness, sadness, fear, dislike, surprise, and anger to stimulate contact by people. AIBO's onboard sensors and data recording capability may allow easier longitudinal behavioral data gathering in home and community settings where obtaining information on the progression of dementing disorders may prove difficult or unreliable.

Tamura et al. (2001) demonstrated that simple baby dolls and toy animals can reduce agitation and increase social interactions among persons with moderate to severe dementia. Tamura et al. (2004) has found that animating the dolls produced significant increases in verbal interaction by demented persons. These investigators presented an AIBO robotic dog dressed in baby clothes or an inexpensive electronic toy dog to 13 severely demented men and women. Patients increased communication with both toys, but more communication was observed with the inexpensive electronic toy dog than with the AIBO. Patients referred to the dressed AIBO dog as either a dog or baby, and the investigators concluded that the robot's ambiguous identity may have reduced patients' communications with it because they were unsure which behaviors were appropriate. In contrast, the simple electronic toy dog reliably elicited behaviors characteristic of pet owners.

Wada, Shibata, Saito, and Tanie (2002) presented a robotic harp seal replica to 26 residents of a nursing facility over a period of five weeks; approximately 38 percent of the residents had some level of dementia. The investigators reported statistically reliable improvements in affect for weeks 2–5 among the residents using the Profile of Mood States questionnaire, and found that persons with prior histories of breeding animals were more likely to benefit from exposure to the robot. Unfortunately, a placebo condition was not included to evaluate the effect of additional attention paid to the residents. A subsequent study by Saito, Shibata, Wada and Tanie (2003) measured urinary stress hormones in nursing home patients interacting with the seal robot or a version having only a minimum set of programmed stereotyped behaviors. Their analysis showed reduced stress levels in elders who interacted with the more lifelike robot compared to elders who interacted only with the simpler version which emitted stereotyped behaviors.

Takanori (2004) has eloquently described these variants of service robots as human interactive robots for psychological enrichment. "Human interactive robots for psychological enrichment are a type of service robot that provides a service by interacting with humans while stimulating their minds and we, therefore, tend to assign high subjective values to them. It is not necessary for these robots to be exclusive, but they should be as affordable as other new luxury products. In addition, accuracy or speed is not always of prime importance. Their function or purpose is not simply entertainment, but also to render assistance, to guide, to provide therapy, to educate, [and] to enable communication. . ." (p. 1751).

CONCLUDING OBSERVATIONS

The receiver of digital communications may eventually find it impossible to distinguish human from machine sources. Some electronic telephone agents to preprocess billing information and make flight reservations are so lifelike and in many cases have such soothing voices and demeanor, that people often prefer them to interacting with humans. Furthermore, the machines never tire, take days off, have a bad day, and almost never make a mistake. Society is poised at the beginning of an era in which most manufactured objects will have some form of communication capabilities, whether in embedded nanotechnologies employing wireless networking or some successor, or machine intelligence capable of human mimicry. Such objects will entertain, serve, guide, and possibly maintain and rehabilitate older persons when their biology begins to fail. These pervasive devices, found in the surrounding environment and perhaps even within persons themselves will form the "ubiquitous computing" environment described by Dishman, Matthews and Dunbar-Jacob (2004) that will gradually enfold the population as it ages. Dishman et al. envision environments whose plasticity allows person-sensitive changes at times, places, and durations of one's choosing to compensate for declining sensory acuity, cognitive, or physical capacity. Communication technology linking human to human, and human to machine, will be the backbone coordinating all such environments. Interfaces may range from simple telephone IVR systems to computer-generated avatars, web interfaces, or possibly even robotic "pets" that serve as wireless interfaces to larger networks of ubiquitous machines.

REFERENCES

Adobe, Inc. (2006). Adobe Acrobat reader. Downloaded from http://www.adobe.com/ on 3/27/06.

Ala, T., Berck, A., & Popovich, A. (2005). Using the telephone to call for help and caregiver awareness in Alzheimer disease. *Alzheimer Disease & Associated Disorders, 19* (2), 79–84.

Benbow, A. (2004). Increasing access to reliable information on the world wide web: Educational tools for web designers. In D.C. Burdick & S. Kwon (Eds), *Gerontechnology: Research and practice in technology and aging* (pp. 86–96). New York: Springer.

Biersdorfer, J. (2006). Typing faster on a mobile phone. *New York Times,* February 23, C-10.

Bigelow, J., Cretin, S., Solomon, M., Wu, S., Cherry, J., Cobb, H., & O'Connell, M. (2001). Patient compliance with and attitudes towards Health Buddy(TM) Downloaded from http://www.rand.org/pubs/monograph_reports/MR1232/ on 1/26/06.

Bluetooth, Inc. (2006). The official Bluetooth wireless info site. Downloaded from http://www.bluetooth.com/bluetooth/ on 3/27/06.

Brodie, M., Flournoy, R., Altman, D., Blendon, R., Benson, J.,& Rosenbaum, M. (2000). Health information, the internet and the digital divide. *Health Affairs,* November/December, 255–265.

Bronswijk, J., van, Bouma, H., & Fozard, J. (2003). Technology for quality of life: An enriched taxonomy. *Gerontechnology, 2* (2), 169–172.

Charness, N. (2001). Aging and communication: Human factors issues. In N. Charness, D.C. Parks, & B.A. Sabel (Eds.), *Communication, technology and aging* (pp. 1–29). New York: Springer.

Charness, N., & Dijkstra, K. (1999). Age, luminance, and print legibility in homes, offices, and public places. *Human Factors, 41* (2), 173–193.

Charness, N. Holley, P., Feddon, J., & Jastrzembski, T. (2002). Light pen use and practice minimize age and hand performance in pointing tasks. *Human Factors, 46* (3), 373–384.

Chen, Y. & Persson, A. (2002). Internet use among young and older adults: Relation to psychological wellbeing. *Educational Gerontology, 28,* 731–744.

Cingular Wireless, Inc. (2006). *TALKS by Cingular Wireless and the Nokia 6620.* Downloaded from http://www.cingular.com/about/talks_program on 1/25/06.

Czaja, S., & Sharit, J. (2002). The usability of telephone voice menu systems for older adults. *Gerontechnology, 2* (1), 88.

Czaja, S., & Lee, C. (2003). Designing computer systems for older adults. In J. Jacko & A. Sears (Eds.), *The human-computer interaction handbook* (pp. 413–427). Mahwah, NJ: Erlbaum.

Dishman, E., Matthews, J. & Dunbar-Jacob, J. (2004). Everyday health: Technology for adaptive aging. In R.W. Pew & S.W. Van Hemmel (Eds.), *Technology for adaptive aging* (pp. 179–208). Board on Behavioral, Cognitive, and Sensory Sciences, Division of Behavioral and Social Sciences and Education. Washington, D.C.; National Academies Press.

Dulude, L. (2002). Automated telephone answering systems and aging. *Behavior & Information Technology, 21* (3), 171–184.

Dunning, T. (2003). Internet and e-mail options. *Activities, Adaptation & Aging, 27* (3/4), 129–131.

Egan, J., Worrall, L. & Oxenham, D. (2005). An Internet training intervention for people with traumatic brain injury: Barriers and outcomes. *Brain Injury, 19* (8), 555–568.

Fox, S. (2004). Older Americans and the internet. Pew internet and American life project. Downloaded from http://207.21.232.103/pdfs/PIP_Seniors_Online_2004.pdf on 2/13/06.

Fozard, J. (2001). Gerontechnology and perceptual-motor function: New opportunities for prevention, compensation, and enhancement. *Gerontechnology, 1* (1), 5–24.

Fozard, J. (2003). Using technology to lower the perceptual and cognitive hurdles of aging. In N. Charness & K. W. Schaie (Eds.), *Impact of technology on successful aging* (pp. 100–112). New York: Springer.

Fozard, J. (2005a). Gerontechnology: Optimising relationships between ageing people and changing technology. In V. Minichiello, & I. Coulson (Eds.), *Contemporary issues in gerontology: Promoting positive ageing* (pp. 241–268). Oxon, England: Routledge.

Fozard, J. (2005b). Impacts of technology interventions on health and self-esteem. *Gerontechnology, 4* (2), 63–76.

Fozard, J., & Gordon-Salant, S. (2001). Changes in vision and hearing with age. In J. E. Birren & K.W. Schaie (Eds.), *Handbook of the psychology of aging* (5th Ed., pp. 241–266). San Diego, CA: Academic Press.

Freeman, E., Clare, L., Savitch, N., Royan, L., Litherland, R., & Lindsay, M. (2005). Improving website accessibility for people with early-stage dementia: A preliminary investigation. *Aging & Mental Health, 9* (5), 442–448.

Gardner-Bonneau, D. (1992). Human factors problems in interactive voice response (IVR) applications: Do we need a guideline/standard? In *Proceedings of the Human Factors Society 36th Annual Meeting Atlanta, Georgia, October 12–16*, pp. 222–226.

Gardner-Bonneau, D. (1999). *Human factors and voice interactive systems.* Dordrecht, Netherlands: Kluwer.

Heeter, C., Gregg, J., Climo, J., Biocca, F., & Dekker, D. (2002). Telewindows: Case studies in asymmetrical social presence. In G. Riva, F. Davide & W.A. IJsselsteijn (Eds.) *Being there: Concepts, effects and measurement of user presence in synthetic environments* (Vol. 5, pp. 279–294). Amsterdam, IOS Press.

Helal, S., Mann, W., El-Zabadani, H., King, J., Kaddoura, Y., & Jansen, E. (2005). The gator tech smart house: A programmable pervasive space. *IEEE Computer Magazine, 38* (3), 64–74. Downloaded from http://ieeexplore.ieee.org/iel5/2/30617/01413118.pdf?arnumber=1413118 on 1/26/06.

Husemann, D., Narayanaswami, C. &. Nidd, M. (2004). Personal mobile hub. In *Proceedings of the International Symposium on Wearable Computers (ISWC'04)*, pp. 43–49.

Jung, J., Do, J. ,Kim, Y., Suh, K., & Bien, Z. (2005). Advanced robotic residence for the elderly/the handicapped: Realization and user evaluation. *Proceedings of the 2005 IEEE 9th International Conference on Rehabilitation Robotics*. Chicago, IL, June 28–July 1.

Karavidas, M., Lim, N., & Katsikas, S. (2005). The effects of computers on older adult users. *Computers and Human Behavior, 21*, 697–711.

Kearns, J.P. (2000) Variable focal length lens. Patent 6,033,070 Downloaded from http://patft.uspto.gov/netacgi/nph-Parser?Sect1=PTO2&Sect2=HITOFF&p=1&u=/netahtml/search-adv.htm&r=44&f=G&l=50&d=ptxt&S1=kearns.INZZ.&OS=in/kearns&RS=IN/kearns on 1/25/06.

Landauer, T. (1995). *The trouble with computers–Usefulness, usability, and productivity.* Cambridge, MA: MIT Press.

Lazar, J., Sponaugle, A., & Greenidge, K. (2004). Improving web accessibility: A study of webmaster perceptions. *Computers in Human Behavior, 20*, 269–288.

Licoppe, C. & Heurtin, J. (2001). Managing one's availability to telephone communication through mobile phones: A French case study of the development dynamics of mobile phone use. *Personal and Ubiquitous Computing, 5*, 99–108.

Lin, D.M. (2003). Age differences in the performance of hypertext perusal as a function of text topology. *Behaviour & Information Technology, 22* (4), 219–226.

Matanda, M., Jenvey, V., & Phillips, J. (2004). Internet use in adulthood; loneliness, computer anxiety and education. *Behaviour Change; Journal of the Australian Behavior Modification Association, 21* (2), 103–114.

Meier, A. (2000). Offering social support via the internet: A case study of an online support group for social workers. *Journal of Technology in Human Services, 17* (2/3), 237–266.

Mihailidis, A., Carmichael, B., & Boger, J. (2004). The use of computer vision in an intelligent environment to support aging-in-place: Safety, and independence in the home. *IEEE Transactions on Information Technology in Biomedicine, 8* (3), 238–247.

Mollenkopf, H., & Fozard, J. (2004). Technology and the good life: Challenges for current and future generations of aging people. In H. W. Wahl, R.J. Scheidt, & P.G. Windley (Eds.), *Annual review of geriatrics and gerontology* (Vol. 23, pp. 250–279). New York: Springer.

Montemerlo, M., Pineau, J., Roy, N., Thrun, S. & Varma, V. (2002). Experiences with a mobile robotic guide for the elderly. In *National Conference on Artificial Intelligence. AAAI*, August.

Morrell, R. (2002). *Older adults, health information and the World Wide Web.* Mawah, NJ: Earlbaum.

Morrell, R., Dailey, S. & Rousseau, G. (2003). Applying research: The NIH senior health project. In N. Charness & K.W. Schaie (Eds.), *Impact of technology on successful aging* (pp. 134–161). New York: Springer Publishing.

Morrell, R., Mayhorn, C., and Echt, K. (2004). Why older adults use or do not use the internet. In D.C. Burdick & S. Kwon (Eds.), *Gerotechnology: Research and practice in technology and aging* (pp. 71–85). New York: Springer.

Morrell, R., Dailey, S., Stoltz-Loike, M., Feldman, C., Mayhorn, C., Echt, K. & Podany, K., (2004). *Older adults and information technology: A compendium of scientific research and web site accessibility guidelines.* Bethesda, MD: National Institute on Aging.

Morrell, R., Park, D., Mayhorn, C., & Kelley, C. (2000). Effects of age and instructions on teaching older adults to use ELDERCOMM, an electronic bulletin board system. *Educational Gerontology, 26* (3), 221–235.

Munson, J. & Gupta, V. (2002) Location-based notification as a general-purpose service. Downloaded from http://delivery.acm.org/10.1145/580000/570713/p40-munson.pdf?key1= 570713&key2=6728038311&coll=GUIDE&dl=ACM&CFID=63489869&CFTOKEN= 97325999 on 1/26/06.

Nokia, Inc. (2006) Show what you mean. Downloaded from http://www.nokiaaccessibility .com/hearing.html on 1/25/06.

Norman D. (1998). *The invisible computer: Why good products can fail, the personal computer is so complex, and information appliances are the answer.* Cambridge, MA: The MIT Press.

Nygard, L., & Starkhammar, S. (2003). Telephone use among noninstituionalized persons with dementia living alone: Mapping out difficulties and response strategies. *Scandanavian Journal of Caring Science, 17*, 239–249.

Omori, M., Tomoyuki, W., Takai, J., Takada, H. & Miyao, M. (2002). Visibility and characteristics of the mobile phones for elderly people. *Behaviour & Information Technology, 21* (5), 313–316.

Opalinski, L.(2001). Older adults and the digital divide: Assessing results of a web-based survey. *Journal of Technology in Human Services, 18* (34), 203–221.

Oticon, Inc. (2006). Hearing loss information and how digital hearing aids provide the best hearing solutions. Downloaded from http://www.oticon.com/ on 3/27/06.

Patterson, D., Etzioni, O., Fox, D., Kautz, H. (2002). The activity compass. In *Proceedings of UbiCog '02: First International Workshop on Ubiquitous Computing for Cognitive Aids,* Gothenberg, Sweden. Downloaded from http://www.cs.washington.edu/homes/djp3/AI/AssistedCognition/publications/compass03tr.doc on 1/26/06.

Philipose, M., Fishkin, K., Perkowitz, M., Patterson, D., Fox, D., Kautz, H. & Hähnel, D. (2004). Inferring activities from interactions with objects. *Pervasive Computing,* October–December, 50–57.

Qian, H.. Loizou, P.. & Dorman, M. (2003). Phone-assistive devices based on Bluetooth technology for cochlear implant users. *IEEE Transactions on Neural Systems Rehabilitation Engineering, 11* (3), 282–287.

Rideout, V., Neuman, T., Kitchman, M. & Brodie, M. (2005). E-Health and the elderly: How seniors use the internet for health information. *Kaiser Family Foundation publication #7223.* Menlo Park, CA. Downloaded from http://www.kff.org/entmedia/7223.cfm on 2/13/06.

Ryff, C. (1989). Happiness is everything, or is it? Explorations on the meaning of psychological wellbeing. *Journal of Personality and Social Psychology, 57* (6), 1069–1081.

Saito, T., Shibata, T., Wada, K. & Tanie, K. (2003). Relationship between interaction with the mental commit robot and change of stress reaction of the elderly. *Proceedings of the 2003 IEEE International Symposium on Computational Intelligence in Robotics and Automation.* July 16–20, Kobe, Japan.

Schieber, F. (2003). Human factors and aging: Identifying and compensating for age-related deficits in sensory and cognitive function. In N. Charness & K. W. Schaie (Eds.), *Impact of technology on successful aging* (pp. 42–84). New York: Springer.

Scialfa, C., Ho, G., & Laberge, J. (2004). Perceptual aspects of gerotechnology. In S. Kwon & D. Burdick (Eds.), *Gerotechnology: Research and practice in technology and aging* (pp. 18–41). New York: Springer.

Selwyn, N., Gorard, S. & Furlong, J. (2005). Whose Internet is it anyway? Exploring adults' (non)use of the Internet in everyday life. *European Journal of Communication, 20* (1): 5–26.

Selwyn, N., Gorard, S., Furlong, J., & Madden, L. (2003). Older adults' use of information and communications technology in everyday life. *Aging & Society, 23,* 561–582.

Sharit, J., Czaja, S., Hernandez, M., Yang, Y., Perdomo, D. Lewis, J., Lee C., & Nair, S. (2004). An evaluation of performance by older persons on a simulated telecommuting task. *The Journals of Gerontology Series B: Psychological Sciences and Social Sciences, 59,* 305–316.

Smyth, K., & Kwon, S. (2004) Computer-mediated communication and its use in support groups for family caregivers. In D.C. Burdick & S. Kwon (Eds.), *Gerotechnology: Research and practice in technology and aging* (pp. 97–116). New York: Springer.

Sohlberg, M., Fickas, S., Ehlhardt, L. & Todis, B. (2005). Case study report: The longitudinal effects of accessible email for four participants with severe cognitive impairments. *Journal of Aphasiology, 19* (7), 651–681.

Sony, Inc. (2005). ERS-7M3. Downloaded from http://www.sony.net/Products/aibo/ on 1/29/06.

Starkey Laboratories, Inc. (2005). Elihearing: Eli with Bluetooth technology. Downloaded from http://www.elihearing.com/UnitedStatesENG/index.htm on 1/25/06.

Takanori, S. (2004). An overview of human interactive robots for psychological enrichment. *Proceedings of the IEEE, 92* (11), 1749–1758.

Tamura, T., Nakajima, K., Nambu, M., Nakamura, K., Yonemitsu, S., Itoh, A., Higashi, Y., Fujimoto, T., & Uno, H. (2001). Baby dolls as therapeutic tools for severe dementia patients. *Gerontechnology, 1* (2): 111–118

Tamura, T, Yonemitsu, S, Itoh, A, Oikawa, D., Kawakami, A., Higashi, Y., Fujimooto, T, & Nakajima, K. (2004). Is an entertainment robot useful in the care of elderly people with severe dementia? The Journals of Gerontology Series A: Biological Sciences and Medical Sciences. 59A(1), 83-85. Downloaded from http://biomed.gerontologyjournals.org/cgi/content/abstract/59/1/M83 on 1/26/06.

Tanie, K. (2004) Industrial Robot Statistics and Industrial Activities. Downloaded from http://ieeexplore.ieee.org/iel5/100/29110/01310934.pdf?arnumber=1310934 on 1/25/06.

Thomas, J.C. (2003). Social aspects of gerontechnology. In N. Charness & K. W. Schaie (Eds.), *Impact of technology on successful aging* (pp. 162–176). New York: Springer.

Thrun, S. (2004). Toward a framework for human–robot interaction. *Human Computer Interaction, 19,* 9–24.

Vodaphone Group, Inc. (2006). Vodaphone speaking phones. Downloaded from http://online.vodafone.co.uk/dispatch/Portal/appmanager/vodafone/wrp?_nfpb=true&_pageLabel=Page_BOS_Content&pageID=AV_0617 on 1/25/06.

Wada, K., Shibata, T., Saito, T. & Tanie, K. (2002). Analysis of factors that bring mental effects to elderly people in robot assisted activity. *Proceedings of the 2002 IEEE/RSJ International Conference on Intelligent Robots and Systems.* EPFL, Lausanne, Switzerland.

Yoshimi, T., Matsuhira, N., Suzuki, K., Yamamoto, D, Ozaki, F., Hirokawa, J. & Ogawa, H. (2004). Development of a concept model of a robotic information home appliance, Apri-Alpha. *Proceedings of 2004 IEEE/RSJ International Conference on Intelligent Robots and Systems.* September 28. October 2, 2004, Sendai, Japan

Ziefle, M. (2002). The influence of user expertise and phone complexity on performance, ease of use and learnability of divergent mobile phones. *Behavior & Information Technology, 21* (5), 303–311.

Chapter 14

GERONTECHNOLOGICAL ONTOLOGY: HUMAN EXPERIENCE WITHIN EXTRAORDINARY FRAMEWORKS

GARI LESNOFF-CARAVAGLIA

PREAMBLE

The concrete world of felt experience has softened its contours and taken on the malleability of a dream. Such subtle alteration has left the individual in an emotional vacuum that strongly resembles the numbness succeeding a tragic event. Perceptions are sharpened in unexpected ways; senses are dulled imperceptibly; the world is as different as a haunting nostalgic reminiscence.

Identification of the source of these alterations elude the individual as elements of change predate the person, emerge with the consciousness of the individual, and engulf future vision. Thus, past, present, and future meet, mingle, and provide the cause or framework for the continuity of ineffable change. Although such change is both intrinsic and extrinsic, distinctions are muted and as soft as the formation of clouds.

Introduction

Projections into the future have one common failing. Such projections can only be based on what is already known or upon what experience of the world had been heretofore based upon a framework anchored in the present. In addition, it is difficult to forecast a future which derives from a present that is, in itself, in constant flux and change. Since future developments in technology rest largely upon what has already been developed in the past and is only being fostered in the present, future aspects of such possibilities are often beyond the scope of the imagination. Much of present day technology, for example, has its roots in developments which originated in ancient Greece and Rome (Lesnoff-Caravaglia, 1999).

In assessing the impact of an aging population upon developments in technology and upon societies of the future, it is a common error to assume that elderly populations of the future will exhibit characteristics similar to those of the present day, such as withdrawal from the work force, declining health, increased needs for hospitalization and nursing care, and other characteristics that suggest a highly dependent older population. Improved health care, however, buttressed by the increased understanding of the physiology of aging, as well as advances in technology, may well alter the characteristics of the elderly of the future.

The conventional view of the life cycle allowed for a specific time span for each age category, along with expectations that particular life events such as educational patterns, marriage, or entrance into the work force would occur at particular points in time. Such fixed categories and expectations as to life events have lost much of their rigidity in the present age (Lesnoff-Caravaglia, 2000). Further, with the gradual loss of distinction between the roles of the sexes, even gender is rapidly losing much of its traditional importance.

The traditional point of view is further eroded by the increase in life expectancy, as well as the extension of what has been regarded as the human life span to 125 years. The growth in numbers of centenarians throughout the world is without historical precedent.

The Concept of Time

The historical conception of time is an ordered progression of events that moves forward according to the observations of physical changes in the environment, the cycles of seasons, and alterations in human development. Such changes were viewed as inexorable and probably under the control of mystic forces. Although later scientific explanations challenged many of these convictions or beliefs, such ordered movement over time continued to provide a comforting structure for human knowledge and physical orientation.

Such ordered placement of persons within time and place have been obviated by the exposure to speed within time and the rapidity of movement of persons from place to place, resulting in the consequent oblivion of the actual space traveled. The relationship of the person to space and time has been virtually dissolved leaving in its wake an uneasy perception of the self as an insignificant participant within a personal experience. The experience itself takes on the aura of fiction, and the sterility of way stations, such as airports, contribute to the unreality of the experience.

Such abstractions of the person affect the ability to discriminate between the real and the dream, between fiction and fact. The realm of knowledge is additionally without mooring as it suffers from the interplay of special interests, political interests, and the field of entertainment. Due, in part, to the presence of such ambiguity and confusion, individual thought subsumes a leveling pattern resulting in uniformity of thought and reaction as the result of such public manipulation (Virilio, 2000).

Following World War II the link between economic, political, and social power engendered by the presence of technology was seen as potentially altering humanistic perspectives regarding persons and the environment (Montemagno & Roco, 2004). The natural world and its inhabitants might well be perceived as solely instruments for profit and gain. It was feared that the form of human thought would be subsumed to meet the requisites of industrialization. Human thought could fall into more calculative modes at the expense of moral considerations to the detriment of persons, cultural constructs, and the natural world (Heidegger, 1977; Sheehan, 1974; Tipler, 1994). By being overshadowed by the technological and mechanical, the humanitarian aspirations tied to the development of technology might be diminished. Thomas Edison, an exemplar of modern American technology, often voiced this fear.

The Altered Human Horizon

The initial introduction of technological innovation occasions both positive and negative reactions. A new technology inevitably carries in its wake the possibility of the unforeseen in the form of malfunction and unexpected outcomes. The potential for accident or malfunction is inherent in the invention. The development of the ship carried with it the potential for shipwreck, while the invention of the railway paved the way for train disasters. In much the same fashion, the plane introduced the plane crash, and the automobile the automobile accident (Virilio, 2000). Primary emphasis was generally placed on the invention itself without foreseeing the potential for malfunction or accident.

Some disasters, such as nuclear accidents, can have global effects resulting in mass destruction. Some inventions such as air travel render geography insignificant (Virilio, 2000). More recent inventions such as devices to create explosions in the electromagnetic field can cause civilizations to regress for a century or more. The crippling of the interconnected communication systems on a variety of levels could effectively bring the world to a halt.

In describing the antecedents of science, philosophers were quick to point out that the sciences would never have originated and grown if the way had not been prepared by magicians, alchemists, astrologers, and witches. It was the promises and pretensions of such groups that first created the impulse to search for hidden and forbidden powers (Nietzsche, 1974).

The penetrating of new worlds built upon imagination and fantasy led the way for media technology. Human frames of reference have been altered by supplanting the real world with floating inconstant images. Medical technology has the capacity to make physical encroachments, such as the taking over of biological functions (the pacemaker, for example). The human body through the procedures of transplants can be regarded as being controlled by technology (Armitage, 2000). Such alterations can be viewed as a technological colonization of the human body.

Choices across the life span are often portrayed in the form of a funnel with the broad end facing the beginning of life and youth, and the narrow tip pointing toward old age (Lesnoff-Caravaglia, 1988). No organization or institution seeks to promote old age as a desirable state. Instead most agencies that deal with the older population have as their mission ameliorative functions or ways to alter, change, or endure old age. Due to the ambiguity of the assignment of roles in old age, choice and decision-making as persons age can appear as empty gestures.

Increases in life expectancy can also potentially embody the notion of the unforeseen as accidents in that advances in technology are largely responsible for increases in life expectancy. The advent of legislation in some nations that permits persons to choose their time of death may lead to a reevaluation of what constitutes life and ways to encourage the prolonging, ending, or continuation of life. Advances in technology may uncover or be the cause of totally new diseases and disabilities in the future. There may well be future references to the "accident" of old age.

The Human/Technology Interaction

Early applications of technology were viewed with enthusiasm as they were seen as methods to control and to conquer the natural environment. The domination of the natural world would provide unlimited opportunities for industrial progress. One such example was the development of the train (the iron horse) and the frenzied speed by which the railroad spanned the North American continent.

The nature of the thinking that inspired the creation and utilization of technology appears to have resulted in the capture of human beings on both the intellectual and physical levels, causing human beings to become subservient to the very machines they created. While not ignoring the beneficial nature of many of the current technologies, the nature of such thinking is guided by such machine domination. Technological presence, thus, has inevitably provided systems which ultimately control human behavior (Marglin & Marglin, 1990).

Much in the same way that the stethoscope provided physiological information circumventing the need for patient interrogation, smart fabrics can now go beyond the person and provide information about a person's physical state while ignoring the individual. The person is totally objectified while the clothing describes his or her health status.

In the fabrication of materials for use in clothing, new fibers consisting of a series of microsensors are inserted which allow one to monitor the physiological parameters (vital signs) of a body. They are housed in a morphogenic fabric that is so soft it can be used in health care settings. Athletes have benefited from another innovative type of clothing that inflates or swells prior to or upon impact, preventing bruises and fractures. The added development of sensors that can activate clothing without the intervention of the wearer, allows for clothing to act on the person's behalf. It is the clothing that prompts the move, not the individual.

The current ecological crisis, the dangers of technological weaponry, the use of technologies by terrorist organizations, and the growing sense of frustration felt by those who are the prey of giant amorphous corporations and complex nameless bureaucracies contribute to the growing uneasiness experienced by individuals with respect to their elusive grip over the control of their lives (Gilleard & Higgs, 2000). Technology, in this sense, rather than enhancing, has effectively diminished the role of the individual person.

On the other hand, the presence of technology has led to increased sensitivity with regard to the humanitarian aspects of science and technology in terms of their responsibilities with regard to human existence and the environment. The freedom of continued life through radical medical interventions continues apace. Alterations of aspects of the environment are also conducive to life enhancement and increased life expectation with robotic capabilities assuming the role of the extension of self (Kaplan, 2004).

The word "robot" was invented in 1920 by the Bohemian writer Karel Capek. In Czech, the word "robota" signifies work. Following World War II and the advent of electronics, the myth of the robot that would free the world of mundane tasks, both in the workplace and the home, took form. Films and books proliferated describing the science fiction world in the most boring and fatiguing tasks of life were taken over by robots (Lesnoff-Caravaglia, 2001; Staudenmaier, 1989)).

A prominent author of fiction of that period, Isaac Asimov, predicted that by the year 2000 robots might rebel against the human race. Robots would rise up shouting slogans based on the statement by Descartes: Cogito, ergo sum (I think, therefore, I am). If this was the case, why should robots remain subservient? Nonetheless, revolutionary utilization of robots has continued apace particularly in settings such as industry and medicine. The effects upon the lives of average citizens have not been as telling. The myth of the robot that does the housecleaning and prepares the meals has been perpetrated for some 40 years, with few concrete results.

Machines continue to be simple creations, but they embody the potential of maturing into something transcending everything currently known. At some future point they may well be viewed as human descendants, while potentially the humans of today become anachronisms and as remnants of technological evolution gradually disappear (Moravec, 1988).

The industrial revolution of several centuries ago initiated the artificial substitution by mechanical means of human body functions such as lifting and transporting. The computational power of mechanical devices has risen a thousand-fold every 20 years since then. The time is approaching when virtually no essential human function, physical or mental, will lack an artificial counterpart. The embodiment of this convergence of cultural developments can result in the intelligent robot, a machine that can think and act as a human, however inhuman it may be in physical or mental detail (Kurzweil, 1999). Such machines could carry on the cultural evolution, including their own construction and reproduction and increasingly rapid self-improvement, without human presence or the benefit of human genes. The evolutionary process will have moved on to a new competitor or form (Moravec, 1988). The culture will then be able to evolve independently of human biology and its limitations, passing directly from generation to generation of ever more capable intelligent machinery.

Many of the human biological traits are out of step with the inventions of the mind. The uneasy truce between mind and body breaks down completely as life ends. Human genes usually survive death, but grouped in different ways in offspring and other relatives. It is easy to imagine human thought freed from bondage to a mortal body, as belief in an afterlife is common enough. It is becoming patently clear that it is not necessary to adopt a mystical or religious stance to accept the possibility. Just as computer programs and data can be moved from one computer into a physically different computer with no alteration, it is possible to imagine that a human mind might be freed from its brain in some analogous fashion (Moravec, 1988). As innovative a form of immortality this might present, the possibility of a post-biological world dominated by self-improving, thinking machines is equally unimaginable.

Computers are becoming increasingly more powerful. Unfortunately, human-like robots, particularly computers, have difficulty in conducting activities which are natural to humans, such as seeing, hearing, manipulating objects, learning languages, and commonsense reasoning. This dichotomy of the machines as doing well those things that humans find difficult, while doing poorly what is easy for humans, is a significantly troublesome aspect in the construction of an intelligent machine.

The future association between humans and machines may well be in the form of a partnership. It is possible that in time the relationship may devolve into a more symbiotic one with the boundary between the human and mechanical partner less evident (Farah & Wolpe, 2004). Some of this is already manifest in the utilization of artificial organs and other body parts. Such replacement parts are viewed by some as superior to the original. There is the potential to replace everything in the form of a new body (Ferkiss, 1969). Such body part replacement would not be physical in construction, but would be a specially designed robotic substitution.

The Global Environment

The ubiquitous presence of screens ranging from the computer to the television make clear that the development of the current culture is a manufactured product. It is less and less a direct human product built upon individual experience within a personal framework. Furthermore, the programming and sound of television throughout the world has a definite North American bias. Contemporary culture is the result of the interface between the group and the machine.

The computer may well replace the activities of reading and writing, with those who do not adapt becoming the illiterate (Ellul, 1990). As new technologies evolve, older forms of behavior are eradicated and no longer exist as a viable choice. The Amish may still travel by horse and buggy, but they abide by new rules of the road, and the horses they purchase from racing stables have to be retrained to turn right. Making a dental appointment or an airline reservation can be delayed because "the computer is down," and there is no other recourse but to wait.

The technical system has now become strongly integrated within offices, means of production, and personnel. The computer implies networks; it brings an entire system with it. Its proper use helps maintain the order within society. The incorporation of nuclear energy or genetic engineering follows the same pattern. It is the proper or improper use of these technologies that challenges philosophical concepts and ethical positions (Ellul, 1990).

The Virtual Experience

The computer has further supplanted the real world through the development of the virtual experience, with the world experienced intellectually, rather than in an actual sense. This theme has been expanded by Virilio (1997) when he describes a contemporary movement that is intensifying due to remote control and long-distance telepresence technologies. The presence and unremitting use of these technologies can result in an increasingly sedentary society composed of overequipped able-bodied persons living in isolation from one another. Further, there are real similarities between the reduced mobility of the well-equipped disabled person with the growing inertia of the overequipped able-bodied person.

The inert, sedentary lifestyle characterizes much of contemporary society. Telecommunication has led to a transparent horizon that allows one to be physically present in one place and, at the same time, to be a phantom witness to events on the opposite side of the world. Physical action is no longer required to alter aspects of one's life space. Drapes, lights, room temperatures, doors, and appliances can be instantaneously controlled through remote control (National Research Council, 2003).

Being hurtled in a chair through space between points of "Arrival" and "Departure" also describes the standard method of travel. The rapid movement of persons from one place to another across the globe is an accepted characteristic of contemporary society. It appears, however, that "Departure" and "Arrival" bear greater significance than the trip itself. People are moved from one point to another via airplanes and bullet trains in a state of passivity that borders on unconsciousness as they sleep, watch films, or daydream as they are hurtled through space. The space intervening the "Departure" and "Arrival" are ignored and are devoid of content. It is the "Arrival" only that has greatest significance. It is the speed of arrival of persons, messages, and television reporting that is of paramount interest (Virilio, 1997).

Having been placed in the position of being a constant recipient of technological interventions, internal as well as external, human experience is inevitably tied to a sedentary life. The end result is that the body appears to be wired to its life space (Virilio, 1997).

Personal Identity

Human aging can be likened to a battle of resistance. There is the resistance to the physical outward appearances of age with regard to changes of the integumentary system, the social stigmatization and ostracism (particularly in the case of women) the decline in power and influence, and the onslaught of disease as aging advances. The redefinition of self is an individual project often restricted by cultural and ethical parameters. Future developments in technology may well play an increasing role in reframing this definition.

One can recover fading beauty, aspire to beauty never possessed but always longed for, recover from melancholy and even depression through the acquisition of beauty, and regain one's self-esteem. That is, one can treat the body by way of the soul (the mind), and one can cure the soul (the mind) via modifications of the body. Over the past ten years the market for plastic surgery has doubled, and its price has exceeded billions of dollars. Such intervention has been sought at fairly equal rates by both men and women.

The body can be treated by restructuring its form and proportions; reducing fat deposits; restoring physical elasticity and vigor; and by modifying the breasts, the posterior, and the abdomen. One can treat the face by eliminating unpleasant lines or imperfections, and one can conquer baldness. These can all be accomplished through mediations that range from surgery to various injections provided by a wide range of cosmetic and health care agencies. For example, increases in height for super hostesses for international events are commonplace. Such procedures require careful selection of subjects and call for long planning. The subsequent reformation of the hostesses can take years.

The cult of narcissism runs apace. Physical attractiveness has become a commodity that is available for purchase much like any desired item. Such advanced technologies have incited societal changes which have altered the roles of males and females. The male has emerged as a sex object parallel to that of the female (witness the popularity of the exhibits of the "Full Monty"). Due to genetic alterations, parents can now predetermine the color of their offsprings' eyes and hair.

In the end, if everyone has the capacity to model or remodel his or her self into carbon copies of figures in advertising copy or the spheres of entertainment, beauty will become standardized, and the malformed may become the beautiful. Or perhaps beauty will be newly defined as charm or charisma—an attribute too ephemeral for packaging and marketing.

In response to alterations in the physical environment, the human body experiences alterations that are in concert with environmental demands. Some such alterations are transplant procedures or the implanting of devices deep within a human body. The arrangement of the domestic environment facilitates the consolidation of the person to the smart house. In the near future there may well be an increased fusion of the biological and the technological. It is already predicted that the majority of surgical procedures in the future will be on the order of organ transplants and the implanting of a variety of prostheses. The goal of such prostheses may include the enhancement or ameliorization of sensory functions such as vision and hearing beyond normal capabilities. Night vision, distance hearing, and specialized gloves for tactile discrimination are increasingly part of the technological armamentarium.

The most durable conquests of the machine, however, lay not in the instruments themselves, but in the modes of life made possible via the machine and in the machine (Mumford, 1963). The refrigerator and the automobile are but two common examples of machines that have altered existence. Few would willingly return to the days of the icebox or travel by foot.

The clue to modern technology was the displacement of the organic and the living by the artificial and mechanical. In the past, the irrational and demonic aspects of life had invaded spheres where they did not belong. It was a step forward to discover that bacteria, not evil elves, were responsible for curdling milk and that an air-cooled motor was more effective than a witch's broomstick for rapid long-distance transportation (Mumford, 1963).

Cent'anni or Long Life

The traditional goal of one hundred years of life (cent'anni--the traditional Sicilian toast) is no longer an unachievable prospect. Life is first spent as an infant and a child, with the second quarter as an adolescent and adult, but 50 percent of life is lived as an older person. Much of this extension of life can be attributed to the advancements in technology, health care, and medical research.

This second half of life has led to some revisions of lifestyle to accommodate this additional premium of long life. Intimate human experiencing, such as the role of sex, has resulted in a new emphasis: sex not as procreation, but sex as recreation.

In addition, the "virtual love" permitted by the sensory feats of cybersex may well have unexpected consequences for human demography by diminishing birth rates. The computer, in this sense, can be regarded as "a universal condom" (Virilio, 1997, p. 67). A further result is a loss of tangible reality that has had its echo in high divorce rates and the growth of single-parent families, and a focus on sexual activity which does not require another human being. "To prefer the virtual being . . . at some remove . . . to the real being close-up . . . is to take the shadow for the substance . . ." (Virilio, 1997, p. 103). At a time when innovations are occurring in artificial fertilization and genetic engineering, with the aid of biocybernetic accoutrements using sensor-effectors distributed over the genital organs, conjugal relations between opposite sexes have been short-circuited and coitus interrupted. Touching at a distance—tactile telepresence—allows partners in virtual love to engage in a cybernetic process in which the operator console is no longer satisfied just to synthesize images or sound, it can also orchestrate sexual sensations.

Virtual sex can potentially provide sensations and experiences that currently do not exist. It is also a form of safe sex as it carries no risk of pregnancy or transmission of disease. Virtual prostitution can be freely practiced and be exempt from legal or regulatory proscriptions. The risks of disease, rape, and other forms of violence can very likely decrease.

If the virtual pleasure of sexual telepresence were eventually to outstrip the real pleasure of embodied love, those societies left to ensure the continuation of the human race will be those that are underdeveloped and, worse, media-deprived (Virilio, 1997). The boundaries between biology and technology, humans and machines, are being effaced one by one.

For some older men the drug Viagra has meant continued participation in sexual activity. For older women, the possibility of artificial insemination and uterus transplants hold promise for continued procreativity even in advanced years. The drop in fertility rates among younger persons can potentially in the future be balanced by families formed late in life by sexually active older couples with the assistance of technology.

In another context, sexuality can become truly age irrelevant through available expediencies such as the Internet. Persons can adopt whatever age they please and can assume attributes that will make them sexually desirable. A woman of 70 can portray herself as being 35, or can imagine herself in the guise of a much younger version of herself, thus reliving her past in the present. Cosmetic surgery also allows for such incursions into the past by permitting persons the opportunity to turn back the years through reframing or reshaping the body. Technology thus can permit choice as to when and how one ages.

New Prospects for Life and Death

The processes of birth and death have been submitted to significant alteration including the virtual survival by way of cryogenics to the feats of virtual transplants and nanomachines, to in vitro and in vivo bio-cultures. Further modifications have occurred by applying to the human organism the standard of switching parts which applies in the mechanical world, the interchangeability of new transhuman beings and the consequent suppression of the pain of living. In fact, by a possible substitutability of cloned bodies, human beings could still cherish the hope of surviving themselves, while at the same time having ceased to exist (Virilio, 1997).

The technologized world can take on a character of its own and operate entirely without human interference. For example, a short story by Ray Bradbury describes the scenario of an automated home that is completely operated though mechanical devices which continue to perform their functions long after the occupants of the home have died, including keeping itself tidy and preparing and serving meals.

The potential freedom that technology can provide may well extend beyond current imagining. Each human sense performs an essential function. Human eyes see what is in front of them; ears, however, can detect sounds coming from the front and behind, left and right, above and below. It is possible to provide robots with numerous eyes and any number of legs and arms. A person fitted with an artificial arm would be presented with some limitations of action. On the other hand, it is also possible that the artificial arm could provide new and unexpected powers. For example, the artificial arm could withstand extremes of heat and could even be immersed in boiling water. In this sense, the new or artificial arm is superhuman (Mori, 1981).

Cohabitation: Humans and Machines

Human beings are, in themselves, imprecise machines. The body itself is a sort of microcosm of the machine. The arms are levers, the lungs bellows, the eyes lenses, the heart a pump, the fist a hammer, and the nerves a telegraph system connected with a central station. On the whole, however, the mechanical instruments were invented before the physiological functions were accurately described (Mori, 1981).

In addition, a drafting machine can draw a hundred or more perfect circles all the same size, but a human has difficulty in drawing even one. People cannot use gases or liquids with their hands, but machines can handle them through the use of pipes and pumps. Repetitive or odious tasks can be performed better by machines. Machines, however, are incapable of analyzing the nature of a complicated problem or grasping the total meaning of a particular line of reasoning (Mori, 1981). Those who argue the obsolescence of humankind overlook the essential difference between humans and machines: A machine has neither instinct nor will and cannot change the course of its action even in the presence of danger.

Ethical dilemmas do arise in the cohabitation of humans with machines. It is almost unavoidable that the human environment and the humans living within that space undergo change (Hughes, 2004). Human beings develop attitudes and behaviors which did not exist prior to the mechanical age. The nature of the combination of technologized human beings and the machines can be viewed as positive or negative, but it is certain that the mix will continue to form and reform itself over time (Gadamer, 1976).

Technology and aging are very similar in one respect--they both have an onward or forward movement. There is no going back. Once a technology is invented and it proves to be useful, it is changed only to become even more complex and does not disappear. Aging also moves forward in an inexorable fashion. In this sense, technology and aging are both structured by time. In technology, the reliance has been on the inventions of the Romans and the Greeks; in human aging, the foundation is built upon infancy and childhood.

The Gerontocracy

It may well occur that societal power in the future will reside in the elderly. It is possible that the day of Plato's philosopher king has arrived.

> Should power reside in age, one might well find in vogue the trembling hand and shuffling gait, spectacles and hearing aid. The young feigning sensory loss and graying the hair or attempting its removal in an effort to appear venerable.

If the pace to be emulated is slow and measured, then the impatience and haste of youth is put to shame. When caution is preferred over imprudence, and deliberate action over trial and error, then youth is a lament and old age a herald.

When age is feared–not because of the proximity of death, but as the centrifugal force of life–then idolatry of youth will fade as will smoked glass and candlelight as fitting accoutrements for women of age. (Lesnoff-Caravaglia, 1984, p. 9)

REFERENCES

Armitage, J. (Ed.). (2000). *Paul Virilio. From modernism to hypomodernism and beyond.* Thousand Oaks, CA: Sage.

Ellul, J. (1990). *The technological bluff.* Grand Rapids, MI: Eerdmans Pub. Co.

Farah, M.J., & Wolpe, P.R. (2004, May–June). Monitoring and manipulating brain function: New neuroscience technologies and their ethical implications. *Hastings Center Report,* 35–45.

Ferkiss, V.C. (1969). *Technological man: The myth and the reality.* New York: George Braziller, Inc.

Gadamer, H. (1976). *Philosophical hermeneutics.* (D. Linge, Trans.). Berkeley, CA: Univ. of Calif. Press.

Gilleard, C., & Higgs, P. (2000). *Cultures of aging. Self, citizen and the body.* Harlow, England: Prentice Hall.

Heidegger, M. (1977). *The question concerning technology and other essays.* (W. Lovitt, Trans.). New York: Garland Pub., Inc.

Hughes, T.P. (2004). *Human-built world: How to think about technology and culture.* Chicago: University of Chicago Press.

Kaplan, D.M. (Ed.). (2004). *Readings in the philosophy of technology.* Lanham, MD: Rowman & Littlefield Publishers, Inc.

Kurzweil, R. (1999). *Age of spiritual machines.* New York: Penguin Putnam Inc.

Lesnoff-Caravaglia, G. (Ed.). (1984). *The world of the older woman.* New York: Human Sciences Press.

Lesnoff-Caravaglia, G. (1988). Aging in a technological society. In G. Lesnoff-Caravaglia, (Ed.). *Aging in a technological society* (pp. 272–283). New York: Human Sciences Press.

Lesnoff-Caravaglia, G. (1999). Ethical issues in a high-tech society. In T. Fusco Johnson (Ed.), *Handbook on ethical issues in aging* (pp. 271–288). Westport, CT: Greenwood Press.

Lesnoff-Caravaglia, G. (2000). *Health aspects of aging. The experience of growing old.* Springfield, IL: C. C Thomas, Pub.

Lesnoff-Caravaglia, G. (Ed.). (2001). *Aging and public health. Technology and demography: Parallel evolutions.* Springfield, IL: C. C Thomas, Pub.

Marglin, F.A., & Marglin, S. (Eds.) (1990). *Dominating knowledge: Development, culture, and resistance.* Oxford: Clarendon Press.

Montemagno, C.D., & Roco, M.C., & (Eds.). (2004). *The coevolution of human potential and converging technologies.* New York: New York Academy of Sciences.

Moravec, H. (1988). *Mind children. The future of robot and human intelligence.* Cambridge, MA: Harvard University Press.

Mori, M. (1981). *The Buddha in the robot.* (C. S. Terry, Trans.) Tokyo: Kosei Publishing Co.

Mumford, L. (1963). *Technics and civilization.* New York: Harcourt, Brace & World.

National Research Council (2003). *Technology for adaptive aging.* Washington, D.C.: The Washington Academies Press.

Nietzsche, F. (1974). *The gay science.* (W. Kaufmann, Trans.) New York: Random House.

Sheehan, T. (Ed.). (1981). *Heidegger: The man and the thinker.* Chicago: Precedent Pub., Inc

Staudenmaier, J.M. (1989). *Technology's storytellers: Reweaving the human fabric.* Cambridge, MA: The Society for the History of Technology.

Tipler, F. (1994). *The physics of immortality.* New York: Doubleday.

Virilio, P. (1997). *Open sky.* New York: Verso.

Virilio, P. (2000). *Polar inertia.* (P. Camiller, Trans.). Thousand Oaks, CA: Sage.

INDEX